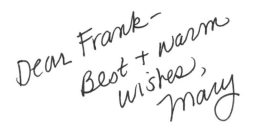

Dear Frank—
Best + warm
wishes,
Mary

Service Automation
Robots and the Future of Work

Service Automation
Robots and the Future of Work

Leslie P. Willcocks
and
Mary C. Lacity

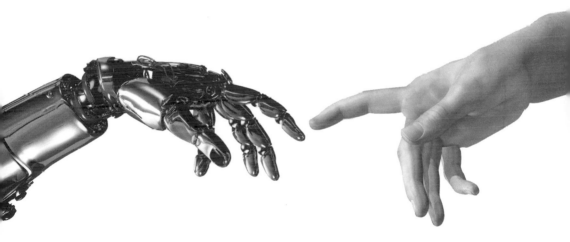

Steve Brookes Publishing
United Kingdom

A 'Steve Brookes Publishing' book
www.stevebrookes.com

Cover design:
Nick Sample
www.nicksample.com

Cover images:
The Great Machine by Giorgio de Chirico, Italian, 1888-1978
1925, oil on canvas
By kind permission of the Honolulu Museum of Art,
Gift of the Friends of the Academy 1945 (390.1)

The Creation of Adam by Michelangelo, Italian, 1475-1564

Authors:
Leslie P. Willcocks and Mary C. Lacity

Published in 2016 by:
Steve Brookes Publishing
60 Loxley Road
Stratford-upon-Avon
Warwickshire CV37 7DR
United Kingdom
Tel: +44(0)1789 267124

A CIP catalogue record for this book is available from the British Library
ISBN 978-0-956414-56-4

Printed and bound in Malta by Latitude Press Ltd.

About this book

The hype and fear blown around automation and robotics need to be punctured by in-depth research. This book captures a year's worth of learning about service automation based on a survey, in-depth client case studies, and interviews with service automation clients, providers, and advisors. The authors embed today's empirical lessons into the broader history and context of automation, as a key to understanding the fast-rising phenomenon of service automation.

The authors, Leslie Willcocks and Mary Lacity, are world experts on information technology and global sourcing. Their work shows how companies and service providers in diverse sectors – including energy, insurance, telecommunications, health care, transport, media and financial services – have adopted service and robotic process automation, the challenges they faced, and the multiple benefits gained. The lessons learned address defining a service automation strategy, launching successful service automation initiatives, preparing the organisation for the changes service automation induces, and building enterprise-wide service automation capabilities.

The study finds that the possibilities for automation and robotics are set by human imagination – and humans also establish the social and political boundaries. While the case studies found that service automation produced multifaceted business benefits, the authors address the bigger picture of where advanced technologies, robotics and automation will lead, examining

About this book

concerns and anxieties over acceleration, employment, security, privacy and environmental sustainability. On employment, they found that service automation replaced routine, repetitive tasks and freed up humans to focus on more interesting work. Will this human-robot-machine complementarity continue into the future? Contrary to today's worst fears, robotics could facilitate the rise – not the demise – of the knowledge worker if managers use their imagination.

The authors give a balanced, informed and compelling view on gaining the benefits and managing the downsides of present and future technologies. On a ten year horizon, they see dramatic changes as automation and robotics, in combination with mobile internet access big data, the Internet of Things, digital fabrication and cloud computing, create massive impacts on individuals, organisations, and on business, economic and social life.

Contents

Contents

Contents

Figures

Tables

Preface

"The only thing that is constant is change." **Heraclitus**

"Never before in history has innovation offered promise of so much to so many in so short a time." **Bill Gates**

"It has become appallingly obvious that our technology has exceeded our humanity." **Albert Einstein**

Powerful thoughts! Humans have constantly strived to make the human experience better than it was in the past and enable all humans to experience a better life. The fact that humans will continue to drive with their inherent curiosity, hope and will to live is still a struggle. The constant innovation of technology has been a great enabler of achieving our human experience and will continue to be limited only by our imagination.

The very recent past has seen some truly astounding advancements. We've mapped the human genome, discovered over 1,000 planets outside of our solar system, and connected over 25 billion devices and over one billion people to the Internet.

Underpinning many of these breakthroughs is a unique set of technologies. Cloud computing has democratised access to world-class technology; mobile devices and networks have put what was once a supercomputer in the hands of millions; advances in database and analytics technologies have enabled us to store unthinkable volumes of data in near-real time, and social platforms have connected producers and consumers in ways unthinkable just a decade ago.

But this technology has also massively increased complexity. While computers are no match for humans at things like reasoning and pattern recognition, humans are no match for computers when it comes to speed and storage. Both business and consumer processes that require doing things quickly, or that require the interrogation of lots of information   big data analytics – are increasingly becoming automated. This is already having, and will continue to have, a profound impact on our global economy as we increasingly work side-by-side, or are replaced by, software.

The authors, Dr. Leslie Willcocks and Dr. Mary Lacity, world-renowned authors on the subject of Outsourcing, have invited some of the world's most influential leaders in the innovation and usage of technology, to input into the development writing of this book.   The insights of these leaders and the authors' in depth analysis will provide you invaluable perspective to apply to your own endeavours.

ISG had the privilege of participating in the development of this book and is excited to see the findings and other insights shared to enable the future that is possible.

Best wishes to you and your organisation's success. We look forward working with you in achieving your Knowledge Power Results!

Steve Hall, ISG Partner, Emerging Markets

About ISG:

Information Services Group (ISG) (NASDAQ: III) is a leading technology insights, market intelligence and advisory services company, serving more than 500 clients around the world to help them achieve operational excellence. ISG supports private and public sector organisations to transform and optimise their operational environments through research, benchmarking, consulting and managed services, with a focus on information technology, business process transformation, program management services and enterprise resource planning. Clients look to ISG for unique insights and innovative solutions for leveraging technology, the deepest data source in the industry, and more than five decades of experience and global leadership in information and advisory services. Based in Stamford, Connecticut, US, the company has more than 900 employees and operates in 21 countries. For additional information, visit www.isg-one.com.

Endorsements

"Lacity and Willcocks have consistently demonstrated a well-renowned, respected, collective experience and wisdom studying the fields of business operations and the future of work in recent decades. Their approach to studying the critical topic of intelligent automation has balance, depth and a great perspective on how this will unravel in the future. The future impact of cognitive computing, driven by major advancements in robotic automation tools, predictive analytics solutions - all driven by the socially intelligent worker is the future, and for many organisations only just realising this, it may already be too late. However, we must remember that all these advancements in automation and analytics technology are useless without the human factor to drive it. This book fleshes out these issues in spades and is a must-read."

Phil Fersht, Founder & CEO, HfS Research

"Yes, robots are coming to take our work away – even the knowledge work we've invested in high levels of education to be able to perform. In the midst of mounting anxiety, Profs Willcocks and Lacity have done us all an invaluable service: taken a clear-eyed, in-depth look at exactly how 21st century automation is reshaping workplaces, and found humanity still winning in the end."

Julia Kirby, Harvard Business Review editor and coauthor,
Only Humans Need Apply: Winners and Losers in the Age of Smart Machines

"Robotic Process Automation and Cognitive Technology are dramatically reshaping the business landscape of today, and the pace of change will only continue to accelerate tomorrow. It will not be the strongest or the most intelligent companies that will survive, but those most adaptable to change. Service Automation: Robots and the Future of Work is a must-read for those seeking not only to survive but to thrive in the world of smart machines."

Chip Wagner, CEO, Alsbridge

"Service Automation is a well-structured and thoughtful book on a topic top-of-mind to professionals and executives alike. Once again, Drs. Lacity and Willcocks deliver the definitive guide."

Debi Hamill, CEO, International Association for Outsourcing Professionals

"This is a must-read for business leaders. Willcocks and Lacity peel back the layers in the rapidly changing world of software automation. They show what is real today, what is still hype, and provide synthesised experience from early adopters that will accelerate your ability to put robots to work in your organisation."

Lee Coulter, CEO, Ascension Ministry Service Center

"Robotic Process Automation is truly the game changer of our time. This goes way beyond cool tech. It's more about digital labor and will forever change how work gets done. Willcocks and Lacity have created a timely must-read for all business and technology leaders who want to ride the wave and not get crushed by it."

Frank Casale, President of Arago USA and Founder, The Institute of Robotic Process Automation

"If you want to know about the most important trend in technology today, there is no better place to start than Service Automation. Willcocks and Lacity provide a well-researched and engaging account of the state of the art in business process robotics and what it means for the changing nature of work."

M. Lynne Markus, The John W. Poduska Sr. Professor of Information and Process Management, Bentley University

Professional Credits

Portions of the Survey in Chapter 1 were initially published as Lacity, M., Willcocks, L., and Yan, A. (2015), *Are the robots really coming? Service Automation Survey Findings*, *Pulse Magazine*, Issue 17, pp. 14-21.

Portions of Chapter 2 and 3 were initially published as Lacity, M. and Willcocks, L. (2016), *Robotic Process Automation at Telefónica O2*, *MIS Quarterly Executive*. Reprinted with permission.

Notes on Contributors

Andrew Anderson serves as the Chief Executive Officer of Celaton Limited. An entrepreneur with over 20 years' experience within the IT industry, Andrew has extensive knowledge of communications, messaging and information systems in sales, marketing and technical roles. Following seven years with The Parachute Regiment, Andrew gained experience as Communications Consultant with Copymore Systems plc, followed by six years at Amba Communication Systems Ltd as Technical Director. He founded RedRock Technologies in 1993 and, through acquisition and organic growth, built one of the UK's best-known brands in communications and messaging software. Andrew steered the company through IPO and public listing in 2001. RedRock was acquired by Netstore plc in 2002 and he joined its management team as Vice President of Product Development. In 2004, Andrew led and funded the management buyout of RedRock Technologies from Netstore plc. In the same period, RedRock acquired DG Tech Ltd and was subsequently renamed Celaton Limited. In 2009, Celaton successfully launched its first learning tools and today the business is recognised as one of the leading companies in the world for its development of cognitive learning technology.

Alastair Bathgate is CEO of BluePrism. Alastair's career spans manufacturing, retailing, banking and enterprise software which has given him a unique understanding of operational business processes and how technology can be used to improve efficiency and service. Setting his sights on the white collar back office, and realising that there was an enormous unfulfilled need in the 'long tail' of automation, he co-founded Blue Prism to provide a new business-led, more granular and economic approach that today we know as Enterprise Robotic Process Automation. A thought leader in this space, Alastair remains CEO of Blue Prism and holds an MBA from Leeds University Business School.

Raymond (Rob) Brindley II has over 30 years of information technology (IT) experience, of which 20 years has been focused on outsourcing. Rob, as the Information Services Group (ISG) practice lead for IT Automation, and the North American Media vertical, is a highly knowledgeable and experienced strategist in the disciplines of Application Development and Maintenance (ADM) and Infrastructure. His clients benefit from his long-term experience in sourcing advisory services, where Rob has delivered advice to senior executives for more than ten years, and has advised on more than 18 successful sourcing initiatives totaling more than US$4 billion of contract value.

Sarah Burnett is a research vice president at Everest Group where she leads the company's Service Delivery Automation (SDA) research globally. Based in London, she also serves European clients across Everest Group's global services research areas. Sarah offers more than 20 years of experience in the industry, having served in a variety of capacities, including in-house practitioner, outsourcing provider, and research analyst. She has also worked in the field of technology to automate processes including food manufacturing, payments processing and e-catalogue formatting for uploading to multiple e-procurement portals. Sarah's latest research reports include European Finance and Accounting Outsourcing and SDA technology assessments.

Michael Chet Chambers has been in the IT field for 25 years. He started off in desktop support trading out a 286 for a 486. He grew into network support LAN and WAN, then was an AS400 operator for a while. Then everything changed when EDI came into his life. He loved it, and spent many years growing a career and building out several teams. His life has changed again now that RPA has arrived. His journey continues …

Christian Clarke is Head of Customer Relations for Virgin Trains. Clarke did not find Virgin Trains – they found him. Having undertaken a Degree in American Studies at the universities of Hull and North Carolina Greensboro respectively, he started working with Virgin Trains Customer Relations as a temp. Bitten by the company-centric bug, he stayed for three years in order to secure a permanent position. Christian has since worked at every level of the department, until becoming Head of Department in 2013. His greatest achievement is successfully facilitating the shift from a complaints department to a resolution centre, and shaping the leaders of tomorrow by guiding and empowering them today.

Chetan Dube has served as the President and CEO of IPsoft since its inception in 1998. During his tenure, he has led the company to create a radical shift in the way IT is managed. Prior to joining IPsoft, Chetan served as an Assistant Professor at New York University, where his research was focused on deterministic finite-state computing engines. Chetan is a widely recognised speaker on autonomics and utility computing and serves on the board of numerous IT-related institutions.

Lou Ferrara is a Vice President at The Associated Press, where he oversees sports, business and entertainment news, while also leading many of the agency's innovations and transformative changes. He implemented automation technologies to write stories about corporate earnings reports in 2014, and has built on that innovation to make it a key part of AP's future operations. A former reporter and city editor, Lou now works across all formats to ensure that AP continues to transform to the mobile and social landscape while harnessing technologies that will allow the AP's modern newsroom and its journalists to flourish.

A.J. Hanna is the Sr. Director Operations Support at the Ascension Ministry Service Center in Indianapolis. He has more than 20 years of experience in operations management, business process standardisation and shared services. In four years at Ascension, A.J. has led the implementation of foundational programs used in the areas of training, continuous improvement, productivity measurement, data analytics and business process optimisation for a center of nearly 900 associates. Most recently, A.J. has led the establishment of the Ministry Service Center's automation initiative. He has been interviewed by InfoWorld magazine and spoken on the topic at industry events.

Cliff Justice is the leader of KPMG's U.S. Shared Services and Outsourcing Advisory practice. He has more than 20 years of experience in helping enterprises deliver improved business performance. Cliff has an extensive background in shared services delivery model design and operations. As a management consultant, he has led strategy, transformation and operational improvement initiatives for numerous enterprises spanning IT, HR, Finance and other corporate services. Cliff and his team have developed KPMG's Global Business Services (GBS) framework, which provides KPMG's clients with the market perspective, data, tools and resources to source, integrate and transform back and middle office functions to improve overall operating effectiveness. He is a frequent contributor to industry research and innovation initiatives. Cliff leads KPMG's innovation efforts to integrate disruptive technologies such as robotics and artificial intelligence into back and middle office operations.

Pravin Rao is Chief Operating Officer and Chairperson at Infosys BPO. He is responsible for driving growth and differentiation across the portfolio. In addition, he is responsible for Global Delivery, Quality and Productivity, Supply Chain and Business enabling functions. Pravin has over 28 years of experience. Since joining Infosys in 1986, Pravin has held a number of senior leadership roles such as Head of Infrastructure Management Services, Delivery Head for Europe, and Head of Retail, Consumer Packaged Goods,

Logistics and Life Sciences. He holds a degree in electrical engineering from Bangalore University, India.

Charles Sutherland is the Chief Research Officer at HfS Research. He is responsible for the overall research agenda for HfS across the 'as a service' economy and personally covers the areas of automation, business platforms, supply chain, procurement and various vertical processes. Charles has been in the business services market for 20 years including previous roles as the Chief Strategy Officer for a BPO service provider and the Managing Director, Growth & Strategy for Accenture's Operations Growth Platform. He has an MBA from INSEAD in Fontainebleau, France and an Honors BA in Economics and Political Science from the University of Toronto. Charles can contacted at charles.sutherland@hfsresearch.com and followed on twitter @cwsuther.

Derek Toone is Managing Director, Robotic Process Automation, Alsbridge. He has been with Alsbridge for 11 years and currently leads the firm's global Robotic Process Automation practice. Derek is a licensed attorney and member of the State Bar of Texas. He has spent the majority of his tenure at Alsbridge delivering ITO, BPO and shared services advisory services to Fortune 500 clients in the banking, financial services, healthcare, manufacturing, distribution and consumer packaged goods verticals. These client engagements encompassed strategy development, vendor selection, contract negotiation and vendor management for a broad array of IT services, business processes and software packages.

Authors' Introduction and Acknowledgements

Welcome to the results of our year-long exploration into what was initially Robotic Process Automation (RPA). This still forms a central piece of our findings and lessons. However, during the course of the year we found ourselves observing further developments and applications in technology, and becoming part of a bigger debate about automation and the future of work. Ultimately we decided that it was going to be difficult, less interesting, but also much less useful, to write a book 'just' about robotic process automation. We took this decision even though RPA has been seeing accelerated take-up from 2015, and has highly significant implications, not least, as we discovered, for certain types of jobs, for business benefits, and for outsourcing and offshoring.

In this book you will find a richness of experiences, insights and lessons on the 'what' and the 'how' of service automation – what it is and how it can be implemented for business advantage. However, we also provide a bigger framing in terms of time – a ten year horizon – and also scale of impact – on society and economy, as well as on the individual business.

The bigger framing takes into account our deep-seated relationship with technology, on-going since pre-historic times. For our purposes we see technology as the collection of techniques, skills, methods and processes used in the production of goods or services or in the accomplishment of objectives, for example scientific investigation. Technology can be the knowledge of techniques, processes, or it can be embedded in machines, computers, devices and factories, which can be operated by individuals without detailed knowledge of the workings of those machines. The term 'technology' arose in the period 1840-1914, during the Second Industrial or Technological revolution. This period saw the building of railroads, large-scale iron and steel production, widespread use of machinery in manufacturing, greatly increased use of steam power, use of oil, the beginning of electricity, and of electrical communications.

The boundless Promethean power that is associated with human-created technologies has always been linked with both awe and anxiety in equal measure.[i] With the coming of the Information Age, driven by the rise of information and communications technologies, age-old questions are being asked once again. In our book we engage with these questions in the first and last chapters to give context to the service automation technologies that, in combination with a group of related technologies, we believe will have enormous impact over the next ten years. These questions, dilemmas and challenges also led us to choose a distinctive symbol for the front cover. It is time to briefly explain why.

The Great Automaton – Questions for Our Times

At some point, after picking up this book, you probably considered its cover. You will have seen a painting – in fact a 1925 masterpiece by Giorgio De Chirico called *El Gran Automata* – literally 'The Great Automaton' or 'The Great Machine'. *"Very pretty"*, you probably thought. We would ask you now to return to the cover and linger a little longer over that image. One author has had this painting on the office wall for a decade now. With every, admittedly increasingly obsessive, glance, we both have pondered deeply about its significance to the day job – researching and providing insight into advanced information and communication technologies and their relationships to, and

---

[i] Recall that Prometheus was a Titan in Greek mythology. He created mankind, was its greatest benefactor, and gifted humans with fire stolen from Mount Olympus, home of the gods. In the myth, he was eternally punished for this sacrilege.

impacts upon organisations. It raises important question we will deal with in this book, but does not provide answers. It is for the stakeholders in the technological future to provide the answers. For us, the painting never loses its compelling enigma.

All great art is a representation of something, whether it be, for example, a concept, an abstraction, a person, an event, or a landscape. But what is this painting a representation, a sign, of? Great artists like De Chirico leave their viewers work to do, and, in creating metaphor, tension and ambivalence, De Chirico's painting invites several interpretations. Here is one.

Historically De Chirico (1888-1978) had little time for Futurism, a contemporary Italian-borne art movement whose eleven point Founding Manifesto poet Filippo Marinetti published in Le Figaro on 20th February 1909. Its macho creed reads as a hymn to struggle, technology and transformation. Futurists, like Marinetti, rejected the past, and gloried in what they saw as the infinite speed and progress made possible through scientific and technological advances for which there are always signs in the present. De Chirico's 1925 painting is, amongst many other things, a considered, highly enigmatic rejection of this techno-vision of the past, present and where we are headed. It can be read as a prediction, but is perhaps better seen as a warning, an icon in a public space, a monument to the possible future if it accelerates out of our control.

The art of De Chirico displayed in *The Great Automaton* centres upon the antithesis between classical culture and modern mechanistic civilization. These two elements are locked in a desperate struggle, and the tragic quality of this situation exudes an aura of melancholy, enigma, and static contradiction of which De Chirico was a prime exponent. Between the lengthening shadows of a deserted town square in the afternoon stands a classical figure, neither human nor merely an object. But De Chirico's new person has no face; he/she is perhaps a dummy, at best a mannequin (from the Dutch meaning 'little man'). The statue is a human-technical 'mash-up' in tension with the sign system of a classical setting – arches, towers, sailing ships, piazza, a bright sky (reminiscent of Giotto or Piero della Francesca paintings) – in which it stands and over which it presides.

The painting represents, metaphorically, a possible future scenario that would see people eliminated by machines, or so developed in their faculties by an infinity of physical, mechanical and digital metamorphoses, as to be recognisable as human in form only. Is the person trapped inside, or do they become the machine? De Chirico wrote, in a letter in 1913, that *"original man must have wandered through a world full of uncanny signs. He must have trembled at each step."* Here he wants us, too, to pause and tremble, and consider, before we move on.

This Book

Reading a book is, amongst many other things, an opportunity to set aside time for reflection, by gaining knowledge and insight that is useful as well as hopefully, enjoyable and interesting. We wrote this book with these aims in mind.

As we said, the bigger framing, in terms of timeline, history and context, begins in Chapter 1, which looks succinctly at the history of automation and robotics, and at the more recent four eras of computing. From this technological trajectory, we make some predictions, and raise three major dilemmas about where we are headed with automation and robotics. Within this positioning, the chapter then discusses where we are with service automation – one, and the latest of, six levers used to create high performing service organisations. We argue that service automation will be enormously impactful, and at the moment we are seeing only the early versions of the tools that can be developed and applied. The chapter also points out that we are still at the early stage of commercial adoption, but that robotic process automation, for example, was ramping up very quickly across 2015, and into 2016. The chapter fleshes out where we are; survey data gives insight into organisational appetite for service automation, the sourcing decisions being made, and the perceived effects.

In the course of our research we found quite a lot of confusion about automation generally, and RPA in particular. There is much hype, much loose use of terms, and the vocabulary can be obfuscating rather than helpful. Chapter 2 tries to set this straight by providing an exposition, with examples, of what RPA and other types of automation tools are, what they do and why they are being adopted.

Three chapters follow, each of which is an in-depth case of business service automation. As evidence, these are at the heart of the book. Early adopters of RPA are finding that automation can radically transform back offices, delivering much lower costs while improving service quality, increasing compliance (because everything the software does is logged), and decreasing delivery time. But as with all innovations, organisations must learn to manage RPA adoption to achieve maximum results. In these case studies, we describe implementations of RPA and share the lessons the clients learned. Two cases are particularly interesting in being clients who were early adopters, and who have matured their RPA capability over a long period. The third case is of more recent RPA adoption by a service provider – Xchanging – who implemented successfully, scaled to group-wide use, then also developed an RPA practice as a new line of business offered to clients.

In Chapter 6 we address a strong, emerging finding that the IT function needs to be onside early in any adoption of service automation and robotics. As found with other uses of 'lightweight' IT, service automation tools have implications for IT governance, security, IT architecture, infrastructure and business continuity that should not be ignored. We point out that such service automation tools can fit very easily into existing IT governance regimes and technology platforms, but that the long term development of those tools into an organisational automation capability requires them to be consistent with IT policies and modes of operation. The chapter details an RPA operating model derived from the experiences of early adopters.

One of the innovations we made in our 2014 book, *The Rise of Legal Services Outsourcing* (Bloomsbury), was to publish structured interviews with senior executives from clients, service providers and advisors 'in their own words', unfiltered and unedited. The innovation was very well received, and so, for this book and topic, we consulted 13 senior, highly experienced executives, and organised their responses into three chapters: one chapter for client respondents, one chapter for provider respondents, and one chapter for advisor respondents. These chapters provided very rich insights and in each chapter we cross-analysed their responses to derive common findings.

In the final chapter we bring things together by looking across all the evidence we have assembled. We provide an analysis and summary of 30 lessons on service automation. The book could have ended at that point, but it became clear, from the many presentations we made during the year, that audiences wanted us to address broader questions, and that the awe and anxieties about where technology – in this case automation and robotics - was headed are very much still with us. For this reason we address in detail present anxieties, and whether it is different 'this time.' With the technologies now and soon to be at our disposal, we ask the question whether 'can' translates into 'should'? We find that there are invariably optimists, pessimists and relativists when it comes to assessing the future development, benefits and downsides of technologies. This is definitely true in five areas of major concern – acceleration, employment, security, privacy and environmental sustainability – to which we give due weight. However we focus in much the greater detail on the future of jobs and work, and in reviewing all the major research studies and comparing them to our own findings from this book, we arrive at some major conclusions and predictions for the short term and long term. We envisage much transformation in the nature of work, but all developments will be at human instigation, and so we do have choices to make. Not all developments will be all good or all bad, but the newer technologies will be very pervasive, and the level of connectivity may cause them to escape much human oversight, or lead to unpredictable outcomes. In terms of design, application and control, as stakeholders in the technological future, we will always have work to do.

Acknowledgements

Since 1989, we have interviewed thousands of private and public sector clients, providers, and advisors in North America, Europe, Australasia, Asia, and Africa on the topic of sourcing business and information technology services. We therefore first and foremost thank the now over 3,000 executives across the globe who have participated in our research over the past 25 years. Without them our work just would not have been possible. Due to the sensitive nature of many of the topics we have chosen to study, some participants over the years have requested anonymity and so cannot be individually acknowledged. Participants who did not request anonymity in our most recent study of service automation are acknowledged in the appropriate places throughout this book.

For the present book, we would very much like to thank all the interviewees and people who have so generously contributed their time and information so willingly. We only have limited space to name anyone specifically but we do owe some enormous debts and would like to acknowledge them here.

Firstly, we thank the clients, providers and advisors who participated in the formal interviews conducted for this book. We thank the International Association of Outsourcing Professionals (IAOP), particularly CEO Debi Hamill and Michael Corbett, for working with us on surveys and presentations on Robotic Process Automation (see Chapter 2). We thank ISG, especially

Author's Introduction and Acknowledgements

Steve Hall, Rob Brindley, Paul Reynolds and Will Thoretz, for supporting the book's publication, and for the valued endorsement in the Preface. A very special thanks to all at Blue Prism, but especially CEO Alastair Bathgate, Chairman Jason Kingdon and CMO Patrick Geary, who had the confidence in us to support our research at a very early stage, and opened up many new research avenues. Special thanks to Patrick Geary for facilitating access to in-depth case studies, and for being a willing mine of information on every subject we threw at him.

We are ever thankful for the supportive research environments of our respective institutions. Mary thanks Dean Charles Hoffman and her colleagues at the University of Missouri, St. Louis. Leslie thanks his great colleagues at London School of Economics and Political Science for their patience, kindness and moral and intellectual support over ten years now.

Work is pleasurable only in the context of a fuller life. Leslie would like to thank his circle of family and friends for their forbearance and humour, and especially George, Catherine and Chrisanthi, not least for the getaway nights at the opera, and Andrew for persisting with the tennis, against odds. Above everything, love to his beloved wife Damaris, who brings joy to all life holds.

Mary thanks her parents, Dr. and Mrs. Paul Lacity, and her three sisters: Karen Longo, Diane Iudica, and Julie Owings. She thanks her closest friends, Jerry Pancio, Michael McDevitt, Beth Nazemi, and Val Graeser. Finally, her son, Michael Christopher Kuban, to whom this book and all things in her life are dedicated.

Lastly, many thanks to everyone at Steve Brookes Publishing, especially Stephanie Lester and Steve Brookes, for their superb quality, great service ethic, high speed, and competitive pricing. The very model of what automation and software, complemented by intelligent, cheerful, well-directed humans, can accomplish.

Chapter 1

Service Automation: The Bigger Picture

What's inside: *While the focus of this book is automation of business services using software, the current state of service automation is best understood by appreciating its broader historical context. In this chapter, we note that automation is not new but can, in fact, be traced back through history. We remind readers that all technologies raise ethical dilemmas. Jumping to the twentieth century and beyond, four eras of information and communication technologies provide the context for the rise of software robots used today to transform back office services. Presently, service automation comprises a variety of technologies, ranging from robotic process automation to cognitive intelligence. Recent surveys, including our own survey, show that business leaders see huge opportunities for the transformative possibilities of automation, but that the market is immature and needs educating on automation's real capabilities.*

1.1. Introduction

This book is about the transformation of services – including customer support, accounting, financial, human resources, information technology (IT) and many other business services – through software automation. We believe that the current state of service automation is best understood by appreciating its broader, historical context. Automation is not new and indeed it dates back to ancient times. Automation has always raised perennial issues about how far human capability can be enhanced by machines without adverse social, economic, political, and, increasingly, ecological consequences. At the heart of our relationship with technology is the question: *"Cui bono?"* For whose good? Who gains, or more crudely who wins, and, by implication, who loses? Another way of posing the dilemma: With technology capability, how far do we convert a 'can do' into a 'should do'? These are questions that have been asked throughout history, whether referring to examples such as gunpowder, the printing press, the steam engine, the machine gun, or nuclear power. And, of course, even the same person may answer the question differently depending on the role they inhabit at any one time – for example, as citizen of a city, of a country or of the world; as an employee or owner of a business; as a consumer or provider of products or services; as an inventor or user of the technology concerned. It is a question we will return to often throughout this book, including in the last chapter where our focus will be on the future consequences for work, of advances in information and communications technologies.

This chapter takes the reader from the ancient Greeks to 2025, focusing on the contexts for service automation. Software 'robots' used today to transform back office services lie on the shoulders of four eras of information and communication technologies (ICTs) – the System-Centric Era, the PC-Centric Era, the Network-Centric Era, and the Content-Centric Era. Today, service automation comprises a variety of technologies, ranging from robotic process automation (RPA) to cognitive intelligence (CI), that piggyback on the enabling technologies that were produced during these eras.

Recent surveys, including our own survey, show that senior leaders in charge of sourcing strategy and back office services see huge opportunities for the transformative possibilities of automation, but that the market is immature and needs educating on automation's true capabilities. We wrote this book to fill that need.

1.2. A Brief History of Automation

"It is unworthy of excellent men to lose hours like slaves in the labour of calculation which could safely be relegated to anyone else if machines were used." **Gottfried Wilhelm Leibniz, mathematician, philosopher, and inventor, 1685**

According to the *Encyclopedia Britannica*, a robot is *"any automatically operated machine that replaces human effort, though it may not resemble human beings in appearance or perform functions in a humanlike manner."* The word *'robot'* can refer to both physical robots and virtual software agents (or bots). Robots can be autonomous or semi-autonomous and range from humanoids such as: *"TOSY's Ping Pong Playing Robot (TOPIO) to industrial robots, medical operating robots, patent assist robots, dog therapy robots, collectively programmed swarm robots, UAV drones, and even microscopic nano robots. By mimicking a lifelike appearance or automating movements, a robot may convey a sense of intelligence, or thought, of its own."* (Wikipedia)

Many take the history of automation and robotics back to ancient times. To give a flavour, Archimedes (287-212BC) did not invent robots but he did invent many mechanical systems that are used in robotics today. The Hero of Alexandria, a mathematician, physicist and engineer wrote a book entitled *Automata* (in Greek meaning 'moving itself') detailing a range of devices, including an odometer mounted on a cart for measuring distance, a wind-powered organ and animated statues. In medieval times automatons - human-like figures run by hidden mechanisms - were used to impress church worshippers into believing in higher powers. Jumping ahead, as early as 1936, Alan Turing was already at work answering the question *"Can machines think?"* while his article *On Computable Numbers, with an application to the Entscheidungs problem*[1] provided a system for handling massive volumes of information at amazing speeds. In 1942, Isaac Asimov[2] wrote the *Three Laws of Robotics* – a fourth was added later (see last Chapter). While all this is very interesting, here we are going to focus on developments since the

1960s with the corporate and societal arrival of information communications technologies.

1.2.1. Eras of Computing

An understanding of the fundamental information and communications technology (ICT) shifts from the 1960s to the future of 2025, provides major context for exploring automation, robotics and their challenges and implications for organisations. David Moschella (1997) identified the four main eras in ICT in his book, *Waves of Power: The Dynamics of Global Technology Leadership, 1964-2010,* which the lead author applied in Willcocks, Venters and Whitley (2014) (see Figure 1.1).[3]

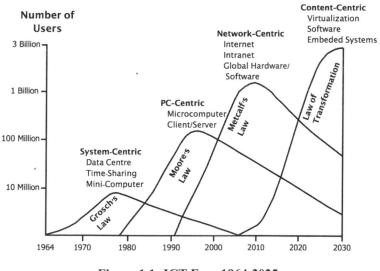

Figure 1.1: ICT Eras 1964-2025
(Adapted from Moschella 1997)

The Systems-Centric Era (1964-1981) began with the IBM S/360 series – the computer industry's first, broad group, of steadily upgradable, compatible, systems. The dominating principle through most of this period was that of Grosch's Law. Arrived at in the 1940s, this law stated that *"computer power increases as the square of the cost"* – that is, a computer that is twice as expensive delivers four times the computing power. This law favoured large systems development. From about 1975, a shift from centralised to business unit spending accelerated, aided by the availability of minicomputers and falling software and peripheral costs.

The PC-Centric Era (1981-1994) began with the arrival of the IBM PC in 1981. The sale of personal computers (PCs) went from $2 billion in 1980 to $160 billion in 1995. This period saw Grosch's Law inverted. By the mid-1980s the best price/performance was coming from PCs and other microprocessor-based systems.

The underlying economics was summarised in Moore's Law, named after one of the founders of Intel. Moore's Law stated that semiconductor price/ performance would double every two years for the foreseeable future. The prediction has remained fairly accurate into the 2000s, helped by constantly improved designs and processing volumes of market-provided rather than in-house developed microprocessor-based systems. The PC-centric era saw shifts from corporate, mostly proprietary, to individual, commodity computing. Technical advances provided business unit users with enormous access to cheap processing. ICT demand and expenditure were now coming from multiple points in organisations. From 1988 onwards, technical developments in distributed computing architecture, together with organisational reactions against local, costly, frequently inefficient microcomputer-based initiatives, led to a client/server investment cycle. The PC-centric era saw a massive explosion of personal computing, with, for example, some 63 million PCs built in 1995 alone. From the late 1980s one increasing response to rising computing costs – especially mainframe, network, telecommunications and support and maintenance – was outsourcing. This was mostly selective, but in some cases 'total' – that is handing over computing, representing over 80 percent of the IT budget, to third party management.

The Network–Centric Era (1994-2005). Though the Internet has existed for over 25 years, it was the arrival of the Mosaic graphical interface in 1993 that made possible mass markets based on the Internet and World Wide Web (www). This era was defined by the integration of worldwide communications infrastructure and general purpose computing. Restricting www. graphical capabilities as it does, communications bandwidth began to replace micro-processing power as the key commodity. Attention shifted from local area networks (LANs) to wide area networks, particularly Intranets. Even in the late 1990s there was already evidence of strong shifts of emphasis over time from graphical user interfaces to Internet browsers; indirect to on-line channels; client-server to electronic commerce; stand-alone PCs to bundled services and from individual productivity to virtual communities.[4] Economically, the pre–eminence of Moore's Law was being replaced by Metcalfe's Law, which states that *"the cost of a network rises linearly as additional nodes are added, but that the value can increase exponentially"*. Software economics have a similar pattern. Once software is designed, the marginal cost of producing additional copies is nearly zero, potentially offering huge economies of scale for the supplier. Combining network and software economics produces vast opportunities for value creation. At the same time the exponential growth of the number of Internet users from 1995 suggested that innovations that reduced use costs, whilst improving ease of use, would shape future developments, rather than, as previously, the initial cost of IT equipment.

By 1998 fundamental network-centric applications were email for messaging and the World Wide Web –the great majority of traffic on the latter being information access and retrieval. Transaction processing in the forms of electronic commerce for businesses, shopping and banking for consumers and voting and tax collection for governments, were also emerging. There were real challenges for the Internet's ability to provide levels of reliability, response times and data integrity comparable to traditional on-line transaction processing expectations. Dealing with these challenges had large financial implications. Markets were also developing for audio and video applications. A key technological change throughout was that most of the existing PC software base would need to become network-enabled. As more people went online, the general incentive to use the Internet increased, technical limitations notwithstanding. One possibility mooted at the time was that IT investment would lead to productivity. The breakthrough would be when corporations learned to focus computing priorities externally – on reaching customers, investors, suppliers, for example – instead of the historical inclination primarily towards internal automation, partly driven by inherited evaluation criteria and practices.

The Content-Centric Era (2005-2025). In 1997, David Moschella[5] made predictions about a fourth era. He outlined shifts from electronic commerce to virtual businesses; from the wired consumer to individualised services; from communications bandwidth to software; information and services – from on–line channels to customer pull – and from a converged computer/communications/consumer electronics industry value chain to one of embedded systems. A content-centric era of virtual businesses and individualised services would depend on the previous era delivering an inexpensive, ubiquitous and easy to use high bandwidth infrastructure. For the first time, demand for an application would define the range of technology usage rather than, as previously, also having to factor in what is technologically and economically possible. The ICT industry focus would shift from specific technological capabilities to software, content and services. The industry driver would truly be 'information economics', combining the nearly infinite scale economies of software with the nearly infinite variety of content.

Metcalfe's Law would be superseded by the Law of Transformation. A fundamental consideration is the extent to which an industry/business is bit (information) based as opposed to atom (physical product) based. In the content-centric era, the extent of an industry's subsequent transformation would be equal to the square of the percentage of that industry's value-added – accounted for by bit – as opposed to atom processing activity. The effect of the squared relationship would be to widen industry differentials. In all industries, but especially in the more 'bit–based' ones, describing and quantifying the full IT value chain would become as difficult an exercise as assessing the full 1990's value chain for electricity. At the time he wrote, Moschella's was an inspired guestimate about the future. As we detail in our 2014 book *Moving To The Cloud Corporation*[6], a lot has happened since to give his overall vision a great deal of plausibility.

1.2.2. The Rise of Automation and Robotics

Where do automation and robotics fit into this complex, technological trajectory shaping an emerging digital age?[7] The answer is they sit within, depend on, run parallel to and help form that technological trajectory. In 1964 the first artificial intelligence research laboratories were opened at MIT, Stanford and Edinburgh universities, while, in 1965, Carnegie Mellon established its Robotics Institute. Since then, we have seen increasing applications of robots across the developed economies in fields such as the military, energy, medical work, manufacturing, and industrial safety, to name just a few. Recent books like Martin Ford's The *Rise of the Robots* (2015), and Nicholas Carr's *The Glass Cage* (2015) chronicle well the increasing robotic usage in these spheres and also in traditional, as well as more digitally-based, service industries.[8] Citing self-driving cars, *Jeopardy!* champion supercomputers, and a variety of useful robots, Erik Brynjolffson and Andrew McAfee, in *The Second Machine Age* (2014), provide convincing evidence that we may well be at an inflection point with automation and robotics.[9] Crucial technology, in the form of microcontrollers, actuation, machine vision, sensors for motion and position tracking, image and voice recognition software and component miniaturisation has reached critical mass in terms of processing speed, connectivity, efficiency and cost effectiveness. These advances have dramatically increased the number of functions, and industries, that can be effectively served by robotics and automation. According to a 2015 ETF

Securities report[10], while robotic density in non-automotive industries is still low, the convergence of robot costs and wages encourages adoption. Moreover: *"automation and robotics are a critical necessity if the world is to maintain and improve its living standards as populations age and workforces shrink."*

Let's widen the focus further. In our view, based on several research streams through 2011-2016, six technological developments will, **in combination with cloud and each other,** create massive impacts over the next ten years on individuals, organisations, and businesses, and society. These six technological trends are (1) mobile Internet access, (2) the automation of knowledge work, (3) big data, (4) the Internet of Things, (5) robotics and (6) digital fabrication.[11] With an even bigger framing, a 2015 Ernst and Young report[12] posits six megatrends. Significantly, the first is the digital future, *"Fuelled by the convergence of social, mobile, cloud, big data and growing demand for anytime anywhere access to information, technology is disrupting all areas of the business enterprise."* The report, correctly in our view, suggests that digital is closely intertwined with expected transformations across the other five megatrends of: rising entrepreneurship, health reimagined, urbanisation, globalisation of marketplaces, and sustainable uses of planetary resources. For example, the report states *"big data, sensors and social applications will underpin the reimagining of health management. Digital technologies will drive the realisation of tomorrow's 'intelligent cities'. Digital oil fields will lead to increased savings and output in the energy space, while 'smart grids' will revolutionise the production, delivery and use of electricity worldwide. The ability to create digitally-based business models has lowered the barrier to creating new and innovative ventures for entrepreneurs around the world."*

1.3. Automation and Robotics: No Limits?

Faced with these impressive developments, it is important not to sell out to a technological determinism, that would see us carried along by waves of technology and the path dependencies they bring – increasingly beyond our control. Even if not yet known (though authors such as Nicholas Carr, Geoff Colvin, Wendell Wallach and Nicholas Agar have made many thoughtful suggestions) there will be important limits to how far these technologies can be developed, and what these technologies will be able to perform.[13] (We will focus again on this issue in our last chapter when looking at the future of technology and jobs). Moreover, all technologies originate in and pass through economic, business, social and political filters. As we have found in our many studies of ICTs across the four computing eras, with a few notable exceptions, the diffusion of technological innovation is rarely seamless; it is invariably a long road indeed from idea to adoption, usage, then institutionalisation.[14]

Technologies create great pathways and opportunities, yet three dilemmas – the digital technology enframing dilemma, the technology solutionism dilemma, and the great singularity dilemma – seem unavoidable.

1.3.1. The Digital Technology Enframing Dilemma

Our present automation and robotic capacity sits in the middle of, and has grown rapidly with, the exponential and on-going explosion of technological capability, widely predicted to show no sign of slowing over the next decade.[15] Gill Pratt,[16] in his 2015 article *Is a Cambrian Explosion Coming for Robotics?,* accurately and usefully details eight technical drivers: (1) the exponential growth in computing performance, (2) improvements in mechanical design tools and numerically controlled manufacturing tools, (3) improvements in electrical energy storage and (4) electronic power efficiency, (5) exponential expansion of the availability and performance of local wireless digital communications, and exponential growth of (6) the Internet, (7) worldwide

42

data storage, and (8) global computation power. It makes for a formidable and impressive list. In the middle of such developments, 'Can Do' for automation and robotics has become accelerated and exponential. A digital/technological enframing, to include automation and robotics, of how we operate in business, and indeed the world, seems unavoidable for the foreseeable future. But how do we manage this, step outside and make judgments about what the limits can and should be? We might call this the **Digital Technology Enframing** dilemma.

1.3.2. The Technology Solutionism Dilemma

Increasing ICT use and widespread process automation have both been partial solutions to an exponential data explosion challenge that they – ironically – have also been helping to create and accelerate. Will the increasing use of automation and robotics merely change the type and heighten the scale of the problems we have to solve? Relatedly, at the level of economic sector, automation and robotics will likely be experienced in the same way as previous technologies we have researched.[17] Starting as tools for competitive advantage, they may well become heavily adopted, thus levelling the playing field, but at a higher level, for the sector and its competing businesses. A competitive-edge weapon evolves instead into a defensive, commoditised, minimum entry requirement to compete. Put forward as a panacea, in practice automation and robotics may create as many new problems as they solve. Following Eugeny Morozov in his 2013 book *To Save Everything, Click Here*[18], we might call this the **Technology Solutionism** dilemma.

1.3.3. The Great Singularity Dilemma

The exponential acceleration in technology and data shapes a future where business activity shifts beyond human capacity to operate within the relevant work processes. Machines will increasingly be needed to work with machines, while cloud computing will allow a much higher degree of connectivity between those machines, be they computers, sensors, robots, pieces of software, or assembled systems, for example. Just looking at robots: the ability to interconnect robots through developments in cloud robotics will revolutionise robot capabilities. Gill Pratt sees the potential gains summarised in four big ideas. Firstly, memory-based autonomy becomes possible through the exponential growth in computing and storage performance. Robots can search and match large numbers of memories of prior experiences to guide response. Progress on fast search algorithms for Internet information has accelerated memory-based approaches. Secondly, high speed sharing of experiences with other robots is enabled. Thirdly, a cloud computing robot 'brain' could learn from imagination, using simulation to explore circumstances that may be faced by a robot in the future and to experiment with solutions, remembering only those that worked. Finally, robots may learn from people – as we shall see with robotic process automation, they already do. Perception remains a challenging component of robot autonomy. But large data sets now available to catalyse perception have proven highly useful. And the online repository of visually recorded objects and human activity is a vast resource that robots are already exploiting to improve their ability to understand and interact with the world, including interactions with human beings.[19]

Where is all this headed? Ray Kurzweil's 2005 book[20] *The Singularity is Near: When humans transcend biology* follows a line flowing from John von Neumann in the 1950s in believing that the first truly intelligent machine will be built in the late 2020s. Extending this idea, one of his important predictions is that we will inevitably merge with machines in the future. For example, brain implants will dramatically enhance human intelligence. Techno-sapiens indeed. But such cognitive amplification will be needed if we are to understand and maintain control of technology beyond the Singularity – the disruption point at which the human era will end, due around 2045. This remarkably techno-utopian view of the future needs balancing, as Singularians, like Kurzweil, rarely addresses the challenges, problems and the *cui bono* questions inherent in such a positive techno-vision. With humans imprisoned and diminutive within our machines, while also seemingly in control and enhanced, De Chirico's great painting El Gran Automata (see book cover and Introduction) provides a vital counterpoint. Steering between Kurzweil and De Chirico leads us to posit a third dilemma for automation and robotics, and indeed the management of technology as a whole. We will call this, the **Great Singularity** dilemma.

We have suggested here important limitations and dilemmas inherent in the belief that technology is, and will be, an unmitigated good for individuals, organisations, business and society. With the caveats noted, we proceed with where service automation is mostly happening today: back offices.

1.4. Technology in Play: Transforming Back Offices with Service Automation

Service automation is having its most profound effects on 'back offices' and it is seen as one of six levers used to create high-performing service organisations. Back offices are where the operational support systems for services are created, managed, and delivered. Back offices from highly competitive industries like telecommunications, utilities, financial services and health care through to government agencies worldwide are ever under pressure to contain costs. But cost efficiency must be balanced with other performance imperatives such as service excellence, business enablement, scalability, flexibility, security, and compliance. From 25 years of research, we learned that low-performing back offices can be transformed to high-performance through five main transformation levers: **centralise** physical facilities and budgets, **standardise** processes across business units, **optimise** processes to reduce errors and waste, **relocate** from high-cost to low-cost destinations, and **technology enable** with, for example, self-service portals.[21] Further developments in automation, including software robots, have added a sixth lever (see Figure 1.2.).[22]

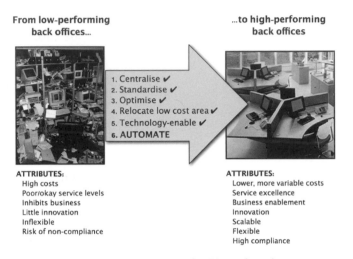

**Figure 1.2: Six Levers for Transforming
Back Office Services**

For the past 15 years, large companies have widely adopted the first five transformation levers to the point that they have become *institutionalised* – that is, an accepted and normal part of managing back offices. However, only in the last three years has the real power of service automation been unleashed. Furthermore, it is important to understand that service automation comprises a number of different technologies with, often, puzzling terminologies. While conducting this research, for example, the clients, providers, and advisors used the following terms to discuss service automation: scripting tools, robotic process automation (RPA), cognitive intelligence (CI), machine intelligence, artificial intelligence, cognitive learning technology, autonomic platforms, cognitive computing, and business process management (BPM), as some common examples. To help clarify the service automation space, a number of advisory firms have organised the variety of tools along a service automation continuum. HfS, for example, offers a rich picture of what it calls the Intelligent Automation Continuum in the *In Their Own Words: Provider Responses* chapter of this book. HfS maps the service automation tools based on the character of the process and the character of the data. As another example, the Everest Group usefully distinguishes the tools by its 'intelligence', generating three classes of tools: rules-based automation, knowledge-based automation, and artificial intelligence.[23]

Using the client examples we gather for this book, we thought about the service automation as a Cartesian plane with the volume of work and degree of work complexity as a good way to classify the examples of service automation we studied (see Figure 1.3). Process complexity increases as the data and rules become less structured, as the number of steps increases, and as the amount and variety of data increases.

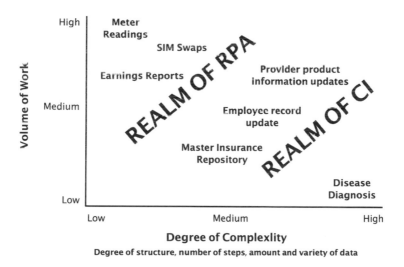

Figure 1.3: Service Automation Landscape

The majority of our service automation case examples in this book adopted Robotic Process Automation. Some of the examples listed in Figure 1.3 will be covered in detail in subsequent chapters, including the examples of meter readings in Chapter 2, SIM Swaps in Chapter 3, master insurance repository updates in Chapter 4, corporate earnings reports, employee record updates and provider product information updates in the clients' contributions for the *In Their Own Words: Client Responses* chapter. These clients adopted RPA for processes characterised by a medium to high volume of transactions and a low to medium degree of process complexity. In contrast, Cognitive Intelligence – defined here as software that finds patterns amongst a vast amount and large variety of data – is well suited for highly complex tasks with low daily volumes (as of 2016). From what we have seen, IBM's Watson is the 'übermaschine' in this CI class. One application of IBM's Watson is cancer disease diagnosis – a highly complex task with perhaps hundreds of thousands of inputs with various levels of structure, but with only a few dozen transactions per day. As of 2013, Watson had access to over two million pages from medical journals, more than 600,000 pieces of medical evidence, and 1.5 million patient records.[24] Watson has an unparalleled natural language interface and ranks its top answers with confidence intervals and the ability for humans to query Watson about where and how it got those answers. The capability differences between RPA and CI are reflected in its prices and maturity, as discussed next.

By early 2016, back office service automation using RPA was still a small market (under $3 billion revenues[25]), though RPA usage was ramping up very quickly in major companies and service providers alike[26]. The main concerns surrounding its reception were: Are the business benefits worthwhile? (It turns out that they are very much worthwhile). How far does service automation adversely impact job types and numbers? (Our researched cases show no great effects at the early stages of use, but during 2014 and 2015 some service providers announced very large headcount reductions, which they attribute to their adoption of automation). How quickly and easily can it be adopted? (Our research shows rapid implementation and easy use). At the same time we, along with other studies, found a lack of client knowledge and/or buy-in being a major barrier to RPA deployment.[27] Clearly at this moment in time, most of the major technology questions we asked in previous sections will apply more seriously only as RPA scales and combines with other technologies, especially cloud. However, RPA will certainly affect the economics of service delivery. One source estimates that the salary of a BPO worker may be $60,000 onshore and $23,000 offshore, but RPA software performing the work of one full time equivalent (FTE) may cost as little as $7,500.[28] Consequently, we believe RPA will have a profound effect on sourcing decisions. We will pick up in more detail the early and likely impact of RPA in our cases (see especially chapters 3, 4, and 5) and in surveys by ourselves and others.

As of late 2015, RPA was still only at the early majority stage of adoption. Meanwhile, more advanced forms of CI were still either being piloted at client sites, or still on the drawing board for future commercial development. CI's price tags reflect its stage of maturity and its ability to deal with highly complex tasks – with implementations costing millions of dollars as of the end of 2015. Future evolution would seem to begin with RPA, which is optimally used with high volume, standardised, rules-based mature stable processes where costs are clear and business value well understood. HfS/ KPMG have suggested a continuum into 'autonomic platforms' – service providers like GenFour and CapGemini already use the term for offering multiple types of automation software – followed by 'cognitive computing' and 'true artificial intelligence'.[29;30] These advances will move the focus from automating structured to unstructured patterned then unstructured, pattern-less data/information. Meanwhile the robotic software will increasingly be able to deal with rules-based, dynamic processes, and carry out advanced judgement and decision-making tasks.[31] We anticipate an accelerating take-up of multiple forms of automation across 2016, as executives acquire detailed understanding of specific products and applications, and gain confidence on automation implementability, reliability, and business benefits.

By early 2016, some RPA adopters in our research had automated over 35 percent of their back office transactions. Depending on the existing state of back office finance and accounting operations, Everest Group (2015) found cost reduction through applying RPA in the back office ranging from 15 to 30 percent of additional savings beyond labour-arbitrage (offshore) based savings. Thus the total savings could go as high as 65 percent for onshore operations. Clients and several research studies report significant, multiple, often simultaneous benefits ranging across cost, process efficiency accuracy, security, business continuity, regulatory compliance, speed, reliability, error reduction, and improved customer satisfaction.[32] Once corporate users pilot and adopt RPA, all report greatly expanded RPA usage – both in volume and extension to new processes. The new breed of automation software providers includes Blue Prism, Automation Anywhere, IPsoft, and UiPath. We found many of their tools easy to use. Business operation people, including those with process expertise but no programming experience, can be trained within a few weeks to automate processes. Business operations groups from companies such as the Associated Press, Ascension Health, some major utilities, American Express, Xchanging, Leeds Building Society, and Telefónica O2 have been using RPA to automate processes quickly – often with limited help from centralised IT. But business executives and service professionals need to ramp up quickly on what RPA can and cannot do for their organisations.

1.5. Service Automation So Far: Survey Findings

Having established what service automation is, we will now explore findings on how service automation is developing and being received. HfS Research (2015) found in their survey work that cloud computing and mobile technologies are today's driving forces, while RPA tools and cognitive computing platforms are tomorrow's. They portray a very dynamic marketplace since 2012 suggesting that *"intelligent automation components are central to the strategies of every ITO/BPO service provider and many of the largest shared service center/global business service operations today."*[33]

Deployments are going beyond proof-of-concepts. Service providers have trialled multiple solutions and selected different contextual partners. Focused consultancies and service providers have emerged. Commercial contracts in sole sourced and advised deals consistently include RPA and cognitive automation components. Centralised, cross-contract investment funds are being put aside for robotic process and cognitive automation development. In their larger 2015 study of the shift to what they call an As-A-Service economy, Phil Fersht and Barbra McGann found over 50 percent of enterprise buyers seeing smarter analytics, automation and pro-active operations staff as having massive impact (above all other factors) if they had this combination in action today.[34]

In their 2015 survey work, Everest Group were finding service automation more prevalent and increasing in outsourcing renewals (28 percent of deals in 2014), with adoption in new deals also on the rise (12 percent of deals in 2014). They also found an exponential increase in Service Delivery Automation (SDA) solution launches (1,300 percent) between 2011 and 2014. BPO providers were definitely formalising their strategies to leverage SDA technologies, while new wave providers were also emerging.[35] To consolidate and enrich this emerging picture and to frame the in-depth case studies in chapters 3, 4 and 5 of this book, in 2015 we carried out our own survey, whose results we now detail.

1.5.1. About Our Survey

We surveyed the attendees of the 2015 Outsourcing World Summit (OWS) during the client-only and provider/advisor-only networking sessions. The sample of 143 completed surveys comprises 63 clients, 64 providers, 15 advisors, and 1 provider/advisor. We summarised the results and asked three service automation experts to reflect on the findings: Alastair Bathgate, CEO and Co-Founder of Blue Prism; Rob Brindley, ISG Director, Robotic Process Automation and Media Industry; and Sarah Burnett, Vice President of Research at the Everest Group (all three also contribute additional insight in the *In Their Own Words* chapters later in this book).

The client respondents are senior leaders in charge of sourcing strategy, governance, procurement and provider management. They are responsible for IT Infrastructure, software development, financial and accounting, human resource, logistics, call centre, and/or research & development services and outsourcing relationships within their organisations. Client respondents represented organisations from a variety of industries including financial services, software, technology, engineering services, manufacturing, aerospace, pharmaceuticals, life sciences, healthcare, and other industries (see Figure 1.4).

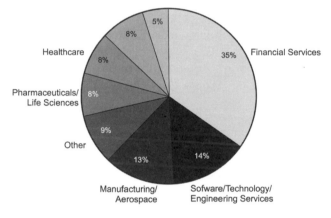

Figure 1.4: Client Industries Represented
(n=63 client respondents)

To get an indicator as to the size of organisations represented, we asked respondents to estimate the number of employees their companies employ world-wide. The size of client firms is found in Figure 1.5. and the size of provider/advisor firms in Figure 1.6. Nearly half the client firms have over 50,000 employees world-wide. The majority of provider and advisor firms employed fewer than 10,000 employees.

1.5.2. Organisational Appetite for Service Automation

Survey respondents were asked to comment on the state of service automation in their own organisations. Specifically, respondents were asked the degree to which they agreed with a statement using a seven point scale, with a '1' indicating 'strongly disagree' and a '7' indicating 'strongly agree'. The mean responses are found in Table 1.1.

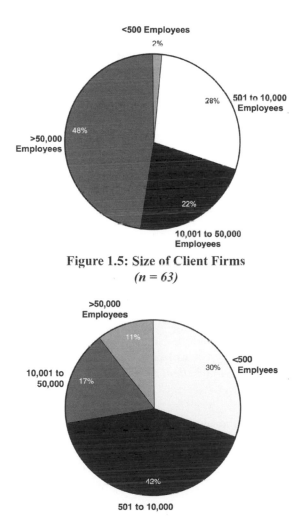

Figure 1.5: Size of Client Firms
(n = 63)

Figure 1.6: Size of Provider/Advisor Firms
(n=76)

Survey Question: Client Version	Average Client Response (n = 63)	Survey Question: Provider Version	Average Provider/ Advisor Response (n = 80)
1. My *organisation* places a great priority on automation of services.	4.5	**1.** My *organisation* places a great priority on automation of services.	4.5
2. My *organisation* increasingly expects services to be more automated.	6.0	**2.** My *clients* increasingly expect services to be more automated.	5.3

(1 = strongly disagree; 7 = strongly agree)

Table 1.1: Perceived Importance of Service Automation

Overall, clients 'slightly agreed' that client organisations place a great priority on service automation and 'strongly agreed' that services will be increasingly automated in the future. Additionally, nearly half of clients indicated that between 26 and 50 percent of their existing services are suitable for some automation (see Figure 1.7). An additional quarter of the clients thought that between 51 and 75 percent could be automated.

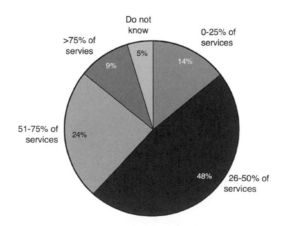

Figure 1.7: Percentage of client services suitable for automation
(n = 63 client responses)

Alastair Bathgate of Blue Prism commented about service automation opportunities, *"It's really interesting to see the range of processes that are suitable for automation in back offices. The RPA programs clients are rolling out grow over time, with more mature clients having 25 to 50 percent of their back office workforce now manned by software robots, representing several hundred FTEs."*

Provider and advisor survey respondents slightly agreed that their organisations place a great priority on service automation. They also slightly agreed that their clients' services will be increasingly automated in the future. We asked Rob Brindley of ISG and Sarah Burnett of Everest Group to discuss what they see as far as providers prioritising automation as a service delivery capability. Rob Brindley increasingly has seen providers incorporate automation into the technical solutions of their service proposal, *"This is particularly evident with top tier providers who have developed or incorporated third-party automation enablement technology to improve the value proposition of their proposals in a highly competitive market, and to drive out cost of their services."*

Sarah Burnett agreed that service providers have accelerated their focus on automation, *"BPO providers are clearly prioritising automation very highly and we are seeing rapid increases in the offerings of automation technologies. Within IT, automation is an older story and not changing as rapidly."*

1.5.3. Automation and Sourcing Decisions

Clients can automate services using several sourcing options – they can do it all themselves, seek the help of an advisory firm, or rely on their service providers to automate for them. Sarah Burnett told us, *"If clients want providers to bundle their tools into the pricing for services, we will see a move to greater output-based pricing. However, if fears of 'technology lock-in' dominate, they will opt for breaking technology apart from services and utilise providers for the skills and expertise, not their proprietary tools and configuration libraries."*

In the survey, we asked clients, providers, and advisors about the effects of service automation on clients' sourcing decisions (see Table 1.2). On average, clients are NOT taking the lead on service automation. Most clients agreed that they rely on providers to automate client services. However, clients indicated that in their sourcing decisions, costs and quality of a provider's staff are more important than a provider's automation capabilities. Talent still trumps technology when choosing among providers.

Survey Question: Client Version	Average Client Response (n = 63)	Survey Question: Provider Version	Average Provider/ Advisor Response (n = 80)
3. My *organisation* is taking the lead on automating business services—we are not waiting for providers to help us.	3.0	3. My *clients* are taking the lead on automating business services—they are not waiting for providers to help them.	4.1
4. My *organisation* needs help in assessing how automation could affect our business and IT services.	4.5	4. My *clients* need help in assessing how automation could affect their business and IT services.	5.0
5. My *organisation* primarily relies on service providers to automate business services.	5.0	5. My *clients* primarily rely on service providers to automate business services.	4.7
6. My *organisation* places heavy weight upon providers' automation capabilities *when choosing among different providers.*	4.0	6. My *organisation* places heavy weight upon our automation capabilities *when selling services to clients.*	4.4
7. My *organisation* is more concerned about the cost and quality of staff than with automation *when making sourcing decisions.*	5.0	7. My *organisation* is more concerned about the cost and quality of our staff than with automation *when selling services to clients.*	4.3

(1 = strongly disagree; 7 = strongly agree)

Table 1.2: Automation and Sourcing Decisions

Rob Brindley of ISG corroborated the survey finding that clients still care more about the provider's people than technology, but added, *"However, clients are continuously looking for providers to demonstrate how they will be more efficient and productive. Initially, this was through process discipline and efficiency, and then labor arbitrage. Providers are now differentiating themselves through the use of technology and automation to create value for the client. Additionally, where clients have sourced, we are seeing providers utilise automation as a method to satisfy their committed innovation requirements."*

Provider and advisor survey respondents shared the same perceptions as clients on these sourcing questions, except for their perceptions regarding client-led automation. Whereas clients reported they were NOT taking the lead on services automation, providers and advisors neither agreed nor disagreed that clients were taking the lead. Our survey showed that, while the average client is not leading the automation charge, clearly some pioneering clients are forging ahead. What does the typical client look like, that comes directly to a software vendor for service automation? Alastair Bathgate of Blue Prism told us, *"The clients are normally large/Fortune 500 companies, but SME organisations are also realising the benefits of the low costs of entry to robotic automation programs. The typical buyer is the senior business management that owns the headcount for these administration roles and is looking for improvements in the efficiency and effectiveness of their operations."*

1.5.4. Perceived Effects of Service Automation

"In the continuing search for business process cost efficiency, automation is truly the next big thing. It not only promises cost savings, but other benefits such as reduced errors, faster operations, and 24/7 coverage."
Everest Group Report[36]

We asked clients, providers, and advisors to step outside their own organisations to reflect more broadly on the effects of service automation (see Table 1.3). Overall, respondents 'strongly agreed' that automation can reduce costs and improve service quality.

Alastair Bathgate of BluePrism said, *"The benefits of automation go well beyond the commercial savings which are very tangible and quickly realised. Clients see dramatic cost savings depending on the types of processes automated and the existing costs of the operation. Most automations pay back in six to 12 months. The other key benefits are increases in accuracy and 'right first-time' processing (with all the downstream benefits as up to 60 percent of work is re-work because of errors), improvements in regulatory compliance, business insight and analytics from automated processes, speed of delivery and operational agility in business operations."*

	Average Client Response (n = 63)	Average Provider/ Advisor Response (n = 80)
8. I think service automation can significantly reduce or avoid costs.	6.5	5.9
9. I think service automation can improve service quality.	6.0	5.9
10. I think service automation is an evolving model that is years away from business reality.	3.5	4.2
11. I think service automation will affect sourcing location decisions by making labour arbitrage less important.	5.0	5.0
12. I think service automation is already altering the underlying economics of service delivery	Not Asked	5.2

(1 = strongly disagree; 7 = strongly agree)

Table 1.3: Perceived Effects of Service Automation

Client survey respondents 'slightly disagreed' that service automation is an evolving model that is years away from a business reality whereas providers and advisors 'slightly agreed' it was years away. The differences are statistically significant. We asked Sarah Burnett of Everest Group to ruminate on this difference, *"The adoption rate of automation is one of the most interesting dynamics facing this market. On the one hand, client organisations that learn about automation are generally eager to embrace it quickly. On the other hand, organisations that have actually implemented extensive automation programs report that it is a multi-year journey. Although some deployments are actually quite easy and require only a matter of a few weeks or months, most programs report that there are many barriers to rapidly scaling an automation program across the myriad of potential processes – lack of skills, other priorities, concerns from corporate IT groups, and the normal resistance to change. This suggests that automation will have a meaningful impact over roughly a five year period – some will see it more quickly, but at an aggregate level across the market it will take some time."*

All survey respondents 'slightly agreed' that service automation makes labour arbitrage less important when making sourcing location decisions. Providers and advisors also agreed with the statement, *"I think service automation is already altering the underlying economics of service delivery"*. Think about this: If 50 percent or more of tasks can be automated, then labour arbitrage becomes a less important factor when selecting between onshore and offshore locations. The onshore team can be highly skilled knowledge workers that deal with complex transactions, handle the exceptions the software cannot execute, and design and onboard new services. Yes, the onshore team is expensive, but the overall cost per transaction remains low when automation is a significant part of service delivery.

1.5.5. Survey Implications

"Automation (RPA) is certainly here to stay, and will continue to evolve to become truly cognitive, with effective application, cost, and reliability to significantly benefit the client." **Rob Brindley, ISG**

So what have we learned? Overall, clients, providers, and advisors agreed that services will increasingly become more automated, that service automation offers a variety of benefits, and that service automation is and will increasingly affect sourcing decisions. Today, most clients expect providers to take the lead in service automation, but they still focus more on costs and quality of staff when choosing among providers.

Considering both the survey results and expert commentaries, clients seem to be in various stages of adoption. Many need help in traversing the hype and realities.

1.6. Conclusion

In this chapter we have described the bigger picture of ICT developments over four eras of computing, to which the rise of service automation and robotics has contributed but also been shaped by. In this framework we pointed out that six technological developments - mobile Internet access, the automation of knowledge work, big data, the Internet of Things, robotics and digital fabrication – will, **in combination with cloud and each other,** create massive impacts over the next ten years – on individuals, organisations as well as business, economic and social life.

However we have questioned whether technological developments can, and should, form a 'no limits' trajectory – not least because all such technologies originate in and pass through economic, business, social and political filters. We also know that the diffusion of technological innovation has been and will be rarely anything approaching seamless. We pointed to at least three major dilemmas that stakeholders in organisations, business and society will confront, and need to deliberate and make decisions on. We called these the Digital Technology Enframing, the Technology Solutionsim and Great Singularity dilemmas. We questioned the degree to which the 'can do' provided by these technologies translates into a 'should do', pointing out five major areas of digital peril highlighted in the literature – acceleration, employment, security, privacy and environmental sustainability.

These major trends contextualise developments in service automation and robotics – the primary focus of this book. The survey findings provide strong evidence that the market as a whole needs much education on service automation and robotics. In the next chapter, we provide an introduction to Robotic Process Automation (RPA), outlining the relevant terminology and definitions, its capability, and its promise, while acknowledging that clients, even more than providers, are mostly still at the low end of any RPA maturity curve.

Citations

[1] Turing, A. (1936), *On Computable Numbers, with an application to the Entscheidungs problem, Proceedings of the London Mathematical Society*, 42 (2): 230-265.

[2] First published as *Runaround* in the March 1942 issue of *Astounding Science Fiction;* Later published in Asimov, I. (1950), *I, Robot,* (New York: Doubleday & Company),

[3] Willcocks, L., Venters, W. and Whitley, E. (2014) *Moving To The Cloud Corporation* (Palgrave Macmillan, London).

[4] Dertouzos, M. (1997). *What Will Be: How The New World Of Information Will Change Our Lives. (*Harper Edge, New York). See also Hagel, J. and Armstrong, A. (1997). *Net Gain: Expanding Markets Through Virtual Communities.* (Harvard Business School Press, Boston).

[5] Moschella, D. (1997) *Waves Of Power: Dynamics of Global Technology Leadership 1964-2010.* (Amacom, New York).

[6] Willcocks, Venters and Whitley (2014) op. cit. especially chapters 8 and 9.

[7] Automation uses technology to replace a series of human actions. We need to distinguish IT automation from Service automation. IT automation improves the core IT functionality and is handled by the IT system management tools, and owned by central IT. Service automation for business processes, which we will focus on in this book, is very different but also highly dependent on IT and software. Service automation combines multiple technologies. As Everest Group (2014) points out: *"Traditional Business Process Management (BPM) technologies can be further enhanced by combining with newer User Interface/robotic process tools. Or a cognitive artificial intelligence tool can help structure and clean data before it is passed through a process tool that will identify exceptions to be handled manually. Further, the entire process need not be fully automated – partial automation is also highly valuable and the most common approach."* See Everest Group (2014) Service Delivery Automation Market in 2014. Everest Group Market Report, October.

[8] Carr, N. (2015) *The Glass Cage: Where automation is taking us.* (The Bodley Head, London). Also Ford, M. (2015) *Rise Of The Robots: Technology and the threat of a jobless future.* (Basic Books, New York).

[9] Brynjolfsson, E. and McAfee, A. (2014). *The Second Machine Age: Work, progress and prosperity in a time of brilliant technologies.* (WW Norton & Co., New York).

[10] Go UCITS ETF (2015). *Welcome To The Age of Automation.* ETF Securities, London.

11 Willcocks, Venters and Whitley (2014) op. cit. especially chapters 8 and 9.

12 Ernst and Young (2015). *Megatrends 2015 – Making sense of a world in motion.* (Ernst and Young, London).

13 See Colvin G. (2015) *Humans Are Underrated: What high achievers know that brilliant machines never will.* (Nicholas Brealey, London). Carr, N. (2015) *The Glass Cage: Where automation is taking us.* (The Bodley Head, London). Agar, N. (2015) *The Sceptical Optimist: Why technology is not the answer to everything.* (Oxford University Press, Oxford). Wallach, W. (2015) *A Dangerous Master: How to keep technology slipping beyond our control.* (Basic Books, New York).

14 See Willcocks, Venters and Whitley (2014) op. cit. chapters 6.

15 See Willcocks et al. (2014) op. cit. chapter 8; Brynjolfsson, E. and McAfee, A. (2014). *The Second Machine Age: Work, progress and prosperity in a time of brilliant technologies.* (WW Norton & Co., New York); Pratt, G. (2015), *"Is a Cambrian Explosion Coming For Robotics?" Journal of Economic Perspectives,* 29, 3, 51-60; Ford, M. (2015) *Rise Of The Robots: Technology and the threat of a jobless future.* (Basic Books, New York).

16 See Pratt, G. (2015), *Is a Cambrian Explosion Coming For Robotics? Journal of Economic Perspectives,* 29, 3, 51-60.

17 See Willcocks, L., Petherbridge, P. and Olson, N. (2004) *Making IT Count: Strategy, delivery, infrastructure.* (Butterworth Heinemann, Oxford).

18 See Morozov, E. (2013) *To Save Everything, Click Here: Technology, solutionism and the urge to fix problems that don't exist.* (Penguin, New York).

19 See Pratt, G. (2015), *Is a Cambrian Explosion Coming For Robotics? Journal of Economic Perspectives,* 29, 3, 51-60.

20 See Kurzweil, R. (2005) *'The Singularity is Near: When humans transcend biology'* (Gerald Duckworth, London); Lacity and Willcocks (2015), *Keys To World Class BPO.* (Bloomsbury Press, London). See also www.lse.ac.uk/ management/research/outsourcingunit for full details and publications.

22 Lacity, M., and Willcocks, L., (2015), *Nine Keys to World-class Business Process Outsourcing* (Bloomsbury, London).

23 Everest Group (2014), *Service Delivery Automation Market in 2014: Moving Business Process Services Beyond Labor Arbitrage*, White paper EGR-2014-1-R-1264.

24 *"IBM's Watson is better at diagnosing cancer than human doctors"*, Wired, February 11, 2013, http://www.wired.co.uk/news/archive/2013-02/11/ibm-watson-medical-doctor.

25 RPA software vendor revenues were around $500 million, but the figure

includes RPA hidden in BPO service providers' broader offerings.

[26] Slaby, J. (2012) *Robotic Automation Emerges As A Threat To Traditional Low-cost Outsourcing.* (HfS Research paper, HFS, Boston).

[27] Everest Group (2015) point to additional barriers in legacy systems and service delivery, lack of adequate process documentation, employee sensitivities, and service provider hesitation (will they cannibalise their own business model?). See Everest Group (2015) *Service Delivery Automation - The business case for RPA in Finance and Accounting.* Everest Group Market report, March.

[28] http://www.operationalagility.com

[29] According to HfS, the key characteristics of autonomics are self-learning and self remediation. See HFS Research (2015) *Autonomics Advances The Conversation Beyond RPA,* July, www.hfsresearch.com/autonomics. By mid 2015, TCS had announced its ignio 'neural automation' platform, Ayehu has entered the market with confined capabilities at reduced licensing costs and Arago announced its international expansion out from its German roots.

[30] According to Cliff Justice of KPMG (2015) Cognitive RPA set to disrupt the knowledge worker market. June 25th www.kpmg - institutes.com, cognitive platforms have the ability to parse context and understand meaning like [IBM's] Watson [supercomputer] did in Jeopardy: *"As that technology merges with robotic task automation... you have technology that can understand your customers and run queries against rules engines. If the response falls within parameters, the technology can inform the robot to carry out a transaction and actually do things that in the past required decisions."*

[31] Sutherland, C. (2015) Presentation on The Intelligent Automation Continuum at the *HfS Intelligent Automation Webinar,* August 27th.

[32] See Burnett, S. (2015). *Overview of SDA, Definitions and the Business Case For SDA.* Everest Group Webinar *Service Delivery Automation: The Next Big Thing.* Webinar, 26th February. Also Everest Group (2014) *Service Delivery Automation Market in 2014.* Everest Group Market Report, October. Also Willcocks, L., Lacity, M. and Craig, A. (2015) *Robotic Process Automation at Telefonica O2* LSE Outsourcing Unit paper 15/03 (LSE, London) and *Robotic Process Automation at Xchanging* LSE Outsourcing Unit paper 15/03 (LSE, London). Also Sutherland, C. (2015) *The Raw Truth About Intelligent Automation.* HfS Research, Boston, September. Those studies of actual RPA implementations mentioned above report additional benefits over time in terms of error reduction, improved governance and compliance, lower recruitment, training and office costs, optimising operations and IT infrastructure, further speeding up processing, and scaling up automation and extending automation to more processes.

33 Sutherland, C. (2015) Presentation on The Intelligent Automation Continuum at the *HfS Intelligent Automation Webinar,* August 27[th,] 2015.

34 Fersht, P. and McGann, B. (2015) *Beware Of The Smoke, Your Platform Is Burning.* HfS Research, Boston, June. The main components of the As-A-Service economy are design thinking, business cloud, intelligent automation, proactive intelligence, intelligent data, writing off legacy, brokers of capability (client staff) and intelligent engagement (with service providers). The survey also shows lack of definitive investments into analytics and RPA so far. This fits with the bigger picture of nearly 70 percent of large enterprises 'kicking the can down the road' when it comes to delivering As-A-Service in the next five years, whereas service providers seem more attuned, and even see themselves already delivering on the concept.

35 Ranjan, R. (2015) *SDA Adoption, Service Providers and Market Outlook.* Everest Group Webinar Service *Delivery Automation: The Next Big Thing.* Webinar, 26th February.

36 http://www.everestgrp.com/2015-02-service-delivery-automation-the-next-big-thing-webinar-16554.html

Chapter 2

What is Robotic Process Automation?

What's Inside: *Robotic Process Automation (RPA) is one type of service automation software. In this chapter, we explain what RPA is, how it differs from other automation tools, and why it is most suited for automating mature, standard, rules-based, and high-volume processes. In particular, RPA is well suited for tasks in which a human being takes data from one form of digital inputs, transforms the inputs following structured rules, and passes the transformed digital outputs to another computer system.*

2.1. Introduction

In the previous chapter, we discussed that service automation covers a continuum of software products, each aimed at automating or supplementing different types of human tasks. The service automation continuum ranged from Robotic Process Automation (RPA) to Cognitive Intelligence (CI). Although CI, as best illustrated by IBM's Watson, is perhaps the more exciting end of the continuum, most organisations begin at the RPA end. Indeed, the detailed client adoption stories covered in the next three chapters are all RPA adoptions. For potential adopters of service automation, it makes sense to gain first a deeper understanding of RPA. This chapter aims to provide that understanding. We examine here the concept of the software robot, distinctive features of RPA, and provide a guide to RPA terminology. We also point to the processes most suitable for RPA.

2.2. The Software Robot Concept

It is important to know that **an RPA 'robot' is not a physical robot**. Although the term 'Robotic Process Automation' connotes visions of physical robots wandering around offices performing human tasks, RPA is a software-based solution, a so-called 'software robot', but not normal software. According to Jason Kingdon, chairman of Blue Prism: *"They call it a robot because it's attempting to have all the characteristics of a virtual human."* However, it is an infinitely scalable virtual human that can be instructed very quickly in order to carry out operational procedures at the speed of a machine, which means the cost line can radically move down, therefore more work suddenly becomes absolutely within scope.

In RPA parlance, a 'software robot' is equivalent to one software license. For business processes, the term RPA most commonly refers to configuring the software to do the work previously done by people. Everest Group (2014) usefully defines RPA as a sub-set of overall business process service delivery automation. It refers to automation that interacts with a computer-centric process through the user interface of the software supporting that process. It processes structured data.[1] RPA software is ideally suited to replace humans for so-called 'swivel chair' processes. These are processes where humans take inputs from one set of systems (such as email), process those inputs using rules, and then enter the outputs into systems of record (like Enterprise Resource Planning (ERP) systems). See Figure 2.1.

Consider, for example, a human resource (HR) specialist who is in charge of onboarding new employees for a large company. The onboarding process likely entails logging on and off a dozen systems to set up a new employee with benefits, payroll, email, voicemail, security clearance, office space, office furniture, computer, parking pass, expense account, identification badge, and business cards using standard rules. Multiply that process by the thousands of employees who are onboarded each year in many large organisations.

Now imagine that RPA software has been configured to do all this work just as the HR specialist did – by logging on and off systems with its own assigned logon ID and password to perform these routine tasks.

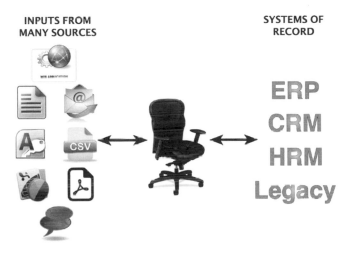

INPUTS FROM MANY SOURCES

SYSTEMS OF RECORD

ERP
CRM
HRM
Legacy

Figure 2.1: RPA is Ideally Suited to 'Swivel Chair' Processes

That's what Robotic Process Automation (RPA) does – it interacts with other computers systems just like a human would. If configured correctly, the RPA software should do the work better, faster, and much cheaper than the HR specialist. The HR specialist in this scenario would be free to focus upon non-routine tasks, such as working with business units to craft job descriptions, suggesting appropriate recruiting outlets, fielding calls from potential applicants, reviewing resumes, and calling references. The HR specialist would also handle all the non-routine exceptions the RPA software could not process. There would be fewer HR specialists needed overall if the volume of work was constant, but those HR specialists remaining should have more challenging work. Next, let's examine a real life example.

2.2.1. RPA example: Resolving infeasible customer meter readings

For a major European electricity and gas utility company, resolving infeasible meter readings for residential customers serves as the business context for this RPA application. Millions of residential customers need to have their meters read four times a year for billing. A customer's meter reading could be self-reported or done by a hired meter reader, but either way, thousands arrive each day. Back in 2008, the legacy mainframe system electronically applied rules to determine whether a meter reading was feasible or not. There could be many reasons to doubt the meter readings. For example, if this quarter's meter reading was lower than the previous quarter's meter reading, it would indicate the infeasible situation that the customer was adding electricity to the grid rather than consuming it. Infeasible meter readings were kicked out of the mainframe legacy system and given to between 25 and 30 people to manually resolve them. Depending on the situation, humans applied rules or judgment to fix errors. Infeasible meter reading resolutions that were highly rules-based were suitable for automation (see Figure 2.2). Humans would continue to process the exceptions that required judgment. The business case called for reducing the FTE count by about 60 percent, improving the quality, consistency, and speed of resolutions.

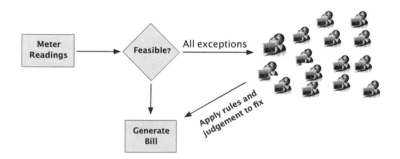

Figure 2.2: Meter Reading Process before RPA

This application was highly successful (see Figure 2.3), but it was targeted to be decommissioned after an Enterprise Resource Planning (ERP) implementation. The ERP system was expected to manage business operations and customer relations and to replace much of the legacy system functionality.

Initially, the European utility company had some naïve expectations that the new ERP system would replace the need for all the robots, but it soon discovered that ERP systems required manual completion of many processes that were still ideally suited for automation. RPA was reinstituted to help with meter reading feasibility again, but this time it was called 'plausibility' to match the enterprise systems' terminology. RPA, in turns out, complemented the ERP implementation.

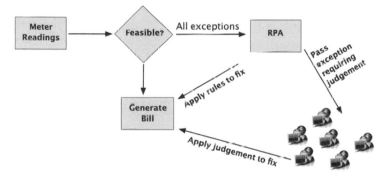

Figure 2.3: Meter Reading Process after RPA

Several observations may be gleaned from this real-life example. Firstly, RPA replaced only the dreary part of the workers' jobs and thus changed the nature of the remaining workers' jobs. Although RPA generated 60 percent in FTE savings, the remaining 40 percent had more interesting work because they performed tasks that required judgement and social interactions.

Secondly, RPA was ideally suited for stitching together computer-to-computer processes. Initially, the European utility company thought that the new ERP would decommission the RPA implementation that interacted with the legacy mainframe system, but it soon discovered that RPA complemented the new ERP system. The European utility, like many other clients in this book, discovered that no ERP system can do everything, and that RPA can automate processes not covered by ERP. Neil Wright, Director of Professional Services for Blue Prism, explained further how RPA complements large enterprise systems: *"As we all know, with a huge enterprise implementation, it doesn't always deliver everything that is was expected to deliver. There are always things around the edges that never get done, so people have to step in. So what we're actually finding as an offshoot is that RPA has become an enabler, a complement to the ERP program because we effectively finish it off."* In the case of the European utility another issue was that the enterprise system had left it understaffed since it had projected huge FTE savings in the initial business case. Rather than hire all the staff it needed to support the enterprise system, RPA was deployed.

Given this typical example, some Chief Information Officers may dismiss RPA as nothing new, thinking, *"We've been automating business processes for years with Business Process Management (BPM) solutions".* They, and other senior executives ask, *"What is distinctive about RPA?"*

2.3. Distinctive Features of RPA

Two things distinguish RPA from other tools like Business Process Management (BPM).

1. *RPA is easy to configure, so developers don't need programming skills.* The RPA interfaces work a lot like Visio, by dragging, dropping and linking icons that represent steps in a process. Figure 2.4 has a screen shot of the development environment from two of the most popular RPA software providers – Blue Prism and Automation Anywhere.[2] As users drag and drop icons to automate a process, code is generated automatically. Business operations people, with process and subject matter expertise but with no programming experience, can be trained to independently automate processes within a few weeks. In contrast to RPA software, BPM solutions require coding expertise.

2. *RPA 'software' is non-invasive compared to typical BPM software.* The second distinctive feature is that RPA technology sits on top of existing

**Blue Prism screenshot
for development environment**

**Automation Anywhere screenshot
for development environment**

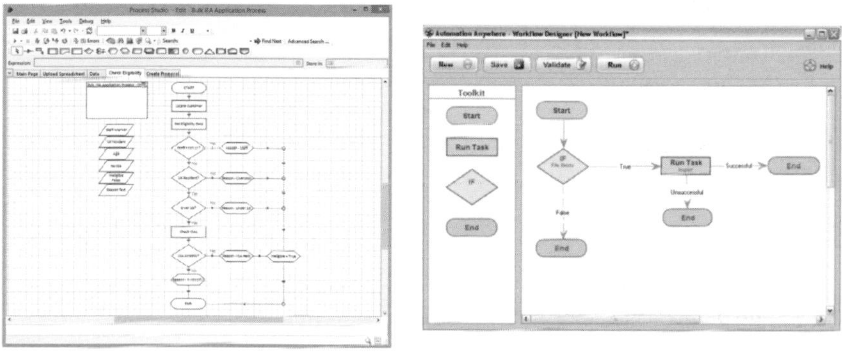

Figure 2.4: User Interfaces for RPA Software

systems – without the need to create, replace or further develop expensive platforms. RPA software accesses other computer systems the way a human does – through the user interface with a logon ID and password. RPA software accesses other systems through the presentation layer – so no underlying systems programming logic is touched (see Figure 2.5). RPA products do not store any data. In contrast to RPA software, BPM solutions interact with business logic and data access layers.

RPA builds robots that then interact in new ways with existing IT systems. In practice, the client does not build a robot, but rather 'teaches' or 'configures' the robot software rules and instructs it to press keys. Furthermore, while IT needs to be involved and there are touch points, on the whole RPA is in fact non-invasive: *"A robot mimics the way that a human being interacts with these underlying security, audit, and access systems. Not only are you getting the interface that is already there because the robot can do the same as a human being can, the security models and the process models are also already in place because you already have a model in terms of the way that you access, that certain systems are allowed to talk to each other, that certain procedures must follow one to the other if you're a human being. All*

of that comes off-the-shelf as part of putting the robot in place because in principle, it is another employee. It just happens to be a virtual employee."
Jason Kingdon, Chairman, Blue Prism

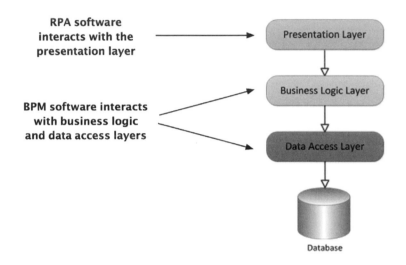

Figure 2.5: RPA as 'Lightweight' IT

Because RPA is non-invasive and does not disturb underlying computer systems, RPA can be considered 'lightweight' IT. Lightweight IT is a term used to describe front-end, commercially available software that supports processes and is typically adopted outside the control of the IT department.[3] We will qualify this understanding in a subsequent chapter when we come back to redefining lightweight IT, since we believe that lightweight IT needs to receive IT sanction to stop it from becoming 'rogue' IT and the risks this engenders.

RPA does not replace BPM, but rather complements it (see Figure 2.6). RPA and BPM are each suited to automating different types of processes. BPM solutions are best suited for processes requiring IT expertise on high-valued IT investments like ERP and Customer Relationship Management (CRM) systems. BPM solutions are developed by IT staff. The two distinguishing attributes of RPA software – it is designed for non-programmers to use and it does not disturb existing systems – means the threshold of business processes worth automating are substantially lowered, as illustrated by the blue tail in Figure 2.6 (or the light grey tail if viewing in black and white). Now, those swivel chair processes that are owned by operations, and are too small to justify the use of IT development resources, can be automated by operations folks. RPA solutions are typically deployed by business operations staff with IT oversight (but not IT developers) for processes that require business and process expertise. The significantly lower IT investment costs now makes automating these processes financially beneficial. Patrick Geary, CMO for Blue Prism, said, *"We are not trying to replace enterprise IT, and we are not really trying to compete with BPMS. It's really this long tail of processes that are typically deployed by humans that are most suitable for RPA. Humans can be redeployed to more intelligent decision-making tasks."*

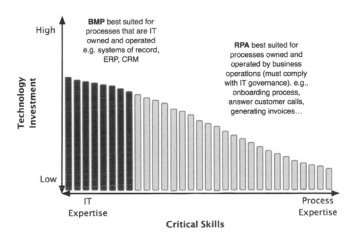

Figure 2.6: BPM and RPA as Complements

Based on interviews in 12 large organisations, Forrester Research[4] found that enterprises benefit from both BPM and RPA technologies (see Table 2.1). It argued that RPA complements BPM: *"The trick is to put them together in the right combination to achieve your strategic goals"*.

Attribute	BPM	RPA
Business Goal	Reengineer processes	Automate existing processes
Technical Outcome	Create a new application	Use existing applications
Integration Method	Access business logic layer	Access the presentation layer of existing
Developers	Software developers	Business operations
Testing Requirements	System testing	Output verification

Table 2.1: BPM versus RPA
(Adapted from Forrester Research (2014))

2.4. Understanding RPA Terminology

RPA terminology can be confusing because it uses some of the same terminology as 'heavyweight' IT. We have attempted to head off some of this problem with the detailed explanation of RPA above. But it is worth pointing to particular misunderstandings that emerged from our research. The words 'developers', 'designers', and 'analysts', in particular, meant different things to different people.

An RPA 'developer' configures RPA software whereas an IT 'developer' writes programming code. The first set of misperceptions comes from RPA using a language normally pertinent to an IT delivery function, in particular the terms 'developer' and 'designer':

"So we have a Robotic Process Automation developer and people automatically think, well it's software development isn't it? Well no it isn't. Similarly, we need a designer to design/document the end-to-end process, but that's all we're doing. We're not designing a software development solution with a number of applications – this misperception is by far the biggest issue. And in some larger organisations where they've got teams of enterprise architects, solution designers, software developers and testers, there is going to be a lot of confusion." **Allan Surtees, Head of IT Delivery, Gazprom Energy**

The confusion leads to the conclusion that RPA people may be doing the work of IT people, when they are not. For example, at Leeds Building Society the in-house IT development team dragged their feet the most, more because they felt that RPA was something potentially within their skill set to deliver in-house.[5] But as one of our respondents put it: *"It isn't just another piece of software. It's a different approach."*

An RPA 'analyst' is a process expert who proactively seeks automation opportunities and typically writes detailed RPA requirements whereas a typical 'business analyst' serves as a liaison between user needs and IT requirements. A further example: A business analyst is normally an expert in the business process, working with the business to understand a set of requirements, resulting in an IT change. In RPA, the analyst is actually someone who goes around and finds processes to automate – a slightly different role. You could use a standard business analyst, but they would not be writing requirements documents, more a document that talks about the end-to-end process.

Neil Wright of Blue Prism said, *"There are subtle nuances about the roles (and indeed the delivery methodology and operating model) that differentiate RPA from traditional IT. The analyst role is a good example – we call the role 'Process Analyst' as opposed to Business Analyst'. The 'Developer' role is a very interesting one. We have toyed with many different descriptions over the years including – modeller, developer, designer and even, configurator. We have found that each of these can be embraced or rejected by clients/ prospects/partners in equal measures but none of the role names have been embraced by all."*

2.4.1. In Practice: Don't change RPA terms – explain them better

In our case studies, RPA terminology invariably caused initial confusion and some trepidation amongst IT departments. Once the business case, and RPA itself, was understood, the fear and opposition tended to dissipate, including amongst Operations staff.[6]

Allan Surtees (Telefónica O2, then Head of IT Delivery, Gazprom Energy) comes from the IT side and has experienced RPA implementations in two different corporations. He comments, *"The terminology needs to change away from trying to use standard IT Delivery type terminology because I think that confuses people. This is because there's a fear factor there in both business operations and IT. From a business operations perspective people say 'Is this going to take my job? Are you going to replace me with a robot?'* *– even though it's a mundane, repeatable, manually intensive task they do not like doing. On the IT side architects ask 'You're going to allow customer service people to develop code?'. I said, 'No, this isn't about development of code.' Then you've got software developers saying 'Well this is going to take my job away.', Well, it's not actually – because it's not software development."*

It may well be that clearer explanations and vocabulary are needed, and that this issue will pass on into the next rounds of automation we flagged in the previous chapter with terms like autonomics, intelligent automation and cognitive automation. But given the long-standing, messy proliferation of new terms in the hi-tech world, a better approach, substantiated by the case evidence we have seen, is educating potential clients as to what exactly RPA is, and how it fits with the IT group and IT systems, and bringing the IT function early into this education process. As Allan Surtees told us, *"It's just getting your head around what it actually is. Though it looks similar – i.e. you use the same rigour that you would in delivery of any IT change – you have to have development/test environments; you have to design the end-to-end process from documentation (if it exists!); you have to develop an end-to-end process using the tool to train a robot and then you have to test that it works before implementing it. It really is NOT an IT delivery, though it does share some attributes."*

2.5. Processes Suitable for RPA

Potential adopters of RPA will want to know how to assess the suitability of RPA relative to their existing processes. Although RPA is new to many organisations, shared services and outsourcing are long-standing practices that can serve as a starting point for understanding the suitability of RPA for existing processes. Based on years of research, we know that processes are most suitable for handing over to shared services or outsourcing (SS/O) when they have high volumes – because high-volume processes provide the most opportunity for reducing costs (see Table 2.2).[7] The easiest processes to move to SS/O have high degrees of process standardisation so that all of the company's business units expect the same service.[8] Processes that are highly rules-based are also easier to migrate to SS/O because rules can be documented, which results in lower knowledge transfer costs compared to processes that require tacit knowledge transfer.[9] Mature processes are easier to move because they are measured, well-documented, stable, and predictable and their costs are known.[10] High levels of process interoperability across many platforms are easier to migrate.[11] Some processes are difficult to move to different jurisdictions because of compliance risks.[12] Highly integrated processes that are tightly coupled and difficult to detach from other processes are also harder to migrate.[13] The degree of business value is also pertinent. Academic research shows that the most critical processes are often insourced close to the business.[14] How does this set of process attributes for SS/O compare to RPA?

	Value recommended for shared services and outsourcing	Value recommended for RPA
Volume of transactions	High	High
	High	High
Degree to which process is rules-based	High	High
Degree of process maturity	High	High
Degree of interoperability	High	N/A
Degree of compliance risk	Low	N/A
Degree of process complexity	Low	N/A
Degree of process integration	Low	N/A
Degree of business value	Low	N/A

Table 2.2: Process Attributes Suitable for Shared Services, Outsourcing, and RPA

Like shared services and outsourcing, *RPA experts and early adopters report that RPA is most suitable for processes with high transaction volumes, high levels of standardisation, are highly rules-based, and are mature.*[15]

However, RPA can deal effectively with complex processes as long as complexity is defined as 'requiring compound steps and the control of many variables'. (Some researchers define process complexity as processes where cause and effect are subtle and dynamic, in which case complex processes would not be ideally suited for RPA.)[16] One of the advantages of RPA is that it is highly interoperable and can readily run on any platform – mainframes, client/server, or cloud systems. RPA only requires access to the presentation layer, i.e. the screens the user sees. RPA software can be configured to logon to many systems and execute tasks. Early adopters have reported that compliance risks are minimal with RPA because every action executed by the RPA software is logged and thus auditable.[17] Finally, Derek Toone, Managing Director at Alsbridge, suggested, *"The degree of business value inherent in the process is worth considering in situations where significantly increasing the speed or accuracy with which a process is executed can yield outsised benefits to the business – for example in terms of enhancing speed to market, product quality, customer satisfaction, regulatory compliance, etc."*

2.6. Conclusion

RPA is a type of service automation that aims to automate 'swivel chair' processes – those tasks in which a human being takes data from one form of digital inputs, transforms the inputs following structured rules, and passes the transformed digital outputs to another computer system. Now that we have explained in more detail what RPA is, how it differs from other service automation software, and the processes for which RPA is most suited, we are ready to share detailed client histories of RPA adoption. The next three chapters present the history of RPA adoption, the business value delivered, and lessons learned by Telefónica, Xchanging, and by a major utility company.

Citations

[1] Everest Group (2014), Service Delivery Automation Market in 2014. Everest Group Market Report, October. Everest Group see RPA as a UI-based/robotic component of service delivery automation. They distinguish this from four other components of SDA – macro or scripted automation, IT automation, business process management, and artificial intelligence. Our research aligns with the usefulness of these distinctions, and also the identification of cognitive automation as a set of tools that build a process related knowledge base and use it in combination with a set of business rules to automate processes. Cognitive tools extend RPA by handling unstructured data, for example the tools provided by Celaton. See our later chapter, *In Their Own Words*, by providers.

[2] Everest Group (2014), Service Delivery Automation Market in 2014. Everest Group Market Report, October. Everest Group usefully conceptualise Business Process Service Delivery Automation as consisting of three different portions. These are: automation of inputs to a process, e.g. content management and screen scraping from websites; automation of the business process, e.g. administering PO and invoices, checking for unusual patterns in transactions, dealing with specific scenarios, especially exceptions; and automation of outputs from the process, e.g. outward contact management, internal notifications, events generated to initiate follow-on processes elsewhere.

[3] Bygstad, B. (2015), *The Coming of Lightweight IT*, 23

[4] Forrester Research (2014) *Building a Center of Expertise to Support Robotic Automation.*

[5] Interview with Kevin Mowles, Head of Business Support, Leeds Building Society, July 21st 2015.

[6] The evidence for this claim can be found in our first three case studies of RPA. See papers by Mary Lacity, Leslie Willcocks and Andrew Craig (2015) on *Robotic Process Automation at Telefonica O2,* LSE Outsourcing Unit paper 15/02; *Robotic Process Automation at Xchanging,* LSE Outsourcing Unit paper 15/03; and *Robotic Process Automation: Maturing Capabilities in the Energy Sector*, LSE Outsourcing Unit paper 15/05. See also chapter 5 of this book.

[7] This study summarises processes suitable for outsourcing: Lacity, M., and Willcocks, P. (2012), *Advanced Outsourcing Practice: Rethinking ITO, BPO, and Cloud Services*, (Palgrave Macmillan, London); This study looks at processes suitable for shared services: McKeen, J., & Smith, H., (2011) *Creating IT Shared Services*, *Communications of the AIS*, Vol. 29, 34, pp. 645-656.

[8] These studies look at standardisation: McIvor, R., McCracken, M., & McHugh, M., (2011) *Creating outsourced shared services arrangements: Lessons from the public sector, European Management Journal,* Vol. 29, 6, pp. 448-461; Sako, M., (2010) *Technology Strategy and Management Outsourcing Versus Shared Services, Communications of the ACM,* Vol. 53, 7, pp. 126-129.

[9] For example, see: Srikanth, K., & Puranam, P., (2011) *Integratin Distributed Work: Comparing Task Design, Communication, And Tacit Coordination Mechanisms, Strategic Management Journal,* Vol. 32, 8, pp. 849-875.

[10] Bidwell, M., (2012) *Politics and Firm Boundaries: How Organizational Structure, Group Interests, and Resources Affect Outsourcing, Organization Science,* Vol. 23, 6, pp. 1622-1642; Lacity, M., and Fox, J. (2008), *Creating Global Shared Services: Lessons from Reuters*, *MIS Quarterly Executive*, Vol. 7, 1, pp. 17-32.

[11] Sia, S., Koh, C. and Tan, C. (2008). *Strategic Maneuvers for Outsourcing Flexibility: An empirical assessment, Decision Sciences,* Vol. 39, 3, pp. 407–443; Tanriverdi, H., Konana, P., and Ge, L., (2007), *The Choice of Sourcing Mechanisms for Business Processes, Information Systems Research*, Vol. 18, 3, pp. 280-299.

[12] Currie, W., Michell, V., and Abanishe, A., (2008), *Knowledge Process Outsourcing in Financial Services: The Vendor Perspective, European Management Journal*, Vol. 26, pp. 94-104; Desai, D., Gearard, G., and Tripathy, A. (2011), *Internal Audit Sourcing Arrangements and Reliance by External*

Auditors, Auditing: A Journal of Practice and Theory, Vol. 30, 1, pp. 149-171; Dunbar, A. and Phillips, J. (2001), *The Outsourcing of Corporate Tax Function Activities, The Journal of the American Taxation Association*, Vol. 23, 2, pp. 35-49; Mathew, S., (2011) *Mitigation of risks due to service provider behavior in offshore software development A relationship approach, Strategic Outsourcing: An International Journal*, Vol. 4, 2, pp. 179-200.

[13] Luo, Y., Wang, S., Zheng, Q., & Jayaraman, V., (2012) *Task attributes and process integration in business process offshoring: A perspective of service providers from India and China, Journal of International Business Studies*, Vol. 43, 5, pp. 498-524; Jayaraman, V., Narayanan, S., Luo, Y., & Swaminathan, J. M. (2013). *Offshoring business process services and governance control mechanisms: An examination of service providers from India, Production and Operations Management*, Vol. 22, 2, pp. 314; Narayanan, S., Jayaraman, V., Luo, Y., & Swaminathan, J., (2011) *The antecedents of process integration in business process outsourcing and its effect on firm performance, Journal of Operations Management*, Vol. 29, 1-2, pp. 3-16.

[14] McIvor, R., Humphreys, P., McKittrick, A., and Wall, T. (2009), *Performance Management and the Outsourcing Process: Lessons from a Financial Services Organisation, International Journal of Operations and Production Management*, Vol. 29, 10, pp. 1025-1047. Ventovuori, T., and Lehtonen, T. (2006), *Alternative Models for the Management of FM Services, Journal of Corporate Real Estate*, Vol. 8, 2, pp. 73-90; Wahrenburg, M., Hackethal, A., Friedrich, L., and Gellrich, T. (2006), *Strategic Decisions Regarding the Vertical Integration of Human Resource Organizations*, in *International Journal of Human Resource Management*, Vol. 17, 10, pp. 1726-1771.

[15] Discussion from The Robotic Automation Advisory Council, Chicago Illinois, April 14, 2015.

[16] For a comprehensive set of process complexity measures see: Day, A. (2009), *On Process Complexity, In Proc. Fifteenth Computing: The Australasian Theory Symposium* (CATS 2009), Wellington, New Zealand. CRPIT, **94**. Downey, R. and Manyem, P., Eds. ACS. 29-34; Shen, W., N.L. Hsueh, N. and P.H. Chu, P. (2011), *Measurement-based software process modeling, Journal of Software Engineering*, Vol. 5, pp. 20-37.Gruhn, V., and Laue, R., *Complexity Metrics for Business Process Models*, University of Leipzig working paper, available at: http://http://czm.fel.cvut.cz/research/BPM Research knihovna/Complexity Metrics for Business Process Models.pdf

[17] Panel discussion, The Impact of Robotic Process Automation on BPO,Automation Innovation Conference, New York City, December 10, 2014.

Chapter 3

Robotic Process Automation at Telefónica O2

What's Inside: *This chapter examines Telefónica O2's pioneering RPA journey. As illustrated through the case study, RPA can produce faster and more accurate service performance, and annual returns on investment of up to 200 percent. The case study offers six major lessons for future RPA adopters: (1) Test RPA capabilities with a controlled experiment; (2) Develop your own criteria for the 'automationability' of processes; (3) Bring IT onboard early; (4) Communicate the intended effect on jobs early in the process; (5) Consider carefully the best sourcing option; and (6) To be an RPA pioneer, you will need to take some risks!*

(This chapter was initially published as Lacity, M. and Willcocks, L. (2016), Robotic Process Automation at Telefónica O2, MIS Quarterly Executive, reprinted with permission.)

3.1. Introduction

To understand the business value achievable with RPA, we begin this case study with the outcomes. As of April 2015, Telefónica O2 deployed over 160 'robots' – i.e. RPA software licenses – that process between 400,000 and 500,000 transactions each month, yielding a three-year return on investment of between 650 and 800 percent (see Table 3.1). For some processes, it reduced the turnaround time from days to just minutes. Subsequently, customer 'chase up' calls have been reduced by over 80 percent per year because fewer customers needed to inquire about the status of service requests. Scalability was another benefit – its robotic workforce could be doubled almost instantly when new products were about to be launched – and then scaled back down after the surge. How did Telefónica O2 achieve such results?

Number of processes automated	Number of RPA transactions per month	Number of Robots (i.e., software licenses)	Number of FTEs saved or redeployed	Payback Period	3-Year ROI
15 core processes	400,000 to 500,000	>160 and growing	Hundreds	12 months	Between 650 and 800%

Table 3.1: Telefónica O2's 2015 RPA Capabilities at a Glance

3.2. Telefónica O2's Pioneering RPA Journey

To put the RPA journey into context, we must explain Telefónica O2's business background. Telefónica O2 is owned by the Telefónica Group. It is the second-largest mobile telecommunications provider in the United Kingdom (UK), after Everything Everywhere (EE), and is headquartered in Slough, located 22 miles west of London. O2 was founded in 1985 as Cellnet, a venture launched by BT Group and Securicor. Fourteen years later, BT Group bought the entire venture and, in 2002, rebranded the company as 'O2'. In 2005, Telefónica bought O2, retained its name, and continued to be based in the UK – keeping both the brand and the management team. As of 2015, O2 had 24 million customers and operated over 450 retail stores.[1] In 2013, Telefónica UK's revenues were €6.69 billion (about £4.8 billion) and it employed 21,580 people. Like all large organisations, Telefónica O2's back offices needed to scale up to match business growth while keeping costs low to thrive in the highly competitive mobile market. This case study explores how Telefónica O2 managed its back offices to accomplish these objectives since 2004.

As with many large organisations, Telefónica O2's ten-year journey of back office transformation began with the transfer of work from the UK to India in 2004. Telefónica O2 initially did a 'lift and shift' of a significant amount of back office work from the United Kingdom to India by engaging a BPO provider with a delivery centre in Mumbai. By 2005, there were 200 Full Time Equivalents (FTEs) working in India, while 98 FTEs remained onshore in the UK. By 2009, the headcount in India swelled to 375 FTEs and headcount in the UK was reduced to 50 FTEs. Telefónica O2 was reaching the ceiling on extracting any more value from offshoring; there was not that much more work that could be moved to India. Furthermore, wages in India were rising. Finally, the contract did not incentivise the BPO provider to innovate. The BPO offshore contract was largely based on hourly wages and the service levels were based on turnaround times and accuracy, not on reducing costs per transaction.

As the volume of work offshore grew from about 400,000 transactions per month to over a million transactions per month, Telefónica O2's back office costs escalated. Wayne Butterfield, Head of Back Office services at Telefónica O2 in 2010 recalled, *"Low cost wasn't so low anymore."*[2] The mandate became: Do more work with less money. His vision was to reduce the FTE count by 50 percent, reduce average response time by 50 percent, and reduce customer calls on back office failure by 50 percent. (Pertaining to this last point, if service is executed quickly and accurately, customers would not need to contact Telefónica O2.)

In 2010, Telefónica O2 managed over 60 core processes (amounting to about 400 sub-processes). To reduce costs further, Telefónica O2 began eliminating non-value added processes and optimising and simplifying the processes that remained. As an example of an eliminated process, Telefónica O2 removed a legacy process that verified order shipments. The order process had become so mature that it was 99.99 percent accurate – the legacy verification process was no longer worthwhile. Butterfield explained, *"The verification was a process in place for people to check hundreds of thousands of orders and they would potentially find one that hadn't gone out. That's a really pointless process. It was there for many, many years and no one had looked at its value."* Verifying bar removal from a customer's account after a Subscriber Identity Module (SIM) swap (process explained below) was a similar example of a legacy process. The bar removal process was automated, so the bar removal verification process made no sense. Telefónica O2 eliminated that process as well.

Besides process elimination, Telefónica O2 also sought to optimise processes by simplifying them, and by bringing the BPO provider onshore to gain a better understanding of Telefónica O2. The entire process rationalisation initiative – which included process elimination, simplification, and optimisation – reduced labour headcount by 10 percent. During this two-year long journey, the possibility of automating processes surfaced when the Head of Finance told Butterfield about Blue Prism software. After an initial assessment of Blue Prism's capabilities, Telefónica O2 decided to conduct two pilot projects to prove the concept.

3.3. RPA Proof-of-Concept

Telefónica O2 needed the answers to three questions: Will RPA integrate with Telefónica's systems of record without breaking them? Will the technology provide quality services? Will the technology provide enough of a return on investment?

In 2010, Telefónica O2 launched an RPA trial on two high-volume, low-complexity processes. One process was SIM swaps – the process of replacing a customer's existing SIM with a new SIM but keeping his or her existing number. The other process was the application of a pre-calculated credit to a customer's account. People using various software systems normally executed these processes. For the pilot tests, Blue Prism's consultants came onsite and configured the RPA software to perform what people normally did to execute the processes. The RPA software was assigned a logon ID and password and the software logged in, executed the tasks on test accounts that used actual data, and logged out of the systems, just as people did. The pilot was completed within two weeks.

Regarding the first question, *"Will RPA integrate with Telefónica's systems of record without breaking them?"*, the trial proved that the technology could seamlessly work with Telefónica O2's systems and it performed tasks as expected. The trial proved so effective that it raised alarms in the IT Security system. The RPA software executed so many transactions in such a short period of time that Telefónica O2's Fraud and Security team tried to hunt down the presumed intruder. When security traced the intrusion to Butterfield's pilot project, he was nearly fired. Butterfield reminisced, *"Although it was scary to be escorted by the Head of Security into a private room, we actually proved the RPA concept quite well!"*

The IT team had already developed very negative ideas about RPA as they had a mature Business Process Management (BPM) system in-house and questioned why additional automation software was needed. The IT team also incorrectly assumed that Blue Prism was a 'screen scraper'[3] package. Screen scrapers were an older technology that recorded users as they moved fields around systems. Screen scrapers only understood that a field located in one specific position on one screen should be moved to another specific position on another screen. If the field was moved without reconfiguring the screen scraper, the technology would no longer function. Butterfield explained, *"[the IT team viewed RPA as] screen scraping, which isn't fit for an enterprise company – unsupported macros created by keyboard warriors in darkened rooms in our offices. People left to their own devices to create macros, running unsupported and quite often needing regular check-ups to keep them running. That was the stigma that we originally received from our colleagues in technology."*[4] In contrast, Blue Prism's RPA software does not rely on X and Y coordinates but instead finds data fields through Html, Java Access Bridge, and surface automation for Citrix.[5]

According to Allen Surtees, a Telefónica O2 Senior IT Project Manager at the time, the biggest challenge IT managers faced was to understand the RPA technology. He said, *"The Architectural Review Board had a fear factor: 'Are we going to let customer service people develop code?' I said, 'No, no, they are not developing code.' It's hard to get your head around what RPA actually is."* Telefónica O2's IT managers thought RPA should be an IT project using existing automation technology. Specifically, Telefónica O2's IT department wanted to test whether BPM could achieve the same results as RPA.

An IT team was assigned to automate two processes with BPM technology. One of the processes was identical to the RPA trial (SIM swaps) and one process was different but with similar attributes. The BPM team successfully automated the two processes within three weeks, which was comparable to the RPA trial. However, when it came to the financials, RPA was the clear winner. The financial discrepancy between the business cases for BPM and RPA was attributed to BPM's additional IT headcount. BPM projects required IT developers and SCRUM teams. RPA projects required just the SMEs from the back office. So the major developmental cost difference was due to the IT labour needed for BMP development. Although RPA had more upfront costs in terms of RPA training for SMEs and short term consulting support, the total cost of development was still lower with RPA. Butterfield said, *"Our projections showed that RPA for 10 automated processes would pay back in 10 months. In contrast, the BPMS was going to take up to three years to payback."* [6] The three-year business cases estimated zero net financial benefits with BPMS and nearly £1 million with RPA. Regarding the last proof-of-concept question, *"Will RPA provide enough of a return on investment?"*, the answer was clearly yes.

3.4. RPA Rollout

After the trials, RPA was selected as the obvious choice over BPM. Before automatically adopting Blue Prism as the software vendor, Telefónica O2 issued a request-for-proposal. Back in 2010, the only truly RPA response was from Blue Prism; the other five responses were BPM solutions. Telefónica O2's IT department eventually became convinced of the value of the tool and Blue Prism became part of Telefónica O2's technology offerings.

Telefónica O2 also asked its Indian-based provider to consider doing the automation on Telefónica O2's behalf. Telefónica O2 understood that the commercials would need to benefit both parties. After a six-month investigation, the BPO provider backed off. Telefónica O2 chose to implement RPA, on their own, with the help of Blue Prism.

Two back office staff members attended a week-long training program at Blue Prism's headquarters. (Since then, Blue Prism's training is mostly online). After the training, a Blue Prism consultant worked alongside the trained staff members for about a month at Telefónica O2. After that, Blue Prism support was reduced to once a week to review the staff member's work. The staff members became nearly 100 percent independent in about 12 weeks. On the ease of which business process people can master RPA, Butterfield said, *"So I think from having never automated a process before or having any qualifications that would even stipulate that they could do this type of thing, to automating processes end-to-end, probably took the guys about three months."*

Telefónica O2 began its rollout with 20 software licenses. The next wave increased the number of RPA software licenses to 75. Eventually, a third staff member was trained. With just a team of three RPA developers in-house, Telefónica O2 automated 15 core processes including SIM swaps, credit checks, order processing, customer reassignment, unlatching, porting, ID generation, customer dispute resolution and customer data updates, representing about 35 percent of all back office transactions by first quarter of 2015.

As the adoption of RPA spread, Telefónica O2 learned that RPA software needs more explicit instructions than humans. When the Apple iPhone was announced, Telefónica O2's customers could preorder the phone. In their exuberance, some customers preordered the iPhone multiple times. Whereas a human would likely recognise that a single customer is really requesting a single phone, the RPA software did not. The software shipped customers multiple phones. Butterfield said Telefónica O2 learned, *"In processes that we felt had hard and sufficient rules around them, we have found that when we put it into RPA and completely remove humans, we had to implement additional 'common sense' type rules not needed previously."*

How many FTEs did automation save? It is difficult to assess the total FTE savings over time because some of Telefónica O2's UK-based people were redeployed to other service areas and the business continued to grow. But the estimated FTE savings are in the hundreds. Butterfield also reported, *"Not only have we saved FTE in the back office, we're now actually saving FTE in the front office as a result of those reduced calls. And then lastly, experience. It's very difficult to measure, from a customer experience perspective, what benefits we've had by using RPA. But with reduced turnaround times, reduced calls, how can experience not be improved?"*[7]

Despite these high levels of automation, Telefónica O2 continued to have a good relationship with its Indian-based BPO provider. Although the provider's FTEs had been reduced on the automated processes by a few hundred, the BPO provider continued to deliver the non-automated back office processes with about 250 FTEs. (Without automation, the offshore FTE headcount would be closer to 500 because of Telefónica O2's growth since 2010.) Beyond the back office, the BPO provider also handled nearly all of Telefónica O2's email and web chat services. In total, the BPO provider had about 900 FTEs supporting Telefónica O2 in first quarter of 2015.

As of 2015, Telefónica O2 planned to continue to automate processes. From a volume perspective, Telefónica O2 was running between 400,000 and 500,000 transactions through RPA each month. It estimated that RPA could increase volumes to 700,000 per month or more. Butterfield said, *"We're certainly not at the end state yet."* [8]

3.5. Lessons Learned

As an early adopter of RPA, Telefónica O2 offers six lessons for other companies considering automation ...

3.5.1. Test RPA capabilities with a controlled experiment

Telefónica O2, back in 2010, did what most companies do when they are considering the adoption of a new technology: they did a proof-of-concept (POC). POCs are small in scale, but aim to test the technical viability and financial value of a product. An interesting twist extended the POC into a controlled experiment when Telefónica O2's IT department claimed that its BPM software could to everything the RPA software could do. A controlled experiment allowed Telefónica O2 to compare directly RPA with BPM. Functionally, the solutions were nearly identical, but RPA delivered better financial value for the types of 'swivel chair' processes Telefónica O2 aimed to automate. As noted in the introduction, BPM would have likely arisen the victor if the automation required re-coding business logic or data access layers. (See Chapter 2 for more comparisons of RPA and BPM).

Some clients, like Telefónica O2 initially did, ask their outsourcing service providers to implement RPA on their behalf. In prior research, we also found that a controlled experiment is the best way to assess provider capabilities.[9] If clients gave two different RPA service providers the same process to automate in a controlled experiment, it would be an excellent way to compare their capabilities.

3.5.2. Develop your own criteria for the 'automationability' of processes

As noted in the previous chapter, potential adopters of RPA often ask how to assess the suitability of RPA relative to their existing processes. In the last chapter, a review of the literature found that *RPA is most suitable for processes with high transaction volumes, high levels of standardisation, are highly rules-based, and are mature.*[10] While these general process attributes offer sound advice, Telefónica O2 developed a simple heuristic – a process is automatable provided automation can save at least three FTEs. Butterfield explained, *"There are a lot of processes that require less than half an FTE a month. And we're probably always going to keep those in back office because even though the commercials are very good for RPA, there's no point in automating a process that saves you less than three FTEs at the moment."*

Telefónica O2's excellent management information (MI) facilitates the ability to identify candidate processes for automation that will save at least three FTEs. Butterfield said, *"The MI that I receive from my BPO provider's work allocation system is phenomenal. I can tell you to the zero point zero zero of an FTE what I'm going to save when I automate a process. I know to the second how long that process has taken to complete over a number of years."*

So, which processes are candidates for saving three FTEs? Telefónica O2 sees volume of transactions and process complexity as guides (see Figure 3.1). To assess process complexity, time serves as proxy. A simple process requires a human to complete it in a few minutes. A complex process may take thirty minutes or more. Although Telefónica O2 tended to select simple processes with around at least 1,000 transactions per week for automation, Butterfield explained how complex processes can be automated to generate savings, *"If you were to automate a complex process, you may only be doing thirty of those a day but automation would still deliver the three FTE savings that you're looking for."*

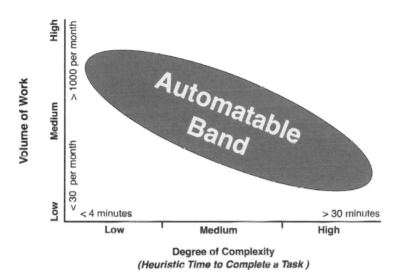

Figure 3.1: Telefónica O2's Assessment of the RPA Suitability

3.5.3. Bring IT onboard early

Telefónica O2, like several other early RPA adopters we have studied, adopted RPA without initially involving IT. Butterfield almost lost his job because he did not inform IT or other parts of the organisation that he was testing new software. In O2 and in other customer cases we have studied, the reasons for excluding IT at the onset were (1) the RPA program was seen as a business operations program since RPA required process and subject matter expertise, not IT programming skills, and (2) fears that IT would beleaguer the adoption with bureaucracy. In all such instances, hindsight indicated that this was a poor approach; customers learned the importance of involving the IT department from the beginning. The lesson to be learned is, *"Bring IT onboard early"*. Certainly this was the lesson Blue Prism took from this experience. Pat Geary, CMO for Blue Prism, said, *"The minute we engage with business owners, we insist on speaking with the IT function. When we talk to IT, we explain that we have a product that is designed to appease their requirements for security, scalability, auditability, and change management."*

Telefónica O2 reported that Blue Prism was resilient and stable. (Butterfield said he could count on one hand the number of times Blue Prism had gone down in five years.) However, Telefónica O2's internal infrastructure that runs Blue Prism had incurred significant launch problems and growing-pains which could have been avoided if IT had been involved earlier.

For the launch, Telefónica O2 decided to run Blue Prism on virtual machines (VM) where a 'lead' VM machine orchestrated all the robots.[11] The virtual machines initially ran two to three times slower than when people were executing the processes. Telefónica O2 had to change server, database, and system locations to increase processing speed. Butterfield explained, *"Having a virtual infrastructure in Glasgow, for example, when your systems are down south in London and Slough, makes a difference."*[12] It took about 16 weeks to optimise the infrastructure.

Once optimised, Telefónica O2 learned that it needed to scale up the infrastructure as the RPA adoption scaled. A 'lead' VM machine worked fine when there were 20 RPA software licenses deployed, but it imploded when the number of RPA software licenses quadrupled. He mused, *"It was like driving a Ferrari with a lawn mower engine."*

Since Telefónica O2's initial RPA adoption, VM desktop technology has advanced considerably and Blue Prism has developed technical guidelines to minimise network latency. Neil Wright, Director of Professional Services for Blue Prism, explained, *"We obviously learn with our clients. We have refined our infrastructure data sheets so that clients coming on board don't experience the problems O2 initially had. We have clients now who are running virtual workforces bigger than O2's without any problems."*

3.5.4. Communicate the intended effect on jobs early in the process

Like any automation technology, some employees can feel threatened by RPA. At Telefónica O2, there was fear initially among the back office and IT staff.

According to to Allen Surtees, a Telefónica O2 Senior IT Project Manager at the time, *"People start fearing that this technology is going to take my job away. It's not only the people in operations, the software developers also think it's going to take their jobs away."* At Telefónica O2 fears were assuaged because it used RPA to reduce FTEs in the outsourced relationship; no internal jobs were directly threatened.

Telefónica O2's internal job security is typical in our research. The operations groups adopting RPA had promised their employees that automation would not result in layoffs. Instead, workers were redeployed to do more interesting work. Once that job assurance was given, knowledge workers have not felt threatened by automation – they embraced it and view the 'robots' as teammates. For example, in our case study of Xchanging in the next chapter, the global provider of IT, business and procurement services, the knowledge workers named the robots, drew physical depictions of them, and even invited them to office parties.[13]

But what if RPA will be used to significantly reduce internal headcount? Prior research on outsourcing and offshoring found that communicating the intended effect on jobs early in the process was by far the best practice.[14] For outsourcing and offshoring, CIOs were reticent to share a sourcing strategy until all the details were planned, reasoning it would be better to have most of the answers prepared before making an official announcement. However, in many case studies, delaying communication caused staff members to panic and to sabotage the outsourcing/offshoring initiatives because many employees overestimated the effects on jobs. The best time to announce outsourcing and offshoring was when CIOs were ready to search for service providers. Extrapolating from that lesson, the best time to communicate that the organisation is considering RPA may be during the POC/controlled experiment.

3.5.5. Consider carefully the best sourcing option

In 2010, Telefónica O2 did not have many sourcing options when it came
to automation. It initially approached its BPO provider to see if it would
develop automation capabilities. Telefónica O2 proposed that financial gains
from automation would be shared with the BPO provider. At the time, the
BPO provider's business model relied primarily on labour arbitrage, so it
ultimately decided to pass on the automation opportunity. But for other
organisations just now looking at RPA, there are more sourcing options to
choose among, including:

- *Insource:* buy RPA licenses directly from an RPA software provider.
- *Insource and consulting:* buy licenses directly from an RPA
  software provider and engage a consulting firm for services and
  configuration.
- *Outsource with a traditional BPO provider:* buy RPA as part of an
  integrated service delivered by a traditional BPO provider.
- *Outsource with an RPA provider:* buy RPA from a new RPA
  outsourcing provider.
- *Cloud-source:* buy RPA as a cloud service (still emerging).

The benefits of insourcing, like Telefónica O2 did, is that the organisation has
high levels of control and keeps all cost savings. At the time, BPO providers
and advisors did not offer RPA services.

Today, many traditional BPO/ITO providers have developed significant
automation capabilities, including Xchanging, Accenture, IBM, Infosys, TCS,
and Genpact. The benefits of engaging a traditional BPO provider include
a full suite of integrated services that combine labour arbitrage, process
excellence, change management maturity and technology expertise. New
RPA providers like GenFour and Symphony are also emerging. GenFour,
for example, is a licensed reseller of Blue Prism, Celaton and Niu-Solution.
Sarah Burnett, Vice President of Research at the Everest Group, commented
on the different sourcing options: *"The open question is whether the service*

providers will be asked to provide the tool sets for automation or if their clients will prefer to license commercial tools themselves and just utilise the service providers' expertise to implement and optimise automation. Fears of technology lock-in may drive a preference to separate tools from services... There is also the rise of the new breed of service providers to consider. These are entirely focused on automated service delivery and could drive growth in consumption-based contract models."

3.5.6. To be an RPA pioneer, you will need to take some risks!

Returning to Telefónica O2's pilot test, Butterfield almost lost his job because he did not inform IT or other parts of the organisation that he was testing new software. In hindsight, Butterfield defended his pioneering behaviours. He said, *"I'd probably do it again. I'd rather apologise for something I've done than seek permission for doing it in the first place. And I think as a pioneer in anything – whether it be RPA or digital customer services which is where most of my passion lies – I think if you seek permission for everything you do, everything slows down. Things can get stuck in governance for years and years."* Pioneers are impatient and seek big results fast. When asked to rate the overall performance of RPA on a scale of 1 to 7, with '1' indicating 'very poor performance', a '4' indicating 'neither good nor bad performance', and a '7' indicating 'exceptional performance', Butterfield only gave performance a 5.5. When asked to explain the moderate rating given the impressive business outcomes, he said, *"I'm quite critical of myself. Although I think we deployed RPA well as an early adopter, I think once we started to deliver benefits, we could have supercharged that and delivered earlier. So we wouldn't be talking about 400 to 500 thousand transactions and 160 robots, we'd be talking about 70 to 80 percent of all transactions and 250 to 300 robots delivering tens of millions of savings – not two, three, or four million of savings."*

3.6. Conclusion

Between 2010 and 2015 Telefónica O2 was something of a pioneer in RPA deployment. It started by automating ten processes and by mid-2015 was using RPA for 35 percent of its back office transactions. As a pioneer, it learned many lessons along the way. Test RPA capabilities with a pilot; develop your own criteria for automationability of processes and communicate the effect on jobs early in the process. Telefónica O2 found its way to discovering the benefits of insourcing RPA capability, but also of automating selected offshore outsourced work. In the early days RPA champions also needed to take some risks, organisationally. As we shall see in Chapter 6, our state of knowledge has matured enough to keep such risks to a minimum and to deploy RPA in a structured way. These lessons have already proved valuable to other companies coming later to RPA adoption. One of these companies has been Xchanging, the subject of our next chapter. Xchanging takes us into new territory because it is a BPO service provider. As we shall see, Xchanging, like Telefónica O2, built a strong RPA capability, and gained multiple benefits from RPA deployment. It also quickly scaled RPA to become an internal group-wide capability, but in a later twist, also came to offer RPA expertise as a global service to external clients.

Citations

[1] http://www.o2.co.uk/abouto2

[2] Quote from Burnett, S. (2015), *A Conversation with Wayne Butterfield, Head of Digital Service Innovation & Transformation at Telefónica*, Everest Group Practitioner Perspectives, EGR-2015-4-0-1422.

[3] According to Neil Wright, Director of Professional Services for Blue Prism, screen-scraping was a poorly executed technology with a fundamentally sound idea to replicate how a user interacted with software. He explained, *"To teach the screen-scraper, all you did was set a recorder and then you navigate around systems and it recorded when the user copied data off of one screen and pasted it into another screen. The recorder remembered everything verbatim."*

[4] Quote from presentation during the Everest Group Webinar, *Service Delivery*

Automation: The Next Big Thing, February 26, 2015.

[5]   As another RPA example, Automation Anywhere software can be instructed to find a field anywhere in a document. To find an invoice, for example, the software can be instructed to find a field next to a text tag that has 'invoice number', 'invoice #' or 'invoice no'. If the RPA software cannot confidently identify the invoice number with the pre-specified search terms, it presents what it thinks the invoice number is as an exception for human intervention. If the human confirms the guess with a touch of a button, the guess is incorporated in the RPA software going forward. Otherwise, the human has to find the invoice number and enter it into the RPA software.

[6]   Op. cit. Burnett (2015)

[7]   Op. cit. Everest Group Webinar, *Service Delivery Automation: The Next Big Thing*.

[8]   Ibid.

[9]   For an example of a controlled experiment of two service providers, see Lacity, Willcocks, and Burgess (2014), *The Rise of Legal Services Outsourcing*, (Bloomsbury, London).

[10] Discussion from The Robotic Automation Advisory Council, Chicago Illinois, April 14, 2015

[11] Blue Prism can run on the cloud, but Telefónica O2 had decided to keep the virtual machines in-house as of 2015 because it had not made the leap away from its own server centres yet.

[12] Op. cit. Burnett (2015)

[13] See Lacity, M. and Willcocks, L. (2015), *What Knowledge Workers Stand to Gain from Automation*, *Harvard Business Review Online*, June 19.

[14] See Practice 4 on pages 20-22 in Lacity, M. and Rottman, J. (2008), *Offshore Outsourcing of IT Work*, (Palgrave Macmillan, United Kingdom).

Chapter 4

Robotic Process Automation at Xchanging

What's Inside: In this case study, we describe Xchanging's successful implementation of RPA using Blue Prism software and share eight lessons it learned to attain significant benefits: (1) RPA needs a sponsor, a project champion and piloting; (2) A culture of business innovation and technology accelerates adoption; (3) RPA should sit in the business; (4) Standardise and stabilise processes before automation; (5) RPA must comply with the technology function's governance and architecture policies; (6) Build internal RPA capability to evolve, leverage scale and increase business value; (7) Multi-skill the robots; and (8) Pay careful attention to internal communications.

4.1. Introduction

To understand the business value achievable with RPA, we begin this case study like the last, with the outcomes (see Table 4.1). As of May 2015, Xchanging had automated 14 core processes, deployed 27 robots that processed 120,000 transactions per month, for an average total cost savings of 30 percent. (Because Xchanging was aiming to build mature RPA capabilities, it invested more human resources than Telefónica O2, so total cost savings were initially more modest than reported in the last chapter.) Besides cost savings, Xchanging reported may other business benefits including improved service quality, faster service delivery, and scalability. A major theme from the case is that the operations teams embraced RPA because it released them from dreary work. By investing early and heavily in RPA, Xchanging is well positioned as a service provider to use its RPA capabilities strategically to attract more clients.

Number of processes automated	Number of RPA transactions per month	Number of Robots	Number of FTEs replaced	Typical cost savings per process	Other benefits
14 core processes	120,000 cases	27	Automation not about replacing people with technology but about continuous improvement	30%	• Improved service quality • High accuracy, low error/ • Exception rates • Faster turnaround time • Multi-tasking • Scalability • Increased compliance • Strategic positioning

Table 4.1: Xchanging's June 2015 RPA Capabilities At A Glance

4.2. About Xchanging

To put the RPA journey into context, we start by explaining Xchanging's business background.

Xchanging is a provider of technology-enabled business processing, technology and procurement services internationally to customers across many industry sectors.

Listed on the London Stock Exchange, at the end of 2014 it had over 7,400 employees (4,600 Business Process Services, 2,000 Technology, 800 Procurement) in 15 countries, providing services to customers globally. Net revenue for 2014 was £406.8 million, of which £282.4 million was from Business Process Services. Expected revenue reductions from exiting the Xchanging Transaction Bank, HR Services business, and London Metal Exchange were partially offset by full first year revenue benefit from MarketMaker4 (MM4) and the first contribution from acquisition of Agencyport Europe. Year-end net cash of £13.7 million (2013: £120.1 million) reflected £90.3 million of acquisitions and £43.4 million of capital expenditure. Adjusted operating profit of £55.8 million in 2014 (2013: £55.5

million), represented a 21.5 percent underlying year-on-year improvement.[1]

Xchanging was founded in 1998, specifically to address the relatively new Business Process Outsourcing (BPO) market. Its founder and first CEO, David Andrews, brought to market an innovative model of enterprise partnership – essentially a 50/50 joint venture model that created a third entity into which the client placed its assets, and Xchanging committed managerial capability in seven business competencies designed to drive innovation and continuous improvement. Xchanging began with four contracts – in HR and procurement with BAE Systems, and in insurance and claims services at Lloyds of London and the London insurance market. By 2007, Xchanging had over 4,200 employees in seven countries, with customers in 34 countries. To capture a variety of customers, Xchanging found it advisable to add four more offerings to its enterprise partnership model – outsourcing (guarantee sustainable savings); products (seeking to offer best solution); straight-through processing (optimising the value chain); and business support. In April 2007, the company went public, and was listed at 240p, at the top end of the quoted price range, and raised 75 million dollars of primary capital. It ended the year with a 17 percent increase in share price since listing and gave a two percent share dividend in May 2008.

However, over the next three years Xchanging began to run into problems – notably after the acquisition, in October 2008, of Indian-based outsourcing and IT group Cambridge Solutions Ltd. for £83 million in cash and shares. By February 2011, Xchanging gave warning that underlying operating profits in 2011 would be *"below the lower end"* of analyst expectations, as it cancelled its dividend and announced the departure of David Andrews, its founder and chief executive of 11 years. Ken Lever became the acting chief executive, taking up the post full time four months later. The new CEO's job was to restore profitability and increase revenues. He addressed quickly the problems associated with The Cambridge Solutions acquisition. A process of transformation ensued.

By 2015 Xchanging specialised in bringing domain expertise and technology-enablement to complex business processing. Deploying technology and innovation, Xchanging aimed to perform customers' non-core and back office functions better, faster and more cost-effectively, allowing customers to focus on strategic activities and adding business value. Xchanging's approach is to combine innovative technology with best-in-class process methodologies to address customers' back and middle office needs. Xchanging uses onshore, nearshore and offshore centres, and works across a wide range of industries building on domain strengths, particularly in insurance. Xchanging invests in product innovation, for example in 2014 with the launch and enhancement of new products such as the Xuber suite of insurance software, Netsett and X-presso. Xchanging's Procurement business has been called a global leader in its field, reinforced by the acquisition of eSourcing specialist MarketMaker4 (MM4) in September 2013, further developing Xchanging's presence in the US market.

In 2015 Xchanging, as a business technology and services provider, consisted of three interrelated divisions. The first was Business Processing Services, which, during 2014, had further simplified its structure with full ownership of German business, Fondsdepot Bank, and Xchanging Italy. Meanwhile in 2014, Technology accelerated strategic development of its Xuber insurance software business with acquisitions of Total Objects (for a consideration of £11.5 million) and Agencyport Europe (for a consideration of £64.1 million), enhancing its ability to offer software products that met international and standardised customer needs. Thirdly, Procurement, by 2015, had repositioned its product and service offerings, underpinned by the MM4 technology platform, and acquired Spikes Cavell Analytic Limited (SCAL) in February 2015. After four exacting years, Ken Lever, Chief Executive, saw 2014 as a challenging year in which the transformation process begun in 2011 was completed, *"To address the future market we have re-defined and focused our range of higher value offerings, based around technology, both in its own right and as an enabler and differentiator, and driven by innovation and insight into our markets."*[2]

"Xchanging is now a business technology and services provider. Our Technology and Procurement businesses offer the potential for higher growth and margin expansion, rebalancing our overall Group significantly in the future. Our foundation Business Processing Services business offers moderate growth, good margins and strong cash generation. Our focus for 2015 is entirely on driving the revenue and profit growth performance of the new Xchanging."[3]

4.3. Xchanging's RPA Journey: Context and Drivers

This chapter focuses on how RPA was adopted in Xchanging's insurance business, as a basis for further usage group-wide. By 2015 Xchanging had two remaining enterprise partnerships, now called shared services, and both in insurance. Xchanging Ins-sure services (50 percent Xchanging, 25 percent Lloyd's of London, 25 percent the IUA) had secured a further five-year contract (in 2012) to run the centralised Insurers' Market Repository (containing the market's claims, premiums, policies and related documentation) and all the back office policy and administration processing for Lloyd's of London and the London insurance market. Meanwhile, Xchanging Claims Services (a 50/50 joint venture between Xchanging and Lloyds of London) had a three-year contract signed in 2014 to continue to manage claims processing. By way of background, Lloyds of London is the world's specialist insurance market providing insurance services in over 200 countries and territories. The London insurance market (LIM) as a whole comprises insurance and reinsurance companies, Lloyd's syndicates, P&I clubs, and brokers. The core of LIM activity is the conduct of internationally traded insurance and reinsurance business. The management and administration of policies, premiums and claims with literally hundreds of London market entities, and millions of end customers is a highly complex, high volume business, in which speed, reliability, consistency and accuracy are vital requisites. An overview of LIM, including Xchanging's role therein, is shown in Figure 4.1.

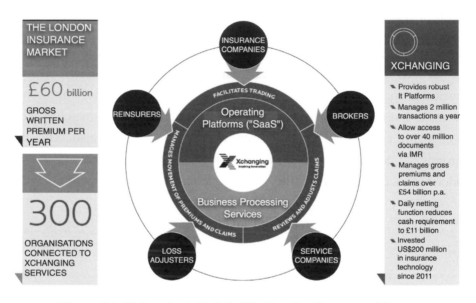

Figure 4.1: Xchanging's Role in The London Insurance Market
(Copyright © Xchanging. Reprinted with permission)

In these ongoing contracts Xchanging had already invested some 13 years of process innovation and continuous improvement. With Xchanging's stress on *"technology at our core"*[4] and with his own deep experience in technology services, for Adrian Guttridge, Executive Director, Xchanging Insurance, the step into RPA seemed obvious, but prototyping was necessary. In early 2014 he placed his data and information manager, Paul Donaldson, in charge of an RPA project to identify and automate ten processes in the insurance business, whilst establishing a long-term governance and support competency for the Group, *"We did not choose an IT person, and it had to be someone who understood process reengineering. Though I have an IT group of over a hundred people onshore and offshore many hundreds more, I put it into the business processing part under the Operations Director."* [5]

Paul Donaldson saw two drivers that RPA seemed to address, *"It wasn't just the customer driver for more business value. It was Xchanging itself having continual improvement embedded in its culture. That's why we have dedicated process black belts."* [6]

Donaldson was a Six Sigma black belt himself, so a suitable champion for the project. RPA also seemed to fit well with Xchanging's core values, including customer focus, innovation, speed and efficiency, and people empowered to make a difference through teamwork.[7] Furthermore, RPA matched with Xchanging's offerings of innovation and technology, but also with the promise of new, valuable expertise working for the customer, together with added service delivery flexibility:

"If you think about flexibility in something like robotics that hits a sweet spot. A robot can scale up and down and switch tasks. You'll train an application, a bit of software once, and if your contracts change, a robot can be trained quickly to adapt. You haven't got human resource type issues like induction time." **Paul Donaldson, Xchanging**[8]

There was another prize. If effective, RPA could also be exploited beyond insurance, thus tapping into Xchanging's relatively new Group-based focus:

"Our deliverable wasn't only towards processes, but to put a framework in place that could be leveraged for the Group – to institutionalise it." **Paul Donaldson, Xchanging**[9]

4.4. The Journey 2013-14: Start Out and Launch

According to the 2013 literature, RPA held out the promise of large cost savings – 20 to 40 percent often being touted – together with faster, more efficient, more accurate, labour-saving process operations and, for a service provider like Xchanging, more business value and more timely and higher quality service delivered to the customer. But all these propositions needed careful checking against what RPA companies were actually providing. At

Xchanging, late 2013 saw a product evaluation of possible suppliers, together with the identification of candidate processes (see Figure 4.2). Xchanging has a huge amount of back office, high volume, repetitive data collection and processing tasks – many of them still manual – and many still taking data from non-integrated legacy mainframe systems. Moreover information is extracted from various sources e.g., Excel, Access, PDF, and input into another system or used to generate reports. There is a lot of manual comparison of information across different screens in a system before netting and closing a transaction can occur. Entry into a target system has to be based on certain business rules. Blue Prism RPA products seemed eminently suitable for addressing these issues and achieving efficiencies from moving data from any source system to one or more destination systems. In particular, a number of claims presented to Xchanging seemed attractive. Robotic FTEs could be one-third the price of offshored FTEs, and could work 24x7 without errors. It took only several weeks to automate, with no need for IT specialists. Super users in operations could train the robots. The robots do repetitive clerical tasks and fit into existing operations. Working in a virtualised environment off a secure, audited and managed platform, the robots could be scaled up and down rapidly while working in any jurisdiction.[10]

4.4.1. Identifying processes for automation

The process of identifying ten candidate processes supported our finding in the Telefónica O2 case: the RPA software seemed most suitable where degree of process standardisation, transaction volumes, rules-based process and process maturity were all high.[11] Xchanging found it challenging to identify what 'high' meant, and made some initial miscalculations. A learning point was that you had to identify suitable processes: *RPA fitted more with high volume, low complex work.* As Telefónica O2 found, there was an automatable band or range beyond which there was little business value. Once this was discovered, Paul Donaldson found that it was not such a good idea to go straight to the business case then glide the processes in.

On the contrary: *"If you define the right process, the RPA business case will naturally follow... the economics will usually add up. It's not going to cost you long-term to deploy."*

2013 Q4	2014 Q1	2014 Q2	2014 Q3	2014 Q4	2015 Q1
Product & Process Evaluation	**Project Mobilisation**	**Project Design & Build**	**Initial Launch**	**Ramp Up**	**Improve**
RPA Product Evaluation	Business Case Approval	Architecture Design	First Four Processes Automated	Next Six Processes Automated	Full DR Introduced
Identification of Candidate Processes	Secure Key Resource	Environment Build	MI Introduced	Advanced Training	Segregation of Run and Change
Creation of Business Case	Mobilise Project	Training	Internal Messaging	Volume Ramp Up	Continuous Improvement

Figure 4.2: The Xchanging Robotic Journey
(Copyright © Xchanging 2015. Reprinted with permission)

4.4.2. Bringing IT on board

The business case was approved in early 2014 and securing the resources and mobilising the project became the main tasks to March 2014. At this stage one of the problems was the relationship with IT:

"There were a lot of skeptics in the technology space; it took a lot of convincing to allow business based-operations to take some form of control over what is a decent sized IT change initiative, and a different way of operating for us as an organisation." **Paul Donaldson, Xchanging**[12]

This was resolved by organising RPA as a technology project with a business driver, being done for, and sitting in, the business. Technology was responsible for delivering the underpinning infrastructure and architecture. This got translated into how the project members were assembled and organised.

4.4.3. Assembling the RPA Team

The RPA initiative had 20 people involved at various times, sitting under the Head of Operational Change – ten from the insurance business and ten from Group technology. Initially, four were developed by Blue Prism to perform the key role of process modeller – basically trainers of the software and system, and owners of the change activity. A separate 'run' function of two people took changes into business operations. From Group technology there was a dedicated systems manager and two support staff, responsible for servers, architecture and technology policy. Project management staff was also involved, along with Paul Donaldson as project lead. Up to August 2014, when the project went live, Xchanging also utilised the RPA provider, Blue Prism, led by their Engagement Manager Richard Hilditch, to educate and support, the plan being to build the in-house capability and become self-sufficient as quickly as possible.

4.4.4. Building the Robotic Operating Model

Xchanging gained implementation speed from selectively applying Blue Prism's robotic operating model (ROM) and Enterprise RPA Maturity Model (see Figure 4.4, and Lesson 6, below)[13] that, together, represented structured, accumulated learning from previous corporate deployments at, for example, Barclays Bank, Shop Direct, the NHS and Telefónica O2.[14] Blue Prism's ROM is particularly strong on building solid foundations for the future:

> *"You have to plan for where this is going to be, not where it is now. You have to build a foundation for a tower block, not a bungalow."* **Patrick Geary, Blue Prism**[15]

As such the ROM covered in detail seven areas: Vision, Organisation, Governance and Pipeline, Delivery Methodology, Service Model, Technology and People.[16] Xchanging drew selectively on this operating model, and Blue Prism's advisory, operating and training resources, together with Xchanging's own extant process/technology knowledge and resources, to create a strong development and implementation roadmap and team.

4.4.5. Training the staff and the robot

During May-July 2014, the RPA group focused on technology design and build, including the architecture, and server and software support, as well as training the process modelers and all staff. A key part was designing and testing processes to get the most out of the robots, and making components efficient, easily maintainable and reusable:

"Once you've trained a robot to do one thing – let's say open or send an email – you could use that logic in tens if not hundreds of processes. You've not got to train the robot for every time you want to use it. But the process expert does need to verify that the robot is actually doing what is required. You give the robot a log-on, on-board the robot in terms of what it needs to do, and then – the big plus – other robots you want to activate will follow suit exactly." **Richard Hilditch, Blue Prism**[17]

By August 2014, preparations were sufficiently advanced to launch four automated processes using ten robots. A notable feature, unusual in other implementations we have seen, was Xchanging's own introduction of Management Information (MI) reports underpinning the operation of the four processes:

"We knew what success should look like and the great thing is that a robot gives you clear concise metrics every single moment. So there's no data capture quality issues at all. It's very black and white. You know exactly how you do, and will, perform. You see the patterns. Because of our Six Sigma background, there's a lot of Sigma-based technology to monitor and to optimise success." **Paul Donaldson, Xchanging**[18]

4.4.6. Automating Example: London Premium Advice Notes

An example will aid understanding here (see Figure 4.3). One new robotised process was the validation and creation of London Premium Advice Notes (LPANs), which insurance brokers use to submit premiums to Xchanging for processing. Once an LPAN is created it needs to be uploaded to the central Insurers' Market Repository. The original process involved the customer sending Xchanging an unstructured data file. The file has to be opened and validated. The operator then has to collect additional data from a system called 'Account Enquiry'. Next, the LPAN is manually created and, with supporting documentation, uploaded to the Insurers' Market Repository. This is a high volume process that the operators did not really like doing, but Xchanging is contracted to do it.

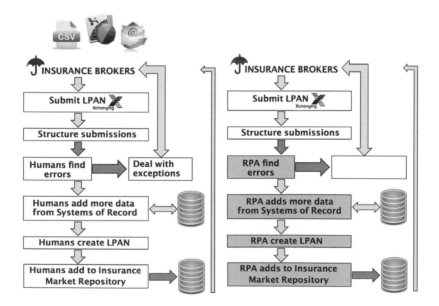

Figure 4.3: London Premium Advice Notices (LPAN):
Before RPA (left) and After RPA (right)
Copyright © Lacity, Willcocks and Craig 2015

Enter 'Poppy', a robot named by Xchanging's PAS technician Amanda Barnes after Remembrance Day 2014 – the day the RPA process went live.[19] In the automated process, brokers still submit premiums, and the human role is to structure this data into a standardised template, and hand it over to a pre-scheduled Poppy which reads the request. After various checks, which a human used to do, Poppy decides whether to complete or make an exception of the request. While Poppy creates the validated LPANs, humans check the exceptions. In this scenario, note that Poppy has to be trained correctly to carry out its tasks. Continuous improvement is also part of the work, with first time completion reaching 93 percent by May 2015. Where a 500 LPAN process previously took days, a properly trained robot can now do this in around 30 minutes – without error.[20] The robot can easily scale up and down to meet changing workloads, without human resource issues, e.g. staff availability, training, overtime cost.

4.4.7. Initial Learnings

What did Xchanging learn from automating this process? Four things:

1. Continuous improvement beyond deployment maximises benefits. The ratio between robot and human process times increases significantly when no web-based applications are involved.
2. High volume, repetitive tasks are better performed by robots, not least due to removal of human error.
3. Operations staff did not fear robotisation, but named and welcomed 'Poppy' as a team member, and indeed, asked if Poppy could be trained up to do more work for them.
4. The robot can outperform a human on quality, speed, and error rate metrics, but can only work at the pace at which the overall process allows it to work.

The launch also saw an intensification of the internal messaging process with many roadshows in the UK and India. Donaldson recognised that people would see RPA as a threat, but Xchanging was never expecting to lose anyone from the business through redundancies, having seen automation coming and planned around it. The message was that RPA gave people the opportunity to move on to other, more interesting, work. The roadshows gave evidence of people taking on new, expanded roles. One example was administering static claims, i.e. claims that have not moved for two years. Previously this was handled by an adjustor who would verify with managing agents that the claim could be purged. Closing the claim involved linking with the CLASS claims system, following London market purging rules and carrying out many validation checks. When this process was automated, the adjustors moved on to customer specific roles, while some became part of the RPA project itself.

While there is a big debate around whether automation would see the repatriation of work from offshore sites, Xchanging argued in its internal messaging that in this case there was no strong rationale for this. Xchanging had no quality problem with its many offshore sites that spanned work in Business Processing Services, Technology and Procurement, and repatriation would not produce a significant cost differential.[21] Offshore processing was already highly efficient. Rather, in practice, automation could be applied in those offshore sites to further improve performance where needed, for example in speed, and may well mean new job opportunities.

4.5. The Journey 2014-15: Ramp Up, Improve and Beyond

In the ramp up period from September to December 2014, the RPA team automated a further six processes. Advanced training for all the operators took place, and volume ramp up occurred across all the ten processes:

"Since really ramping up, we started to upskill our people even more and we've really started to escalate volume. We're working about 70,000 cases per month using our robotic workforce. We leave to human interaction about 7 percent of the processes we've automated – mainly business exceptions, or things process users don't want us to do. System exceptions

are incredibly low, usually down time in the application or an unexpected behaviour." **Paul Donaldson, Xchanging**[22]

By May 2015 the automated processes were achieving a success rate of 93 percent against the original 80 percent target. That came from all the continuous improvement. During 2015 Xchanging started to institutionalise its RPA capability:

"Platform disaster recovery is in, with every robot having a robot friend sitting in another site somewhere; it's as simple as that. We've got an exact copy in a separate site. When we were a certain size it didn't make sense to divide the 'run' and 'change' functions but we're now growing to a stage where it makes sense. 'Run' is now an India-based team. The continuous improvement thing's been quite major for us. We did a whole raft of changes at the start of the year and we've just got more benefits out of the process that we'd never planned to at the start by really tweaking in a controlled manner." **Paul Donaldson, Xchanging**[23]

4.5.1. Automating Example: e-policy

From late 2014 on, there developed a growing demand for RPA from offshore site managers, as part of their continuous improvement efforts. As an example, one offshore process is e-policies, which originally, as a high volume business, took 20 FTEs to administer. E-policies have been in terminal decline, and the process was over-engineered. The RPA team removed waste and automated the process reducing the FTEs from seven to two, with still quite a lot of human resource needed, since e-policies were mainly business exceptions. Offshore automation was happening selectively, where there was a business rationale, but work was not being repatriated through automation.

By June 2015 the RPA team was doing a lot more work in insurance, looking to double what they had already achieved in the first quarter of the year. RPA had also become part of Group operations, reflected in Paul Donaldson's appointment as Group Product Manager for Robotic Automation. Meanwhile the RPA initiative was being extended into the Procurement division of the Xchanging business. The F&A financial services area was also pushing hard to implement RPA.

4.6. Lessons Learned

According to Everest Group, four key factors are driving the need for more cost-effective operations in the insurance market.[24] Macroeconomic pressures include low interest rates, low GDP growth and high unemployment ratios. Meanwhile post-2008, regulatory changes globally have been causing massive upheaval in the insurance sector. Rising fraud incidents are increasing the cost of operations for insurers. Lastly, as the modern consumer moves toward digital experience, insurers need to respond – this being translated into increased pressure for more efficient and cost-effective operations.

Business Process Service providers like Xchanging need to respond to these combined pressures. At one level of analysis, Xchanging had gone as far as it could with existing methodologies and technologies. The company's continuous improvement capability was still strong, but a lot of effort was needed for marginal improvement, while offshoring further work would weaken both the onshore presence, and also Xchanging's image in the London insurance market. Meanwhile RPA fitted extremely well with Xchanging's three-year, 2011-2014, transformation (offering a further improvement lever), and its strategic positioning against major shifts in the Business Process Services market. RPA also fitted well with its innovation and technology capability and messaging to demanding customers desiring those very attributes. Additionally, Xchanging could see, from previous implementations of the Blue Prism's software, that the operational payoffs were considerable, if it took the accumulated learnings, married them to their relevant in-house capabilities, and built an RPA capability for the organisation as a whole, for the long-term. Interestingly, while RPA is sold, most often, on large savings on FTE costs, this did not emerge, in Xchanging's case, as a primary driver. Xchanging seemed to have a mature awareness of the multiple, even strategic payoffs that were possible, and in our view this gave RPA adoption dimensions of innovation, learning, and organisational acceptance – lacking in less successful cases.

In the experience of Blue Prism's Neil Wright, Xchanging shares three key features of success with implementations he saw at Telefónica O2 – cultural adoption across the board, IT engagement to ensure that the IT estate is scalable, and building in-house RPA capability. According to Wright, the first is particularly key for scaling RPA, *"Where it's gone exponential around the organisation is where it's been culturally adopted, and the C-suite is pushing it and driving it forward. Where we see a lack of exponential growth, it's just divisional implementation pioneered at middle management level. The concept and technology are embraced but their breadth of influence over the organisation is just not wide enough for it to go any further."*[25]

At Xchanging this view was digested and acted upon. In our further analysis, Xchanging did not have to face the major barriers to deployment encountered in less successful cases. Drawing on her Everest Group work, Sarah Burnett has outlined these as: legacy systems and service delivery; lack of adequate process documentation; lack of knowledge and/or buy-in; employment sensitivities; and service provider hesitation (to protect their more traditional FTE-based pricing models).[26]

Xchanging has gained multiple benefits from its RPA deployment so far. Cost savings run from 11 to 30 percent depending on the process being automated. Meanwhile there is significant and still improving service delivery in terms of quality and speed, and better ability to manage, in terms of governance, security and business continuity. Processing activity also has become more flexible, scalable up and down, and across activities, within wide ranges. Starting in the insurance business, Xchanging is also extending RPA to Group-wide adoption, and planning strategic, competitive edge payoffs. Xchanging provides rich learning. As a pioneer of RPA with remarkable results, the Xchanging case offers, on our analysis, eight lessons for other companies considering automation.

4.6.1. RPA needs a sponsor, a project champion and piloting

Xchanging's approach and successful experience is consistent with our earlier findings on IT-enabled business projects.[27] Successful RPA projects need a senior sponsor, who might spend only 2 to 5 percent of his/her time on the issues, but who initiates the idea, underwrites the resources, and protects progress into business adoption and use. A project champion – like Paul Donaldson – will provide between 40 and 80 percent of his/her time. The role involves communicating the vision, maintaining motivation in the project team and the business, fighting political battles, and remaining influential with all stakeholders, including senior management. Drawing on its multi-site experience, Blue Prism's early message to Xchanging was:

> *"You need someone who is your head of Robotic Process Automation and that person is going to be the evangelist, the person who owns and is responsible – and is seen as being responsible – within the organisation for establishing this capability and then for growing it out across the Enterprise over a period of time."* **Neil Wright, Blue Prism**[28]

Piloting, using a prototype 'time-box' approach and a suitably chosen multi-functional team, has been a widely accepted, effective approach to delivering IT enabled business projects since the 1990s. Xchanging utilised something very similar for its RPA design and deployment. Project management is needed. RPA users will be trained and assigned full time, along with IT specialist support. External resources may be needed to mentor, advise and fill resource gaps. Certain users and managers from the business may need to be brought in to provide additional knowledge and reaction on an occasional basis. Co-location of team members also helps the key processes of team building, knowledge sharing and mutual learning. 'Time-boxing' gives a short deadline, e.g. three months for a live business deliverable – in Xchanging's case, for example, the first four processes. If this is not feasible, break the project down into smaller 'dolphin', as opposed to 'whale', projects, each with a business deliverable.[29]

4.6.2. A culture of business innovation and technology accelerates adoption

Why was RPA adoption so fast at Xchanging? The answer lies in its fit with business strategy, and the long-standing imbeddedness of innovation and technology in Xchanging's culture. Xchanging's business strategy recognised that the outsourcing market was changing, as were customer demands. In BPO:

"Low-priced service provision is no longer enough. Service providers must add value for their customers. Innovation and technology-enablement are prerequisites for successful partnerships. Providers are turning to analytics and data manipulation to move from data provider to knowledge creator, empowering decision makers within customer organisations. As the business process services market matures, becoming more sophisticated, enterprises are increasingly recognising value in signing deals with specialist, best-in-class providers." **Ken Lever, Chief Executive, Xchanging Annual Report, 2014**

The way forward for Xchanging was to make differentiated offerings through innovation, technology, and customer and industry insight that, together, unlock business value for the customer:

"We have invested significantly in our strategy to put technology at the heart of all our businesses." **Ken Lever, Chief Executive, Xchanging Annual Report, 2014**

Indeed, the title of Xchanging's 2014 Annual Report is *Putting technology at our core*, with Xchanging seeing digitalisation as a significant driver amongst clients, and so offering technology to enhance the value of clients' complex back and middle office business processes. Having technology and innovation at its strategic and cultural core, Xchanging adopted RPA quickly and effectively. Without these prerequisites, other organisations will find RPA adoption more challenging.

4.6.3. RPA should sit in the business

All our respondents at Xchanging and Blue Prism were adamant: **RPA must sit in the business**. Thus Adrian Guttridge, Executive Director, Xchanging Insurance said, *"The technologists will back it up and provide support but it's got to be business driven, otherwise it would be perceived as being done to, not by, the business – not right at all."*

Paul Donaldson, the RPA lead, reinforced the message, *"It's in the innovation/ business part very deliberately. I'm quite protective that it shouldn't sit in the technology arm. My concern would be if you made it a technology project, you would over-engineer the process and you would end up delivering very little."*

For Blue Prism this is totally consistent with previous implementations at a range of clients. Moreover, locating RPA in the business is the underlying premise in their Enterprise RPA Operating Model, representing that distilled experience.[30] The empirical studies of small-scale and major IT-enabled business projects and of IT innovation for business value, also support this finding over many years, across industries and types of technology. Where there is a business goal, the technology is new to the organisation, learning needs are high and a multi-functional participatory team is required, then what Willcocks, Cullen and Craig (2011) call, in their book *The Outsourcing Enterprise,* an 'adaptive/innovative' as opposed to a 'technical' focus, is the way to proceed.[31] IT leadership is best only where the objective is the efficient use of existing technical know-how; the problem is a technical one; the problem definition and the solution and implementation are clear; and a detailed contract can be drawn up specifying requirements and deliverables.

This issue will be discussed in much more detail in a later paper focusing on the role of the IT function in RPA.

4.6.4. Standardise and stabilise processes before automation

In practice, Xchanging encountered initial problems identifying processes that were suitable for automation with the technology and software they wanted to run with. Several processes had to be rejected before the four most amenable processes were chosen. But Xchanging's prior excellence in process reengineering and continuous improvement addressed another element – unstable processes. Applying automation to an unstable and/or inefficient process would not do that much good:

> *"This is a big one for us and one which, I think, a lot of companies don't really understand. Don't automate a process that's not ready to be automated. Stabilise it first. It's a basic Six Sigma principle. There's a lot of 'lifting and shifting' needed just to move a task from a human to a robot. In all of our processes, we keep a delivery lead in the process world, to standardise and streamline before we automate."* **Paul Donaldson, Xchanging**

4.6.5. RPA must comply with the technology function's governance and architecture policies

Xchanging, including its Technology people, needed a lot of convincing internally that RPA was not going to introduce new risks: for example an important piece of data leaking out of the business, high profile IT disconnects, or raising concerns amongst their insurance industry customers, who tend to have a conservative approach to innovation. Paul Donaldson told us two things. Firstly, consider your technology infrastructure as early as possible and implement and stabilise it a few weeks before going live. Secondly, have a dedicated IT systems manager working with a business lead from the start of the journey:

> *"A healthy relationship between IT and the business is vital ... I have a*

kind of 'partner in crime'. He's a systems manager that works in the technology world, and has worked for me from day one. I know the infrastructure can scale up and down. If our processes tripled next week in size, we could probably fulfill that delivery for the processes that have been automated." **Paul Donaldson, Xchanging**

Patrick Geary of Blue Prism extended this point, *"The minute we are engaged with the business owners, we insist on speaking with the IT function. We know that business owners care about the part of the RPA they see. But IT is concerned with the stuff under the water, as it were. We tell them that RPA is data center and enterprise centric; it's designed to meet IT's requirements for security, scalability, auditability and change management".*[32]

As a corollary to Lesson 3 above, it is clear that RPA is not about not building process IT 'bungalows' but building within an overall IT architecture:

"With RPA you can go on a two day training course and be dangerous very quickly, if you aren't doing it in a managed way. There has to be an IT corridor of governance that sits around automation." **Patrick Geary, Blue Prism**

Paul Donaldson was emphatic, *"The way we modelled it was we had a business driver that sat actually as a technology project being done for the business; the technology guys were delivering the underpinning infrastructure and architecture. That's the mistake I see a lot of customers making – going alone as business. They will come unstuck because the technology just won't scale up and down. It will get them to a certain level and they're going to have a big problem to resolve."*

4.6.6. Build internal RPA capability to evolve, leverage scale and increase business value

It is clear that Xchanging did not see RPA as just a case of training the robots to run processes. Richard Hilditch of Blue Prism pointed out the comprehensive approach Xchanging adopted, *"It's the whole framework and capability around leadership, the methodology to select the right processes and prioritise those processes, getting the right governance approval boards in place, through to delivering the process in terms of the right people fully trained and organised, right infrastructure, the right support for that infrastructure and the right operating model to manage this new robotic workforce that they've hired* " [33]

Taking this approach, Paul Donaldson of Xchanging stressed the evolution of both capability and benefits achieved:

"What we launched in August 2014 is very different from what we have now. Anyone that deploys a process and just leaves it will not get the full benefit. It's only from seeing it live in practice where you find the unknowns that happen in the production world. You can simulate tests to your heart's content but can't really get all of those live behaviours. I can show you some great results where we've over-doubled the benefits. Simple tweaks in the process - for example simulating 'if I can save five seconds on that item by not logging out this way and logging in this way' - we can easily extrapolate that up and you can get that extra benefit from the virtual workforce because you can guarantee that behaviour will always be done in exactly the same way." **Paul Donaldson, Xchanging**

Xchanging, guided by the Blue Prism and HFS RPA maturity models, evolved quite quickly to the institutionalisation stage shown in Figure 4.4:

"They needed people dedicated to manage these robots when they're running in production, but Xchanging also need to allow their developers to focus on doing what they were good at and trained to do, i.e. keep developing those processes. From November 2014 through to January 2015, they embedded that and extended their team. They delivered wave two themselves, and so had moved through the industrialisation stage. By April 2015 Xchanging were fulfilling our full Robotic Operating model blue print and so had reached our certification stage." **Richard Hilditch, Blue Prism**

To realize the full potential from Robotic Process Automation requires a focus on building awareness and adapting organisationally as well as building specific RPA skills and capability.

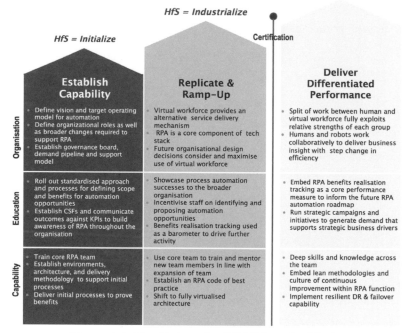

HfS = Institutionalize

HfS = Industrialize

HfS = Initialize

Certification

Establish Capability

Replicate & Ramp-Up

Deliver Differentiated Performance

Organisation
- Define vision and target operating model for automation
- Define organizational roles as well as broader changes required to support RPA
- Establish governance board, demand pipeline and support model

- Virtual workforce provides an alternative service delivery mechanism
- RPA is a core component of tech stack
- Future organisational design decisions consider and maximise use of virtual workforce

- Split of work between human and virtual workforce relative strengths of each group
- Humans and robots work collaboratively to deliver business insight with step change in efficiency

Education
- Roll out standardised approach and processes for defining scope and benefits for automation opportunities
- Establish CSFs and communicate outcomes against KPIs to build awareness of RPA throughout the organisation

- Showcase process automation successes to the broader organisation
- Incentivise staff on identifying and proposing automation opportunities
- Benefits realisation tracking used as a barometer to drive further activity

- Embed RPA benefits realisation tracking as a core performance measure to inform the future RPA automation roadmap
- Run strategic campaigns and initiatives to generate demand that supports strategic business drivers

Capability
- Train core RPA team
- Establish environments, architecture, and delivery methodology to support initial processes
- Deliver initial processes to prove benefits

- Use core team to train and mentor new team members in line with expansion of team
- Establish an RPA code of best practice
- Shift to fully virtualised architecture

- Deep skills and knowledge across the team
- Embed lean methodologies and culture of continuous improvement within RPA function
- Implement resilient DR & failover capability

Figure 4.4: The Enterprise RPA Maturity Model
(Copyright © Blue Prism. Reprinted with permission)

It would seem, therefore that we have, in Xchanging, a strong example of how to go through those first two key stages of the maturity model – establish Capability, then Replicate and Ramp Up – in a structured, controlled and professional manner.

The additional payoffs from this comprehensive approach were many. Once RPA was industrialised, Xchanging could engage hundreds of robots quite quickly if it wanted, because it had put in the right business and technical architecture to support them. Alex Bentley of Blue Prism also pointed out that, now that Xchanging has reached the 'institutionalised' stage, RPA could also be used to contribute to strengthening regulatory compliance, test out new business strategies cheaply and quickly, and address digital pain points in the organisation.[34] Adrian Guttridge, Executive Director of Xchanging Insurance, was thinking even further ahead, *"There is an opportunity for us to do something more and go to market with a robotics automation capability that says: you're not a client of us today, why don't we come in and help automate some processes for you? Alternatively, outsource to us a back office function and we will automate and bring it to a completely different price point. We will underwrite costs and you mitigate risk with the option to take it back after three or five years."* [35]

The lesson? Begin with a larger business goal, as well as a requirement for operational improvements. The strategic benefits of building the capability, and industrialising and institutionalising RPA will come through as RPA expands the reality of what is possible.

4.6.7. Multi-skill the robots

It is important not to implement point solutions per process. This lesson sounds small relative to Lesson 6, but is one Paul Donaldson, in particular, chose to emphasise. Why? Because, if you follow the approach detailed in Lessons 5 and 6, multi-skilling is relatively easy to do and produces notable benefits:

"The team leader makes sure all robots have turned up for work today, i.e. are logged in, and ready, then, driven by SLAs, allocates work and makes sure all the robots are kept busy. At Xchanging, because the first automation wave was well set up, and the robots well trained, they could reuse a lot of components in the new processes. Xchanging picked up quickly on reuse, switching tasks, and multi-skilling the robots, and needed us very little in the second wave." **Richard Hilditch, Blue Prism**[36]

Paul Donaldson of Xchanging is adamant on the value he gets from multi-skilling the robots, *"Multi-skilling: I'm amazed people don't do this. No different from what you do in a human resource pool. Get all robots on your virtual servers able to do any process. You can get them doing stuff when they've got no other work to do, and it doesn't cost you anything extra. It's an easy win that few follow. I think it comes from designing processes and robots upfront and from 'fit' with technology infrastructure. So don't go it alone just because this is a business driven piece of software. Have a healthy relationship with the process and IT people."* [37]

4.6.8. Pay careful attention to internal communications

The most recent studies of the global business and IT services market suggest a rapidly changing market with rising customer demand for new technologies, cloud computing, analytics and for suppliers being closer to business needs, as well as for business innovation.[38] More than ever before modern BPO services providers like Xchanging need, amongst others, what we call a transformation competency, a key part of which is managing simultaneous technical, organisational and work change. With RPA, Xchanging had the advantage of possessing this competency from its original design in 1998, through the staffing of its Lloyds and London insurance markets insurance contracts in 2001, to the present day. More generically, service providers like Xchanging tend to be good at behaviour management and dealing with communications in times of change: with outsourcing contracts it is something they have to deal with routinely, and the costs of getting it wrong can be prohibitive. As a result, with RPA, Xchanging was well set up to manage internal communications, especially given its extant culture favouring technology and innovation:

"I thought there'd be a lot more resistance than there was. Paul (Donaldson) should take a lot of credit for that. Also when we brought in those processes, we've redeployed people – and you have natural attrition anyway so just recruit less. So people have been very receptive, and also recognised it allows them to do more interesting jobs." **Adrian Guttridge, Xchanging**[39]

Xchanging took a very open approach to internal communications, making RPA visible across insurance operations, creating newsletters and road shows, saying in practice *"this is what's happening, this is when it's happening, come and see"*. Donaldson also made sure the operations teams were engaged to support the project and understood what it meant for them six to twelve months down the line, in terms of opportunities. Richard Hilditch of Blue Prism fills out the picture, *"All the Xchanging people I spoke to were very excited. I think Xchanging positioned it very well – they had regular communications. It got very high visibility at senior management because of the benefits it would bring. They have Group-wide communications about where the project is, where they are on this robotic journey and what the robot's doing. They even had a competition to name the robots. You could go into their new, main London office and see a massive screen that shows all the robots working just because they want to showcase what these robots are doing."* [40]

Naming the robots seemed to be a fairly natural process. According to Ann Manning, working in the static claims process, she called the robot Henry from day one, *"He is programmed with 400 decisions, all from my brain, so he is part of my brain and I've given him a bit of human character which works for me, especially when I'm working from home."* [41]

Working in the LPAN process, Amanda Barnes reported similar experiences, and also gave symbolic form to the robot Poppy, as shown in Figure 4.5. Both Xchanging employees said they had a list of further uses for the robots, essentially work they did not want to do, but to which the robots were eminently suited.[42] Clearly, the named robots are an effective input and product of the internal communication process.

The lesson here is that while RPA went smoothly, Xchanging did have prior advantages on transformation capability and organisational culture. Nevertheless the company felt it necessary to be very active on internal communications. Other organisations may not have such prior advantages and will need to be fully alert to the likely issues. Certainly Donaldson remained so, reflecting on jobs and the reorganisation of work, *"There will be a challenge when you get to a certain scale and you cannot pull those levers of natural wastage, job enrichment and reassignment, and that's something we will have to adapt to in time."*

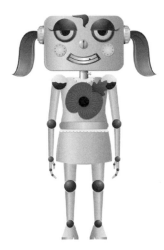

Figure 4.5: RPA at Xchanging: 'Poppy', the robot in the LPAN Process
(Copyright © Xchanging 2015. Reprinted with permission)

4.7. Conclusion

This chapter has provided major insights into the deployment of Robotic Process Automation in the insurance sector, and has detailed eight lessons for those about to embark upon, or already undertaking automation. As such we provide some success benchmarks which, we believe, are in fact applicable across sectors. Adrian Guttridge, Executive Director of Xchanging Insurance is very clear on the business value of RPA, *"I think RPA helps us hugely around error rates, consistency, volumes, speed and price point. For our existing contracts we will end up wrapping a service around it to our clients who can buy off the shelf as it were, but also it is something we can take to market. What's more, it gives us an extra option than just pure offshore labor arbitrage. The other thing it does is to demonstrate a level of innovation to our clients."*

But importantly, he also underlines something we detailed in our parallel cloud computing research, namely that all such technologies need to be placed in a broader context. In our book *Moving To The Cloud Corporation*, we argued that a range of technologies will operate in combination with cloud and with each other to create massive impacts on individuals, organisations and business, economic and social life. These are: mobile Internet access, the automation of knowledge work, big data/analytics, the Internet of Things, robotics and digital fabrication[43]. Adrian Guttridge put it this way: *"If we look at automation more widely, then it isn't just about robotics. If you look at digitalisation, mobility, analytics, and all those moving parts at the moment, RPA is just one part. You need to look at your overall technology strategy of where you're going and how this will figure with it. Businesses will need to clarify their own priorities. For example, is it to make their workforce mobile? Or to put robots in the back office? Both? Or something else again?"* [44]

Citations

[1]   Figures from *Xchanging Annual Report, 2014*.

[2]   *Xchanging Annual Report, 2014*.

[3]   Xchanging release *Xchanging 'Full Year Results, 2014'*, February 2015.

[4]   *Technology At Our Core* is the title of Xchanging's 2014 Annual Report.

[5]   Interview with Adrian Guttridge, Executive Director, Xchanging Insurance, May 18th 2015.

[6]   Interview with Paul Donaldson, Xchanging, Group Product Manager for Robotic Automation, April 22nd 2015.

[7]   Xchanging espouses six core values:

   • Customer Focus – 'We focus relentlessly on the customer. We provide flexible, practical and value added solutions. We deliver results by constantly taking the initiative'.

- Innovation – 'We challenge the status quo and approach our business with creativity, fresh ideas, lateral thinking and a commitment to do things in a new way. We inspire innovation'.
- Speed and Efficiency – 'We act quickly and decisively. Speed is of the essence'.
- Integrity – 'We are dependable and responsible people committed to being open, transparent, honest and direct in all of our activities'.
- Excellence – 'We are dedicated to continuous improvement, which is reflected in our leadership in technology, implementation, operations and quality standards'.
- People – 'We create value, are empowered to make a difference and are responsible and accountable for our actions. We succeed through teamwork based on mutual respect and the desire to invest in each other's success. website www.Xchanging.com accessed May 25th 2015.

[8] Interview with Paul Donaldson, Xchanging, Group Product Manager for Robotic Automation, April 22nd 2015.

[9] Interview with Paul Donaldson, Xchanging, Group Product Manager for Robotic Automation, April 22nd 2015.

[10] Interview with Patrick Geary, Blue Prism, Chief Marketing Officer, January 5th 2015.

[11] See Lacity, M. and Willcocks, L. (2015) *Robotic Process Automation at Telefónica O2*. LSE Working paper 15-03, April.

[12] Interview with Paul Donaldson, Xchanging, Group Product Manager for Robotic Automation, April 22nd 2015.

[13] As can be seen, the model marries well with the 'Horses For Sources' model, which also influenced Xchanging's thinking. See Sutherland, C. (2014) *The Evolving Maturity of Robotic Process Automation*. Horses For Sources, Boston, November.

[14] See Lacity, M. and Willcocks, L. (2015) *Robotic Process Automation at Telefónica O2*. LSE Working paper 15-03, April.

[15] Interview with Patrick Geary, Chief Marketing Officer, Blue Prism, March 15[th,] 2015.

[16] A more detailed account and analysis of the ROP model appears in the fifth paper in this series, published in Autumn 2015.

[17] Interview with Richard Hilditch, Engagement Manager, Blue Prism, April 19th 2015

[18] Interview with Paul Donaldson, Xchanging, Group Product Manager for Robotic Automation, April 22nd 2015.

19 Poppy was named after the day the idea was thought of – Remembrance Day November 2014. Interview with Amanda Barnes, Xchanging May 2015.

20 By May 2015 it was taking the robot five minutes to deal with 25 LPANS, which formerly took a human two hours and five minutes to do.

21 In practice the goal of Blue Prism, who licensed the software, was not to be cheaper than offshore, but cost neutral at worst, but faster, more replicable and accurate and offering greater local control. Interview with Patrick Geary, CMO, Blue Prism, January 5th 2015.

22 Interview with Paul Donaldson, Xchanging, Group Product Manager for Robotic Automation, April 22nd 2015.

23 Interview with Paul Donaldson, Xchanging, Group Product Manager for Robotic Automation, April 22nd 2015.

24 See Everest Group (2015). *Service Delivery Automation: The Business Case For RPA in Insurance Services*. Market Report, March 2015.

25 Interview with Neil Wright, Director of Professional Services, Blue Prism, April 16th, 2015.

26 Sarah Burnett, presentation at the Everest Group Webinar *Service Delivery Automation: The Next 'Big Thing'*, February 26th, 2015. The barriers are detailed in Everest Group (2015). *Service Delivery Automation: The Business Case For RPA in Insurance Services*. Market Report, March 2015.

27 Willcocks, L. Petherbridge, P. and Olson, N. (2004). *Making IT Count: Strategy, Delivery, Infrastructure*. (Butterworth, Oxford).

28 Interview with Neil Wright, Director of Professional Services, Blue Prism, March 27th 2015.

29 Our recommendation on IT-enabled business projects has been to go for 'dolphins not whales'. i.e. small projects based on iterative learning, with quick business payoffs, though the technology used must be consistent with the IT architecture and infrastructure of the organisation. Large 'whale' projects tend to go over budget, experience time delays, and sub-optimise on delivery. See Willcocks et al.(2004), op. cit.

30 A much more detailed discussion of the Enterprise RPA Operating Model appears in later papers, where the model will be compared against our analyses of a series of RPA case studies and their results.

31 See Willcocks, L., Cullen, S. and Craig, A. (2011) *The Outsourcing Enterprise: From cost management to collaborative innovation* (Palgrave Macmillan, London), especially chapter 5: *Collaborating to Innovate: The next phase*. Also Lacity, M. and Willcocks, L. (2014) *Nine Keys To World Class Business Process Outsourcing*, (Bloomsbury, London), especially chapters 8 and 10. Also Cullen,

S., Lacity, M. and Willcocks, L. (2014) *Outsourcing – All You Need To Know*, (White Plume Publishing, Melbourne). The academic findings are remarkably consistent over many years. See for example Willcocks, L. Feeny, D. and Islei, G. (1997) *Managing IT As A Strategic Resource* (McGraw Hill, Maidenhead), especially chapters 6-10.

[32] Interview with Patrick Geary, Chief Marketing Officer, Blue Prism, January 5th 2015.

[33] Interview with Richard Hilditch, Engagement Manager, Blue Prism, April 19th 2015.

[34] Interview with Alex Bentley, Strategy Director, Blue Prism, April 16th, 2015.

[35] Interview with Adrian Guttridge, Executive Director, Xchanging Insurance, May 18th 2015.

[36] Interview with Richard Hilditch, Engagement Manager, Blue Prism, April 19th 2015.

[37] Interview with Paul Donaldson, Xchanging, Group Product Manager for Robotic Automation, April 22nd 2015.

[38] See for example Horses For Sources (2014) *Executive Report: The State of Services and Outsourcing in 2014*. (HFS, Boston), September. Also Willcocks, L., Venters, W. and Whitley, E. (2014) *Moving to the Cloud Corporation*. (Palgrave Macmillan, London).

[39] Interview with Adrian Guttridge, Executive Director, Xchanging Insurance, May 18th 2015.

[40] Interview with Richard Hilditch, Engagement Manager, Blue Prism, April 19th 2015.

[41] Interview with Ann Manning, Associate Adjuster, Xchanging, May 25th 2015.

[42] Interviews with Amanda Barnes and Ann Lamming, May 2015.

[43] Willcocks, L., Venters, W. and Whitley, E. (2014) *Moving To The Cloud Corporation*. (Palgrave Macmillan, London).

[44] Interview with Adrian Guttridge, Executive Director, Xchanging Insurance, May 18th 2015.

Chapter 5

Mature RPA Capabilities in the Energy Sector

What's Inside: *In this chapter, we present a model of a mature service automation operating capability. Although there are several ways to govern a mature capability, we have found that a Center of Excellence (CofE) is a good practice. A CofE works across organisational units to identify, prioritise, and develop automation projects before they 'go live'. Once in production, the CofE's controller team schedules, monitors, and handles exceptions of the live processes. A mature service automation capability has several feedback loops that serve to strengthen the capability over time. The path to building a mature service automation capability is illustrated through a case study of a major European utility.*

5.1. Introduction

Mature service automation capabilities have evolved beyond proof-of-concepts initiated in a single business unit to create an organisation-wide competency. Although there are several ways to govern a mature service automation capability, we have found that a Center of Excellence (CofE) that serves as a shared organisational resource is a good practice. A CofE works across organisational units to identify and prioritise automation projects and houses a team of developers to work with business units to define, design, configure and verify automated processes before they 'go live'. After implementation, the CofE's controller team schedules, monitors, and works with business units to handle exceptions of the live processes. A mature

133

service automation capability has several feedback loops. The first feedback loop continually improves the automated processes as the CofE continues to work with the business units to potentially automate more functionality of a live process. The second feedback loops increases the CofE's productivity as more reusable components are added to and taken from an automation library.

To illustrate how a mature service automation operating capability can be built, we draw on the experiences of a major European utility's successful implementation of RPA and share the lessons it learned to attain results. At the request of the company, we use UTILITY as its anonymised name. After first experimenting with automation in 2005, UTILITY scaled RPA massively and has since built mature RPA capabilities. The RPA account manager for UTILITY promises that would-be RPA adopters will learn many insights from studying the implementation, *"UTILITY has one of the most mature, well-structured, well-oiled, and well-regarded RPA capability among any automation customer. Yes, it has a very impressive scale with 300 robots, but the maturity of their demand management, delivery management and robotic operating model renders their RPA capability truly stunning."*

5.2. The RPA Outcomes and Context

To further convince potential RPA adopters of the business value achievable with RPA, we begin this case study as we did in previous chapters, with the end results. As of May 2015, UTILITY deployed over 300 'robots' to automate about 20 to 25 percent of its back office work associated with meter management, customer billing, account management, consumption management, segmentation and exception processing. The robots process about 1 million transactions each month yielding an average return on investment of 200 percent within 12 months (see Table 5.1).

To put the RPA journey into context, we next explain something of UTILITY's business background. It is one of the big European energy suppliers of electricity, gas, and related services to homes and businesses. It also operates and manages a portfolio of coal, gas and oil-fired power stations. In 2015, UTILITY employed thousands of people and served millions of customers.

Percentage of Processes Automated	Number of Automated Processes	Number of RPA Transactions Per month	Robotic Scale	Payback Period on Typical RPA Project	1-Year ROI on Typical RPA
about 25%	about 25	1 million	2 humans orchestrate 300 robots that perform the work of 600 people	12 months	200%

Table 5.1: UTILITY's 2015 RPA Capabilities at a Glance

As typical in the energy sector, UTILITY had gone through a number of acquisitions, restructurings and shifts in corporate strategy. Under its structure, electricity was generated under a centralised European headquarters, with separate business units operating as retail businesses. Corporate challenges included reducing costs and increasing revenues in a political environment that was increasingly subsidising renewable energies. Both profit margins and utilisation of traditional power generation were in decline across Europe. UTILITY needed to target dramatic savings but was also looking to expand into renewable energies and to modernise its infrastructure.

In one country, the retail business aimed to become number one in customer experience by 2016. This required a number of transformation programs, process redesigns, and large-scale changes in the way the employees worked, and the technologies applied.

UTILITY needed to reduce business operations costs in order to contain consumer prices. Cost reduction became another major strategic thrust. Outsourcing, transformation programs, and information technologies were all deployed to meet this goal. In 2014, more work was moved offshore to India-based service providers and more work was outsourced to domestic service providers. As of 2014, about 50 percent of UTILITY's customer service processes were outsourced.

135

It is within this context of a business strategy to improve customer service and to reduce costs that the enterprise RPA ramp-up took place. Initially, RPA began in the mid-2000s in one division, fizzled out a bit, then RPA was adopted by another division a few years later where its true business value became evident. By 2013, under the new business strategy, RPA was ready to scale up to 300 robots to contribute to these goals; the RPA strategy became aligned with its business strategy. RPA had been enormously valuable in delivering process efficiencies that could be passed on to customers. RPA also allowed employees to focus on value-adding front-office activities, including working directly with customers. In the next phase, RPA would be deployed to an even larger digital workforce, with RPA becoming a fundamental pillar in the future business strategy.

5.3. The RPA Journey

The first few UTILITY people to experiment with RPA in the mid-2000s were from one of the smallest business divisions. The adoption happened so long ago that few remaining employees can remember it. UTILITY automated one process that used a handful of robots, and no more, for the first couple of years.

Most people mark 2008 as UTILITY's first serious adoption of RPA. This adoption occurred within the residential business with its millions of customers. At that time, UTILITY had many bespoke systems and many parts of the legacy processes were still manual. According to one senior executive, the 2008 objective was to find out how to use the technology. The 2008 business case was to license ten robots from an RPA provider, in order to automate a few specific processes that were costing quite a lot of money. A small team picked off very simple processes and proved that the technology worked.

The small RPA team began finding processes to automate, and it learned from early missteps. Initially, UTILITY had some unrealistic expectations about automation and subsequently picked some processes that were not ideally suited for automation. On one pilot process, UTILITY tried to replicate a Management Information (MI) function but soon realised that there were better tools to do MI. Through trial and error, UTILITY learned to better identify processes or sub-processes for automation. Sometimes it was worth automating just a portion of a process. UTILITY learned that the sub-processes (hereafter we use 'processes' for readability) ideally suited for automation have unambiguous rules, require limited exception handling, have high and predictable volumes, and operate in a stable environment (see 5.5 Lessons Learned for more detail). The processes to find, sort, and resolve infeasible customer meter readings were examples that fit these criteria well (see Chapter 2 for a detailed example). One senior manager at UTILITY reported that RPA gives UTILITY the opportunity to look at repetitive human tasks that are actually quite *"mind-numbingly boring"*.

5.3.1. The IT department tolerates RPA

Initially, the RPA pilots were so small that they were under IT's radar. But as RPA began to scale, IT began to notice large volumes of activity running on some systems. IT managers were concerned about the increased risks to corporate systems, since RPA was being conducted by business operations. Without IT's control, how could IT assure system availability, response time, security, and compliance? Suppose RPA caused something catastrophic to happen to the company's corporate systems? Anticipating a barrage of questions from the business to the IT help desk, IT questioned whether it should be running RPA as a major IT program instead of RPA being run by business operations.

The RPA team and the RPA provider demonstrated to the IT department that the software met its requirements for security, scalability, auditability, and change management. They convinced IT that RPA should be housed in business operations because RPA was only doing processes the way a human did – no programming code was being touched. After the initial concerns were assuaged, the relationship with IT improved, with one senior operations manager confirming that they now (2015) have a good working relationship with IT.

5.3.2. RPA adoption spreads

In 2010, RPA adoption accelerated. Word spread among business operations groups about the business value of RPA. More and more business operations groups wanted to automate their processes. People were added to the RPA team to meet increased demands for more automation. The team grew from three people to seven people. The RPA provider account manager recalled that *"It got to a point where demand was almost outstripping delivery supply in terms of their RPA capability to build it."* Business operations groups were increasingly asking the RPA team to examine their process documentation for automation suitability.

RPA spread to the industry supply side of UTILITY's business as revenue management, meter management, and boiler insurance processes were automated. In the sustainable practice part of UTILITY, RPA was applied to solar energy. By mid-2015, 25 percent of their back office transactions were being performed by robots.

5.3.3. Selling the IT department on RPA's Enterprise Worthiness

UTILITY's business operations group had grown the IT infrastructure organically as it scaled to 85 robots by 2012. During the growth, whenever the RPA team wanted to add ten new robots, they had to scramble to get another server. They ended up with a heterogeneous set of servers located in different countries. However, when the RPA team was looking to massively scale RPA to 300 robots, it wanted IT's support in turning RPA into an enterprise-wide system. The RPA team wanted a larger, more homogeneous and robust infrastructure. The RPA provider staff and the RPA team had several meetings with IT leadership and IT middle management to discuss the future expansion of RPA.

5.3.4. RPA scales to 300 robots

At the start of 2013, UTILITY implemented their plan to more aggressively and strategically pursue automation. Rather than buy robots for particular processes, the company decided to buy a robot army that could be deployed anywhere across its businesses. By 2014, UTILITY licensed 300 robots for multiple years. Robotic automation had become part of the strategy to use technology to increase customer satisfaction and help position the organisation as a leading energy provider in Europe. RPA would increase in the domestic retail business unit and would be deployed across even more strategic business areas including finance, administration and HR to increase efficiency and make cost savings.

5.3.5. RPA effects on outsourcing

Automation is not just affecting client adopters; automation is also very much on the minds of executives who lead outsourcing service providers. Offshore BPO and ITO providers aim to massively implement automation in order to stay competitive. For example, Wipro, India's third-largest outsourcing services firm, announced in April of 2015 that it expected to reduce its workforce by about 47,000 people in the next three years because of automation. Over the next few years, we shall see the degree to which clients continue to automate within their own business operations groups or whether they seek to have their service providers automate on their behalf. At UTILITY, both routes were evident.

As mentioned in the section on the business context for RPA, about 50 percent of customer service processes were outsourced, mostly to India. UTILITY had since automated some processes that were run out of India, representing about 5 to 10 percent of the volume of back office work. The work previously done by the Indian-based provider was now being done by domestically-based robots. It was less expensive for UTILITY to build a robot and run it domestically, than it was to offshore the work. While one might say this work was 'reshored', it did not create new jobs domestically.

UTILITY, like other client cases we are studying, was willing to work with its service providers to get them to automate parts of the processes they were performing for the company. UTILITY's outsourcing providers were actually very interested in learning more from the company about how to build a better RPA capability. A key question for a mature RPA adopter like UTILITY is to determine how much of their RPA capability to share with providers.

5.3.6. Strategic RPA Outcomes

UTILITY had two major strategic thrusts: to keep business operating costs low and to improve customer service. Pertaining to business operating costs, RPA projects, on average, yielded a 200 percent reduction in costs compared to the manual process. Pertaining to customer service improvements, RPA helped resolve or prevent the reasons why customers called for assistance in the first place. By 2014, customer service had improved dramatically in some areas. Although it is difficult to calculate the separate contributions of elevated management attention on customer service, the transformation programs, additional staff, additional training, and RPA, all interviewees concurred that RPA had a material impact on achieving strategic goals. Here are two examples:

UTILITY dramatically improved the percentage of customer bills generated on time. The company used to have a real problem generating customer bills on time; some customers were billed as late as two years after service. UTILITY brought in hundreds of additional staff to focus on solving the issues of late bills. It deployed robots to deal with exceptions. The combined efforts of additional human and robotic FTEs proved successful. UTILITY reduced its late bill backlog by over two thirds.

UTILITY improved customer service. As part of a 'customer first' strategy,

UTILITY wanted humans to speak to customers for voice activities on the front end, but RPA was used on the back end. RPA was used to reduce the backlog of requested work and to add additional customer features that would have been cost prohibitive or too slow if performed by humans. RPA was used, for example, to expedite the logging of customer complaints so agents could spend more time solving their problems. UTILITY also added services with automation for activities it couldn't do in the past because of limited staff and resources. For example, the robots issued more frequent notification to customers on service status. As a result of the commitment to customer service, UTILITY reduced total complaints by over 25 percent in 2014 and they were clearing the vast majority of complaints within 24 hours. RPA certainly played a role in this success.

5.4. Mature RPA Capabilities

By 2015, UTILITY's RPA capabilities were very mature compared to most other RPA adopters. It had a well-established Robotic Operating Model in terms of governance, RPA demand management, RPA development, and strategic outcomes. Although it took a few years to reach this level of maturity, client firms just beginning their RPA journey can accelerate learning by examining UTILITY's model. In this section, we describe a Mature Service Automation Operating Model (see Figure 5.1) as illustrated by the UTILITY example. In section 5.5, *Lessons Learned*, we explain more about how clients can move from an initial operating state to *a more mature end-state*.

5.4.1. Federated governance

"UTILITY has RPA ambassadors out in the business offering to collaborate."
Senior executive, RPA service provider

At UTILITY, automation was embraced by the C-suite as one tool to help the company deliver service excellence to customers while minimising price increases through lower operating costs. By 2015, UTILITY had a sophisticated mix of human and robotic workers to meet these strategic challenges. Specifically, the onshore workforce dealing with business process was about 2500 people and 300 robots, with the robots performing the work of about 600 people.

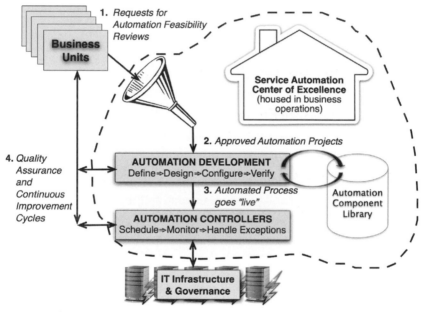

Figure 5.1: Mature Service Automation Operating Model
(Source: Authors)

The RPA governance was structured as a federated model. The centralised team, which we will call the Center of Excellence (CofE), was part of the domestic residential business. Thus, UTILITY's RPA capability was housed in business operations, not as part of the IT department, which was typical among our cases. The CofE helped other divisions with automation. The CofE comprised about nine people, an RPA manager, four developers, two control room staff, a configuration coordinator, and a portfolio analyst. Other RPA teams were housed in three other business units. These were small groups of two to four people.

5.4.2. Demand management capability

The CofE consisted of two main teams. A Development Team did the work of definition, design, configuration and results verification. The Control Room Team then was responsible for operations management and deploying the robotic workforce. Both teams complied with the IT function on governance, security, and compliance.

As a company with mature RPA capabilities, demand for automation could come from anywhere within the company. Demand for automations typically came from customer transformation programs and from operational teams in the business units (see number 1 in Figure 5.1). Demand was quite high, with anywhere between 10 to 30 processes somewhere in the development cycle. Candidate processes for automation were put through the pipeline where the CofE assessed its automation worthiness. First, the CofE gathered local work practices, also known as Standard Operating Procedures. The team also needed transaction volumes and transaction frequencies. It needed to know response time, for example, and whether there were backlogs of work. The CofE, in cooperation with the requesting business operations area, developed a business case if automation looked promising. With clear instructions on how the process worked and what the transaction times were, CofE produced a project initiation document. That document was then signed off by the business users, the automation developers, and any other invested parties before the development started (see number 2 in Figure 5.1).

5.4.3. The typical RPA business case

As UTILITY's RPA capabilities matured, it developed more ambitious business cases to help prioritise the high demand for automation. As of 2015, the business case usually required automation to project a benefit of at least a 200 percent reduction of costs within 12 months compared to the manual process. All costs and benefits were included in the estimates. The costs of RPA included technology costs for software licenses, hardware, IT service costs, and RPA staff costs. The financial benefits of RPA projected FTE avoidance, FTE redeployment, and/or FTE savings. FTE avoidance occurred when UTILITY used robots to complete work rather than employ, recruit, or move internal staff. FTE redeployment occurred when the company used robots to release humans for other work. FTE savings occurred when robots were used to reduce actual headcount in some of the outsourcing relationships. Besides cost benefits, other benefits were projected. RPA also had the ability to work faster and longer hours; one robot deployed at UTILITY could normally do the work of between two and five FTEs. Robots could technically work continuously, but robots at UTILITY typically ran 17 hours per day because of IT restrictions or business process operations.

5.4.4. The development and operation teams

The CofE used RPA developers to build the automated solutions and a Control Room Team to operate the robots once they were in production. The RPA developers were heavily involved with business stakeholders and operations team in the beginning. The RPA developers documented the project, developed the RPA solution, tested the solution by verifying results, then handed it over to the control room team once the robots were live. The Control Room Team then took over full management of the live RPA process, including interacting with the business operations folks to coordinate the daily stream of work, the output reports and exceptions (see number 3 in Figure 5.1). Besides the normal control room work, CofE aimed to continually improve the solution. The Control Room Team also received change requests directly from business operations users, which it handed back to the RPA developers. So the cycle of improvement continued (see number 4 in Figure 5.1).

5.4.5. Skillsets

A mature RPA capability has a well-developed idea of the skillsets needed for the various RPA roles. UTILITY certainly did; it looked to recruit RPA developers from among the operations staff who possessed a strong understanding of the business, a logical mind, and preferably had a systems analysis background. The overriding requirement to be on the RPA team is to be able to extract logical structures from chaotic business data so that prescribed algorithms can be built. IT skills were also valued, but one manager said, *"We're not IT staff but we have staff with IT skills."*

For the control room staff, UTILITY looked to recruit people who were organised, methodical, logical and had a consistent approach to work. Controllers needed to plan the day and organise the workload vis-à-vis other system priorities such that the correct work was sequenced and the correct numbers of robots were activated. The control room staff also needed good communication skills because they interacted with business operations people when they spotted any issues or anomalies.

One astounding fact about the Control Room Team was that there were only two people controlling a workforce of 300 robots. At peak times, these two controllers orchestrated the work output equivalent to 600 or more people. An RPA service provider executive explained, *"You know, when you think of that compared with a typical human workforce structure where you might have a team leader per 10 or 20 people and then you've got an operations head maybe in charge of 50 people, you're replacing seven to ten managers with just two people. That's another interesting cost-saving dimension to robotics really."*

5.5. Lessons Learned

As an RPA pioneer, UTILITY's journey to RPA maturity took a few years because there were no prior trailblazers to follow. It had to learn lessons for itself. Fortunately, the case offers clients just beginning, or even midway through their automation journeys, an opportunity to learn ten valuable lessons.

5.5.1. Strategic RPA requires cultural adoption by the C-suite

One RPA provider we interviewed has found that the clients who get the most business value from RPA have strong support from the C-suite of executives. The Director of Professional Services explained, *"The sites where RPA value has gone exponential is where the organisation has culturally adopted automation in the C-suite, with the C-suite pushing it and driving it forward."* This cultural adoption was evident at UTILITY. UTILITY's CEO was the evangelist for the transformation programs and the role technologies, including RPA, contributed to them. He spoke about RPA to C-suite executives throughout the company's regional divisions. That level of awareness and support is vital to an enterprise RPA capability. So how does one get the support of the C-suite? Initially, some key managers in customer service had prior exposure and experience with RPA. They served as champions of RPA and had the clout to warrant attention at the C-suite level. The C-suite understood that RPA could improve customer service and reduce costs.

Talking about some other RPA adopters, an RPA provider found that RPA delivered less value when RPA adoption was pioneered by middle managers with limited influence. The Director of Professional Services for an RPA provider said, *"Where we see a lack of exponential growth, it's in just divisional implementations where the breadth of influence over the organisation is just not wide enough for it to go any further. People across the organisation look at RPA as some sort of curiosity. Whereas when you've got that C-suite buy-in, that's when you really get the traction."*

5.5.2. Let business operations lead RPA

Who should own RPA programs – business operations or IT? At UTILITY, RPA adoption began in business operations and has remained in business operations since its inception. Our evidence is that this is consistent with previous implementations and true for a range of clients.

At UTILITY, the CofE was confident that the decision to let business operations lead RPA was vital for success. CofE had control over the use and exploitation of the robots within the business and within a good governance framework, which meant IT trusted the CofE. The CofE didn't have to go through an IT governance steering group to get approvals, which would have slowed the process. Over time, the IT department actually realised that housing the RPA program in business operations was advantageous to its own strategy; it could focus on core IT programs like ERP rather than deal with long lists of RPA requests from business operations.

5.5.3. Send the right message to staff

Across our case studies, we have seen clients primarily use RPA to automate very repetitive and boring work, freeing up internal staff to work on tasks that are more varied, complex, and interesting. So far, we have not seen internal layoffs directly attributable to RPA – the internal staff has been redeployed to other business activities or RPA helped to avoid adding headcount. When staff are not threatened by RPA, they welcome the benefits of fewer repetitive tasks into more customer-facing roles. At UTILITY, RPA has been around for so long that it is not perceived as a threat. To the contrary, the staff viewed RPA favourably. The operations staff has seen a legacy of prior automation projects that freed people from tedious tasks to focus on more interesting work. One senior executive told us: *"People see automation as an opportunity to improve what they do."*

In other companies new to RPA there will still be initial anxieties. According to Director of Professional Services at an RPA provider, this can be dealt with: *"How do we remove this fear?: 'I'm going to lose my job'; 'The robots are coming'; 'They're going to take my job off me'. Remove that fear by selling the positives, the values associated with what it'll mean is as human beings you're not having to do the boring mundane jobs anymore, that you can focus on the value-add jobs like interacting with customers."*

5.5.4. Evolve the composition of RPA teams over time

After ten years of adoption, UTILITY had developed a mature, federated RPA governance structure where most of the RPA capability was in-house and relied on the RPA provider for consulting. This mature end-state began with a very different team composition.

When UTILITY first adopted RPA, the provider trained about four client employees and provided mentoring, consulting and co-development for the first set of automated processes. Initially, the RPA team composition comprised about 80 percent RPA provider staff to 20 percent UTILITY staff. By the time UTILITY adopted its fifth process, nine months later, the ratio had flipped. The RPA team ratio became about 20 percent RPA provider staff to 80 percent client staff. Once UTILITY reached maturity, the provider's role became more advisory. An RPA provider account manager, said, *"Most of the consulting time is consumed for expansion and for helping the customer with ongoing best practices, upgrades, migrations, and the occasional complex system they may wish to deal with. So we are a trusted advisor and mentor rather than a body shop."* UTILITY's RPA team composition evolution was typical also among other cases we studied.

5.5.5. Identify process and sub-process attributes ideally suited for automation

In the discussion section, we saw that UTILITY had a mature demand management capability to identify processes that were worth automating. A more accurate description would be that UTILITY and other RPA clients automate sub-processes. An end-to-end process usually will have many sub-processes, with some of those sub-processes being more suitable for automation than others. Within an end-to-end process, UTILITY automated a range of sub-processes from as high as 100 percent of the sub-processes automated to as low as 2 percent of the sub-processes automated.

UTILITY learned that the processes or sub-processes (hereafter we use 'processes' for readability) that were ideally suited for automation possessed the following technical attributes:

- unambiguous rules
- limited exception handling
- high and predictable volumes
- operated in a stable environment
- accessed multiple systems
- known costs

The ideal processes had **unambiguous rules** because robots required precise instructions. The processes needed **limited exception handling** involving analysis, judgment, perceptual, or interpretive skills. These kinds of exceptions were handled best by humans and if there were too many exceptions, it typically was not worth automating the process. At UTILITY, robots handled backlogs of work or enduring business-as-usual volumes. **High volumes** often drove the business case for automating. Computing resources could be allocated in advance when the process had **predictable volumes**. Volumes need not have been stable – they certainly fluctuated with daily, weekly, monthly, or quarterly cycles – but they needed to be predictable within a range for smooth performance. The ideal process operated in a **stable environment**; if the interfaces changed, the robot needed to be reconfigured to accommodate the change. For example, if the robot accessed a system that had new features added, like new menu items or new option buttons, the robot needed to be reconfigured. Robots were very quick at logging on and off **multiple systems,** much faster than humans, which both reduced labour costs and increased speed. UTILITY also needed a clear **understanding of the costs** of a manual process so it could calculate whether the business case was strong enough to warrant automation. Typically, the cost of a manual process was calculated by considering the standard unit of time/average handling time it took a human to complete the process times the resource costs (salary, wages, overhead, etc.).

5.5.6. Prototype continually as RPA expands to new business contexts

At UTILITY most processes are subjected to a phased approach. The CofE does a phase one that gets the process up and running, knowing full well that a secondary development may come along to give further improvement. Since every context was slightly different, and there was always something new to learn, UTILITY was in state of 'continual prototyping'. Whenever RPA was going to be deployed for the first time to a new system, UTILITY recruited a small team to prototype a simple process. Once the simple process was up and running, the team was expanded to add more functionality. An incremental approach allows the CofE to manage expectations and also makes sure that the foundations are robust, secure and actually work as expected.

5.5.7. Reuse components to scale quickly and to reduce development costs

As UTILITY built a library of robotic processes, they were reused on other automation projects. Business operations groups now understood the technology and were increasingly asking the CofE, *"Can you automate this? You've done another one similar and I've seen other departments use automation, can you give us a solution?"*

With RPA, the turnaround time was much faster than for requested changes in the mainframe system. The RPA provider account manager explained further how component reuse lowered the development costs. He said, *"It's a self-fulfilling prophecy, the more processes you automate, the more objects you build in your robotic library, therefore, the more reuse you get, the assembly and delivery costs of those objects into new processes becomes more and more economic."*

As of summer 2015, the development times for implementing an RPA project had been reduced between 30 and 40 percent because of the reusable components.

5.5.8. Bring IT on board early

"IT needs to be involved. As clients build a virtual workforce, they have to make sure that a robot can have access to a system because there'll be someone in information security somewhere that says only humans can access a system." **Director of Professional Services, RPA Provider**

Although the CofE was observant of all IT policies, practices, procedures and governance, it did not, like other early RPA adopters we have studied, initially involve IT. In most customer cases we have studied, the reasons for excluding IT at the onset were (1) the RPA program was seen as a business operations program since RPA required process and subject matter expertise, not IT programming skills, and (2) fears that IT would beleaguer the adoption with bureaucracy. In all such instances, hindsight indicated that this was not the best approach; customers learned the importance of involving the IT department from the beginning to address their quite legitimate concerns.

The most influential evidence to convince IT that RPA was enterprise worthy has been its performance record; the RPA software used by UTILITY had never caused an IT outage in eight years of operations. Even with this performance record, a good relationship with IT must be maintained over time; it cannot be just a matter of an initial green light, because people come and go in organisations. New IT employees at UTILITY, for example, occasionally blamed RPA for network congestion and had to be educated about RPA just as prior IT employees had been educated. As part of stewarding the relationship with IT, the RPA team kept IT informed of any large RPA changes.

5.5.9. Build a robust infrastructure

"Optimisation of virtualisation in the run time environment matters. Poor optimisation can make robots slower than people." **Sarah Burnett, Vice President of Research, Everest Group**

Another IT-related issue is the RPA technical infrastructure. Like most client adoptions that begin in business operations, the UTILITY team loaded the

RPA software on its existing servers. The RPA 'infrastructure' comprised servers with different power, memory, and operating systems, which caused disparate performance and complicated management oversight. Once RPA was elevated to a strategic level, a uniform infrastructure was built (see Figure 5.2). The RPA provider account manager, said, *"They have a brand new shiny infrastructure which is delivered by one of the outsourcers. They've got 300 identical robots on the very latest servers in a shiny new data centre, so that's brilliant."*

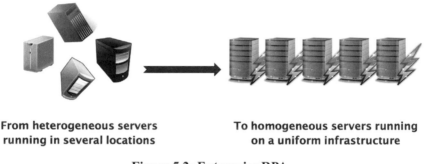

From heterogeneous servers   **To homogeneous servers running**
running in several locations   **on a uniform infrastructure**

Figure 5.2: Enterprise RPA

5.5.10. Consider RPA as a complement to enterprise systems

Initially UTILITY thought that the ERP system would decommission all the robots, but it soon discovered that RPA complemented ERP. UTILITY discovered that no enterprise software package can do everything, so RPA could automate processes not covered by the ERP system. The Director of Professional Services for a major RPA provider explained to us how RPA complements large enterprise systems: *"As we all know with a huge enterprise implementation, it doesn't always deliver everything that it was expected to deliver. There are always things around the edges that never get done, so people have to step in. So what we're actually finding as an offshoot is that RPA has become an enabler, a complement to an ERP program because we effectively finish it off."* Another issue at UTILITY was that the enterprise system left UTILITY understaffed since it had projected huge FTE savings in the initial business case. Rather than hire all the staff it needed to support the enterprise system, RPA was deployed.

5.6. Conclusion - A Future with Robots-on-Demand?

Much has been predicted about the effects of automation on the nature of human work. Some pundits expect that automation will leave very few tasks for humans – other than lawn mowing and hairdressing. Based on our case study research at UTILITY and other client firms, we predict a different future for the automation of knowledge work. In the next five years, we think that workgroups increasingly will comprise both human and robotic FTEs, and each will be assigned tasks for which they are ideally suited. The robots will very quickly extract, consolidate, and re-arrange data for humans to make judgements upon. We are seeing this today, but, in the future, the robots might not need as much pre-configuration or as much structured instructions. UTILITY wanted to next tackle unstructured data with automation. It wanted robots to read unstructured text, such as text messages or emails, and decipher what it means. The benefit is that robots are very fast, and the ability to rapidly process huge amounts of unstructured data and present an interpretation in real time would greatly enhance customer service. In the future, an agent on the phone with a customer might immediately ask a robot to mine a vast amount of data to help complete the customer call within seconds. Imagine when a human worker, in the middle of a task, could just demand a robot when needed – a Robot-On-Demand.

Chapter 6

The IT Function & Robotic Process Automation

What's Inside: *As noted throughout this book, Robotic Process Automation (RPA) is often the first type of tool among the service automation continuum to be adopted. Typically, business operations are the first group to embrace RPA because of its ease of use and non-invasive properties (see Chapter 2). However, when business operations are the prime movers, IT's role becomes muddied. In this chapter, we aim to show why business operations and IT must collaborate in order to get the most out of RPA and indeed, from all service automation tools. We recognise the general challenges facing modern IT organisations (since we are IT professors) as well as the specific challenges RPA seem to pose and the questions RPA raises among IT professionals. We show that RPA can actually alleviate the burden on IT's backlog of requests and suggest IT's specific governance roles that unleash the full potential of service automation.*

6.1. Introduction

In this chapter we focus on the IT function and its role in RPA. Why? Because our in-depth case work and interviews show much misunderstanding about RPA's attributes, and how RPA fits with corporate IT architectures, infrastructures, skills sets, governance and security procedures. In our view this has created unnecessary barriers to adopting RPA, and delays to gaining the large process and business benefits manifestly available – as demonstrated in our case studies.[1] As discussed already, some RPA adopters in our research have automated over 35 percent of their back office transactions. Clients report significant, multiple, often simultaneous benefits ranging across cost, process efficiency, accuracy, regulatory compliance, speed, reliability, error reduction, and improved customer satisfaction. Once corporate users pilot and adopt RPA, all report greatly expanded RPA usage both in volume and extension to new processes. The new breed of automation software providers includes Blue Prism, Automation Anywhere, Celaton, IPsoft, and UiPath. Many of their tools are so easy to use that business operations, including people with process expertise but no programming experience, can be trained within a few weeks to automate processes. Business operations groups from companies we've discussed throughout this book, such as The Associated Press, Ascension Health, Xchanging, Leeds Building Society, and Telefónica O2, have been using service automation to automate processes quickly – often with limited help from centralised IT.

However, therein lies a major challenge. Chief Information Officers and other IT professionals need to ramp up quickly on what RPA can and cannot do for their organisations. They need to know how RPA can be leveraged for the long-term and the critical role IT professionals play in RPA success. In this chapter, we first show how the IT function has immense challenges, but argue from the case evidence that RPA, properly managed, relieves, and can even be a real solution, to these, rather than just an additional problem. We answer four specific questions RPA raises, and show how, in practice (in the researched organisations) these were answered and navigated with relative ease. We then look at six cases in more detail and draw out the lessons learned from the cross-organisational, evolving history of RPA, and the emerging components of an effective implementation methodology.

6.2. Challenges of the Modern IT Function

Our most recent studies covered over 130 IT functions.[2] What emerged?

Today's IT functions experience multiple, often conflicting, pressures and demands (see Figure 6.1). Business pressures are now intense. The high profile area is business-IT alignment. This is very difficult to achieve, with dynamic business contexts leading to constantly changing requirements. IT functions are now judged increasingly on business metrics in terms of quality, responsiveness, business value, end-customer service and satisfaction, cost efficiency, fit with business need, and time to market. IT functions are also judged by increasingly knowledgeable, IT literate and demanding users at 'coal-face' operational levels.

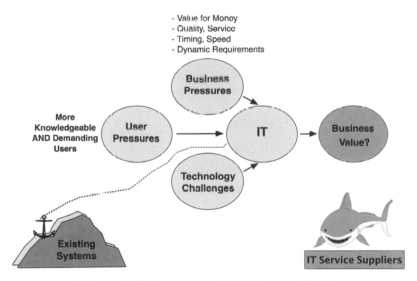

Figure 6.1: Pressures and Challenges For IT

Behind the scenes, IT functions are devoting anything between 30 and 70 percent of their effort and cost on maintaining existing legacy systems.[3] Failure here, and the knock-on effects to internal users and external customers, can become high profile very quickly, as, for example, several UK banks found in summer of 2015. Keeping the technology platform, architecture and infrastructure operational, streamlined, secure, and resilient for the long-term, while not detracting from business performance is a major undertaking now that IT is the engine room of the modern, digitising organisation. Deploying external service providers both onshore and offshore has been seen as one way of relieving the pressure on delivery. But our studies over the years show that outsourcing needs strategic direction, distinctive in-house capabilities, and constant management attention. The threat of further outsourcing may sharpen internal performance, but also creates further pressures on, and attention issues for, IT executives.[4]

Above all, in terms of expertise, advice and decision-making, the CIO and IT function form an organisation's central capability on Information and Communications Technologies (ICT). IT executives are expected to proactively innovate for business value through ICT development, implementation and deployment. Their key role is to navigate existing and emerging technologies, in order to lead/guide the business in piloting, adoption, sourcing, and usage decisions. In itself, navigating through the techno-hype, the capability becoming available, the IT that is merely useful and may be an expensive distraction, through to what will be of real strategic value is, today, an immense challenge. Social media, business analytics, mobile, and cloud as-a-service (SMAC) technologies and applications, as well as software packages, are proliferating at an accelerating rate.

Bigger still, on an eight to ten year horizon, strategically organisations are attempting to shift their existing technology architecture, infrastructures and applications towards digital platforms that can underpin the development, of what we call 'cloud corporations', i.e. digital businesses.[5] The daunting scenario facing the CIO is shown in Figure 6.2. Our most recent work suggests a range of challenges here:[6]

- Adoption of any major new technology is necessarily an arduous process banging up against culture, existing structures and governance modes.
- With cloud computing there are still genuine security and privacy challenges that have to be worked through.

- If governance and sourcing were a challenge in the past, cloud computing introduces new and more rapid risk.
- Integration with legacy technologies, and defining and executing the migration path to cloud computing can become a major obstacle. Many legacy systems are unsuitable for migration to the cloud computing so service integration becomes much more critical to achieving the true benefits from cloud computing.
- Governance and interoperability in the larger cloud computing 'ecosystem' become key.
- The human resource implications of cloud computing are considerable; we are finding digital skills shortages in-house a major drag on making progress on cloud computing.
- With all these challenges, very often the challenge of getting business innovation from cloud computing is being postponed.

Cloud Is Very Challenging For IT Corporates

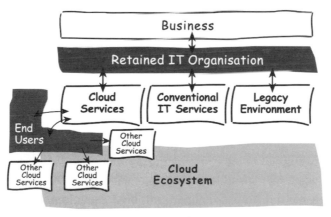

Figure 6.2: Cloud Challenges
(Source: Willcocks et al. (2014) Moving to the Cloud Corporation)

While individually each pressure or demand would seem to be manageable, it is the cumulative interdependent effect that is so daunting. Not surprisingly, with so many difficult challenges, and the likely high – and high profile – costs from 'dropping the ball' as it were, IT executives need in their armoury control, regulation, standards, change management, security policies, and strong governance. If Robotic Process Automation plays outside these, and business operations adopters of RPA seem to be taking over roles IT legitimately occupy, then this adds yet another threat or challenge to the IT estate and IT executives will, understandably, react negatively.

6.3. Answering IT's Questions about RPA

In the context of the overall challenges facing IT managers, RPA raises additional questions and seems to add to IT's burden. In our research experience, IT managers frequently ask five questions:

1. Is this RPA vocabulary misleading? *"It sounds like IT to us."*
2. Does RPA really help IT achieve our business imperative of better, faster, for less?
3. How far is RPA yet more 'shadow' or 'grey' IT, outside permissible limits and creating knock-on threats?
4. Surely RPA should be an IT project, under IT's control?
5. What are the governance, skills set and organisational threats and implications we need to deal with?

In Chapter 2, we answered the first question by explaining RPA's vocabulary and clarifying the terms 'robot' and 'robotic software'. In Chapter 2, we also explained the differences between RPA's roles and traditional IT roles as 'developers', 'designers, and 'analysts'. In this section, we look at the last four questions and how they have been answered in practice.

6.3.1. Does RPA really help IT achieve our business imperative of better, faster, for less?

Today's IT functions are expected to square the circle (or perhaps triangle) on resources, time and quality. Classically, these three project components are seen as trade-offs. If you want to do it quickly, it will cost more and/or quality will suffer. If you want to reduce costs and resources expended, then expect quality to go down and the timeframe to lengthen. In today's corporations, however, senior business executives expect IT to be delivered faster, better and cheaper, simultaneously, and adjudged primarily on business, not IT metrics. One of our very experienced respondents put it another way:

"How do you take a finite IT resource, and map it against the infinite demand that you get from the business. Because, in my experience, they're continually consuming and using IT, and requiring more and more to remain competitive." **IT executive, major utility.**

The pressure, then, arises from the enormous, rising demand for IT. Enter Robotic Process Automation. In our case studies of success, RPA was touted invariably because of a business problem, and/or a huge backlog in IT developments/fixes required by the business. At Telefónica O2, Wayne Butterfield, Head of back office services, had already pulled all the other levers to do more work with less money (see Chapter 3). His vision was to reduce FTE count by 50 percent, reduce average response time by 50 percent, and reduce back office failure customer calls by 50 percent. Servicing the London insurance market, Xchanging had a huge and rising amount of back office, high volume, repetitive data collection and processing tasks, many of them still manual, and many still taking data from non-integrated legacy mainframe systems (See Chapter 4). It is within the context of market pressure and business strategy to improve customer service and to reduce business operations costs, that a utility company's RPA deployment took place (see Chapter 5). RPA seemed a natural fit. For Steve Chilton, IT Director at University Hospitals Birmingham NHS Foundation Trust:

"The majority of areas where we've used RPA is to address what I describe as business conundrums, not necessarily IT conundrums. For example, pharmacy stock control transactions, which we implemented in days not months – and much cheaper than any alternative. RPA has been used to support functions including HR, Recruitment, Financial, Patient Administration, and Logistics, as well as supporting IT automation needs."

At Leeds Building Society, *"We are not unique in terms of experiencing that common frustration in Operations of having a significant schedule of developments and too few being able to get through the pipe at any one time. So there's 101 things to be done and our 'long tail' of change has become even longer. Deploying RPA, therefore, initially as a tactical solution, was very welcome."* **Kevin Mowles, Head of Business Support, Leeds Building Society**

Meanwhile at Gazprom Energy the issue is also meeting sales growth targets with limited people resources:

"We've got large growth targets as part of our mid to long-term business plans, and naturally we are driving sales across all of our customer segments, which can put pressure on the back office function. A lot of our business processes are manual and repeatable so if we can get RPA to work these processes as they come through, it should allow us to meet our targets and take the pressure off our back office teams." **Allan Surtees, Head of IT Delivery, Gazprom Energy**

Whether initiated by business operations or IT executives, in all these cases RPA played straight into IT's 'better, faster for less' dilemma. But with what results?

In Practice: RPA eases IT workloads and delivers high-quality results quickly and inexpensively

We have documented in Chapters 3, 4 and 5 the types and levels of success experienced at three organisations –Telefónica O2, Xchanging and a major utility – using RPA (see also Table 6.1 below).[7] The three cases show in great detail how RPA has been successfully utilised to address the 'better, faster, for less' dilemma. We have gained further insights from three other organisations – Leeds Building Society, Gazprom Energy and University Hospitals Birmingham Foundation Trust. Looking across these, RPA proved to be a good 'squarer of the circle' for business and process problems.

	# Processes Automated	# RPA Transactions per Month	Business Value	ROI
Telefónica O₂	35% of back office (15 core processes)	400,000 to 500,000	- Faster delivery - Better service quality - Higher compliance - Unbeatable scalability - Strategic enablement - FTE avoidance - FTE redeployment - FTE savings	650% to 800% 3-YR
Utility	35% of back office	1 million		200% 1-YR
Xchanging	14 core processes	120,000		30% per process

Table 6.1: RPA Value Delivered in Client Case Studies

Some illustrative examples:

"We have used RPA to significantly enable the organisation in terms of efficiency, ease the burden of overheads, reduce cost, and support the delivery of improved outcomes for our patients. The more that we can do to speed up efficiently designed processes and enhance transactional quality, potentially releases capacity and other efficiencies within the organisation which ultimately go back into patient care activities. It's been an effective vehicle for that." **Steve Chilton Director of IT, University Hospitals Birmingham NHS Foundation Trust**

"I'm utilising my 'small change' manager who has a large backlog of change requests he just can't deliver using standard development on legacy systems. He can probably use RPA to fulfil a significant number of those change requests. Rather than IT do the development on the system, you replace it by just letting the robot perform the same end-to-end process, so releasing the developers to do more value-add work. So does IT do the development on the system, or replace it by keeping the same process

but just letting the robot perform it, so releasing those individuals to do more value-add work? It's an easy decision." **Allan Surtees, Head of IT Delivery, Gazprom Energy**

We found RPA also easing the workloads of the IT function and even being applied within IT function work itself. All our respondents reported big reductions in development time, for example:

"It's been very fast when traditionally, we've been used to seeing nine to 18 month timescales for deployment as opposed to six to eight weeks." **Kevin Mowles Head of Business Support, Leeds Building Society**

Steve Chilton, Director of IT, University Hospitals Birmingham NHS Foundation Trust commented, *"My worry is that IT shops will not embrace RPA for the business, and either see RPA only as a tool to help them address IT issues, or will fail to support RPA appropriately, seeing RPA as a threat. We do use a bit of RPA in IT, for example in end-user experience monitoring, but largely we're using RPA as a real asset (working closely with and in support of business process stakeholders) to address business process proficiency problems within the organisation."*

Commenting on three recent automated mortgage lending assessment and savings application processes, Kevin Mowles at Leeds Building Society said, *"The business results have been excellent. In terms of the first assessments, we've got 98 percent completion rate (by RPA). For electronic ID searches it's not as straightforward, and we have 9 percent business exceptions and 4 percent system exceptions. The savings maturity application has a 70 percent RPA completion rate but it was always accepted that that would be the case. The main other benefits we've seen are significant speed, reliability, accuracy, and of course reduced costs."*

At Leeds Building Society (LBS) they are experiencing annual growth in workloads. However, workflow can be volatile because it is dependent on market pricing of products. At the same time, major investments in the core

IT infrastructure impacted on the business units through reduced organic development:

"So when you are able to introduce changes into the frontline through mortgage lending and through savings, the guys were lapping it up. It had become important for us to find a tactical solution where we could deliver process change." **Kevin Mowles Head of Business Support, Leeds Building Society**

Mowles, as did all client respondents, also pointed to the advantage gained from the reusability of the objects built in RPA. They can be recycled into other processes, so growing RPA capability further. Thus Mowles predicted RPA in ten LBS processes by September 2015, and in a 100 processes by 2017.

To summarise what IT and Operations executives told us in our case research: For the IT department, first of all RPA can give quick, multiple business wins to their business customers, and simultaneously relieve pressure on the IT work backlog. Secondly, RPA costs a lot less than many other solutions. Thirdly, organisations can introduce RPA very quickly with no great effort. Fourthly, RPA is a real asset, extendable to many pressing business conundrums. And lastly, the management problems IT experiences from RPA are trivial, with very little fallout, as long as RPA is subject to proper controls by the IT function. Which brings us to 'shadow' IT question.

6.3.2. How far is RPA yet more 'shadow' IT outside permissible limits and creating knock-on threats?

Shadow IT is proliferating as the attractions of mobile, cloud services, social media, endless new apps and the like, drive purchases and deployments outside corporate IT. Software as a Service (SaaS) provides a case in point. Initial cost-benefit analyses of SaaS may make shadow arrangements look immediately attractive, but losing control of architecture, security, applications and deployment can have far-reaching and damaging consequences. Elsewhere we also point out that, in heavily regulated sectors, such inexpensive, easily available, quickly implemented, seeming low maintenance 'shadow' IT may not be so attractive once regulatory agencies start viewing them as 'critical'.[8]

Is RPA shadow IT? All experienced users we interviewed agreed that, if badly implemented as a very basic tool outside IT sanction, RPA has limited business use, and can wreak havoc with security and enterprise architecture.[9] As 'grey', 'stealth', 'shadow', or even 'user-led' IT, RPA can introduce operational risk, IT insecurities, and create fault lines in applications. Further, it loses the advantage gained from properly developed and implemented RPA (described below) in being un-scalable.

But as we indicated in Chapter 2, as a programme that evolves into an enterprise capability, effective RPA is better characterised as 'lightweight' IT. Our colleague Bendik Bygstad first coined the term in his recent paper *The Coming of Lightweight IT.*[10] Bygstad characterises 'heavyweight' IT as the traditional systems and databases, which are becoming more sophisticated and expensive through advanced integration. There is an on-going effort to integrate IT silo systems into seamless solutions by various technologies, such as service-oriented architecture and cloud computing. We should regard this as a new wave in software development: the technical and management challenges are significant, and the costs are very high. The solutions are quite advanced, but also more complex.

Bygstad portrays 'lightweight' IT as the new paradigm of mobile apps, sensors and bring-your-own-devices, also called consumerisation or the Internet of Things. For him, the key aspect of lightweight IT is not only the cheap and available technology as such, but the fact that its deployment is frequently done by users (or vendors), bypassing IT departments. For Bygstad, the technology calls into existence the possibility of a new socio-technical knowledge regime with IT-based innovation increasingly being conducted by non-IT professionals. He suggests calling the phenomenon 'lightweight'

IT, because it is 'light' in several aspects: It is typically cheap and easy to use technology, it can often be deployed without IT specialists, and it tends to be mobile technology. He defines lightweight IT as *"a socio-technical knowledge regime driven by competent users' need for IT services, enabled by the consumerisation of digital technologies."* He suggests that to preserve the advantages of both lightweight and heavyweight IT, they should be only loosely integrated, in terms of technology, standardisation and organisation.

There is a problem with this argument, as Bygstag recognises himself when he says that lightweight IT *"presents organisations with a whole set of new challenges concerning use, security and IT governance."* He also talks approvingly of the concept of 'bimodal IT', coined by Gartner (2014), who suggest two different IT departments: one for traditional IT, focused on stability and efficiency, and one experimental and agile, focused on time-to-market and tight co-operation with business units. For him, lightweight IT extends this perspective. However, while Gartner suggest two different IT departments – or perhaps an IT department operating in two different modes – Bygstad suggests that lightweight IT should only be loosely coupled with mainstream IT, that the IT function will often be bypassed, and offers no practical solution to the risks he recognises in doing so.

Our studies of RPA implementation present an interesting test case for Bygstad's definition of lightweight IT. We suggest strongly that the definition is best modified to, *"a socio-technical knowledge regime driven by competent users' need for IT services, enabled by the consumerisation of digital technologies, and consistent with IT governance, security, architecture and infrastructure."*

This means that the level of coupling depends on the non-invasiveness of the lightweight IT, and how far it is to be evolved into an enterprise capability. Lightweight IT, as such, can still be an IT-enabled innovation in the business. It can still operate largely outside 'heavyweight' IT resources. Moreover, it can be implemented quickly, as a business project, using a different approach from that used for heavyweight IT projects – as we shall see more precisely in the next section. In the case of RPA, its non-invasiveness depends on how it has been designed, while in our cases at least, all clients wanted to build RPA into an enterprise capability. Implemented within this definition, RPA becomes lightweight IT, and avoids the perils IT executives rightly associate with 'stealth', 'shadow', 'grey' and 'end-user' IT.

In Practice: RPA is 'lightweight' IT that benefits from business-IT cooperation

In Telefónica O2 (Chapter 3) and at a major utility (Chapter 5), RPA was initiated outside the IT department and operated at low scale under the IT function's radar, until alarm bells began to ring. It was only once the IT department became significantly involved, and satisfied that RPA met compliance requirements, that RPA use escalated, and an enterprise RPA capability began to be built, supported by both business unit and IT resources. In the case of Xchanging, a service provider with a mature reengineering and IT capability, RPA was initiated by senior executives in its insurance business, but IT was quickly involved, and though some IT people were, at first, skeptical, the business and IT cases for RPA proved convincing. IT had to be involved because:

"Our deliverable wasn't only towards processes, but to put a framework in place that could be leveraged for the Group – to institutionalise it."
Paul Donaldson, Xchanging

At Leeds Building Society:

"To start with this was very much outside of IT. However, once we'd decided that this was the route that we wanted to go down (in the middle of 2014) and we reached internal agreement on a pilot and the money had been assigned, then from that point IT have been firmly involved."
Kevin Mowles Head of Business Support, Leeds Building Society

At University Hospitals Birmingham NHS Foundation Trust, RPA always fell under the control of Steve Chilton, the IT Director, who initiated RPA there. While at Gazprom Energy, Allan Surtees, Head of IT Delivery, had previous RPA experience at Telefónica O2, and understood the importance and role of the IT function in its adoption and how to build RPA into an enterprise capability.

The weight of evidence suggests that RPA is lightweight IT as we have redefined it. But if it is lightweight IT how is it best implemented?

6.3.3. Surely RPA should be an IT project, under IT's control?

For the last 15 years business executives, and many CIOs, have recited the mantra that *"there are no IT projects anymore, only business projects that are IT-enabled."* Our own research into 26 IT-enabled innovation cases suggests that more precisely they mean that most projects with a business imperative – and all IT-enabled business process innovation – need to be business/user led rather than IT led.[11]

RPA can be characterised as an IT-enabled business process innovation. How should RPA be managed? Our colleague David Feeny helps us enormously by delineating two fundamentally different ways of dealing with IT projects in the modern organisation – 'specialist focused' and 'business/ user focused'.[12] A specialist-focused approach is useful where there are clear technical problems, known solutions, the work required is in the technology platform, the technology is relatively stable and mature, and business user input required is trivial. Such projects can be primarily led by IT specialists. Detailed requirements and time-scales can be established and the outcome will be increased IT efficiency and improved technology platform (see the Technical approach column in Table 6.2). Much heavyweight IT may be handled in this way, though more often these days with an agile-informed rather than a waterfall development philosophy.

On the other hand, projects embodying IT-based business innovation are firstly business projects, and secondly are inherently unstable. They present adaptive/innovative and not just technical challenges (see Table 6.2). Detailed business requirements, as opposed to the overall business objective, are unclear and subject to rapid change. Flexibility for further learning and innovation is required. Additionally the technology itself (less so RPA) may be underdeveloped, lacking stability, and detailed technical specification. Alternatively, it will be a developed technology or piece of software, but being used in a new organisational setting (the case with RPA). Here it is unwise just to contract development and delivery to IT specialists, whether these be in-house or external service providers. Instead a multi-functional team drawn from users, operations, IT and suppliers needs to engage with defining the problem, and arriving at and implementing a solution. Learning is vital, innovation is usually necessary, and a general business goal rather than precise metrics point the way forward. Buy-in by multiple stakeholders – in the case of RPA, business executives, operations staff, end-customers as well as the IT function – is vital. Such projects, especially when they have strategic business value, or, like RPA, will become an enterprise programme, require a high-level sponsor and a project champion, both taken usually from the business, not the IT side.

Such approaches invariably embody some form of 'time box' philosophy. Business needs the solution quickly. A time discipline is placed on the project. The 80/20 rule is applied to functionality. Development proceeds through prototyping and learning, and the project is broken down into multiple projects or stages, each with a business deliverable – digestible chunks, as it were, or as we have called such projects 'dolphins, not whales'. Thus with RPA, we found adoption decisions highly influenced by the speed with which RPA could be implemented and produce business results. An important finding on time-box projects, however, is that though the development will be usually within the business, what is delivered must not be a 'portakabin', i.e. a building outside the IT architecture and infrastructure blueprint.

Analysing what people told us about successful RPA implementations, it is clear that, depending on the IT maturity and needs of the organisation, RPA falls somewhere between the techno-adaptive and adaptive-innovative approaches shown in Table 6.2.

ISSUE	APPROACH		
	Technical	Techno/Adaptive	Adaptive/Innovative
Problem definition	Clear	Clear	Unclear; Requires learning
Solution and Implementation	Clear	Requires learning	Requires much all-party learning
Primary Responsibility	Specialists	Specialists and user; participatory	User with specialists; multi-functional teams
Type of Problem-solving	Technical	Technical-adaptive	Technical-innovative
Contract with IT/External Services	Requirement based	Time/materials resource based	Shared risk-reward; outcomes-based
Objective	Efficient use of existing technical know-how	Effective implementation of existing solution in new setting	Effective business solution
Primary Leadership	Specialist	Collaborative	Business sponsor/ champion

Table 6.2: Specialist-Led, Collaborative and
Business-Led Approaches

In Practice: Business operations leads RPA

In most of our cases, RPA was manifestly both a response to a business problem, and to the IT function being under terrific pressure to deliver on multiple business priorities while looking after the IT plumbing - our Figure 6.1 becomes real, as it were. The emerging truth is that in many cases RPA is a response to business problems that have been low on the long list of IT priorities, or which the IT function cannot deliver on quickly and cheaply enough, despite the business value.

In the successful cases we have investigated, RPA was accepted as an Operations programme, with IT collaboration and scrutiny. This can be seen for example in the Telefónica O2, Xchanging and in other cases.[13] The only exception was where RPA was initiated by a senior IT executive who kept control on a temporary basis, to allow the Operations people to mature their understanding and capability in the area. At the University Hospitals Birmingham NHA Foundation Trust, RPA was initiated by the IT Director, Steve Chilton, who nevertheless commented, *"RPA is an operational asset that needs to be mobilised and led run and led by business process stakeholders working closely with IT, process subject matter experts, and process efficiency experts. IT use RPA as an enabler for business process stakeholders working as part of a wider programme group."*

At Leeds Building Society, Kevin Mowles, Head of Business Support, also endorsed that RPA had to be business/operations led, *"Whilst it is Operations led, IT supported the delivery through the provision of a Business Analyst and Project Manager. Internally we have a projects portfolio, and all central change is coordinated through IT. The identification of the pilot processes and subsequent development have all been operations led."*

Our cases establish that RPA must be managed as a business and operations project and programme, not an IT project (unless an IT department uses RPA software to automate IT processes, in which case the IT department would lead the effort). But what are the resulting implications for RPA governance, skills sets and organisation?

6.3.4. What are the governance, skills set and organisational threats and implications we need to deal with?

IT governance can be defined as *"specifying the decision rights and accountability framework to encourage desirable behaviour in using IT."*[14]

According to Weill and Ross, the experts in this area, top-performing enterprises generate returns on their IT investment up to 40 percent greater than their competitors, and IT governance explains a big part of these differing results. The important components of IT governance are: IT Principles – clarifying the business role of IT; IT Architecture – defining integration and standardisation requirements; IT Infrastructure – determining shared and enabling services; Business Application Needs – specifying the business need for purchased or internally developed IT applications; and IT Investment and Prioritisation – choosing which initiatives to fund and how much to spend.

Weill and Ross found that, for most organisations, IT principles, IT architecture and IT infrastructure strategies should be primarily the domain of the IT function. Meanwhile the corporate centre and the business units tend to be much more involved, or even the primary arbiter on business application needs and IT investment decisions. This was particularly the case in highly competitive, dynamic markets, with the business driving for high growth and fast responses to the market. Here, in fact, the IT function may have few decision rights, and a 'Business Monarchy' may prevail also on IT principles, architecture and infrastructure decisions.

RPA initiatives walk straight into many dilemmas here, especially in contexts where IT executives are nervous on having few decision rights in areas for which they feel responsible and exposed. But the actual clear answer emerging from the cases we have studied is that, to be organisationally effective, RPA needs to enter the existing IT governance processes for all five decision areas as soon as possible.

6.3.4.1. Skills Sets

Once we have navigated through the misleading vocabulary (see Chapter 2), the skills sets to deliver RPA, and build RPA into an enterprise capability, seem intuitive and well known. We will deal with these in more detail in the next section, but they need to be, initially, a combination of business process reengineering, lean development, business change, operational skills, business analysis, and IT development and IT audit skills. Subsequently, as RPA grows, RPA may well become a Centre of Excellence in the organisation (see Chapter 5), with, in large corporations, some distinctive capability in the business units utilising RPA. In all cases it will have good links with the IT function.

6.3.4.2. Organisation

The organisation challenge – where to locate RPA – was one of the lesser problems emerging from our research. We found skills sets and capability building much more important influences on levels of success. We conclude that it is not crucial where RPA sits in the organisation structure, though symbolically it is probably best located outside the IT function and within Operations or the business units whose processes have been automated. In truth, we found a variety of organisational arrangements, (which we will map in more detail below) together with the rationales for them. None of the arrangements we saw, however, seemed to detract from the effective usage of RPA.

In Practice: RPA governance fits within existing IT governance or may evolve to a Centre of Excellence

On governance we found various approaches, depending on the history of IT in the organisation, whether existing governance structures could continue to fit RPA decisions and management within them, and the understanding and maturity of RPA in the business at any one time. Most RPA adopters manage to fit RPA within the existing governance structure, then evolve the governance as RPA expands into new business processes and across the business units. In the early stages of adoption, though business-led, RPA is often small, seen as tactical and fits comfortably within existing governance processes. Thus at Leeds Building Society:

174

"Irrespective of where the activity is across the Society, whether it's just regulatory, process or systems, the project portfolio is managed through IT. So as soon as the RPA pilot was agreed in the middle of 2014, IT provided the structure and the support in terms of making sure that the pilot progressed against the project objectives and milestones. So RPA fitted into the normal governance structure." **Kevin Mowles, Head of Business Support, Leeds Building Society**

On skills sets, there was more common agreement across our successful RPA adopter cases, and we shall codify the findings below. On organisation, we found a variety of practices. For example, The University Hospitals Birmingham NHS Foundation Trust started from within IT function and kept it there for over eight years. Xchanging started in Operations but with a strong relationship with their IT department. A major utility experienced some problems with locating it first in Operations, but subsequently kept it there while developing a strong relationship with the IT department. As Patrick Geary of Blue Prism confirmed from his own client experiences, *"Not everybody does it in the same way. Some have more of an IT bias. One of our clients has a Centre of Excellence which sits entirely in IT with some business support. You have other organisations that are virtually all business with a small amount of IT and then you have ones that sort of sit between the two."*

Bringing skills sets and organisation together, one interesting development we encountered was a global financial services organisation that formed an RPA Centre of Excellence (CofE) from the start. According to one of our respondents, they did so *"because they recognised the business value of RPA, but wanted to balance the need for speed and agility on the business side with control and governance on the IT side."*

Clearly, the organisation in question had learned a great deal from earlier implementations at other organisations. The CofE of nearly 30 people (mostly RPA developers) sits between Operations and IT, and contains a set of roles and responsibilities from the Operations side and also the IT side. The CofE forms a cross-functional team with the clear objective of rolling out RPA automation on a global basis as quickly and as safely as possible.

6.4. Lessons from the RPA Case Studies

"The biggest lesson is about starting the journey with a conjoined IT and business collaborative approach. It's got to work as a partnership. If you don't involve IT upfront, you're doomed to failure because they'll just resist it for many good – and not so good – reasons." **Allan Surtees, Telefónica O2 and then Head of IT Delivery, Gazprom Energy**

"Once IT is on board very early, and you've got the right people looking at it, then it will go well. The problem, I suspect, is where people do it more off-the-cuff – they don't have the right level of governance, controls, and segregation of duties and then that can leave organisations a little bit exposed." **Kevin Mowles, Head of Business Delivery, Leeds Building Society**

"Robotic Process Automation is one of the best investments I ever made as a director of IT. I continue to see lots of opportunities on behalf of the business for sustaining this approach. The thing to be cautious about is to ensure you continue to grow and respond in a pragmatic, careful and structured way so that in the near future we're not looking at RPA as a problem we've created for ourselves." **Steve Chilton Director of IT, University Hospitals Birmingham NHS Foundation Trust**

Having focused on challenges to the IT function, in this final section we bring together the learning and thinking available from our case studies and interviews, and point to effective practice and ways forward.[15] The central issue we address is: How do you balance the needs of IT in terms of governance, security, and resilience, with the business demand for quickly delivered, cheap, automated solutions against pressing business imperatives such as better information, process improvement, improved customer service, the ability to respond to changing market conditions? From the IT angle: What do you have to put in place, in terms of an operating model and functionality, to evolve and support an enterprise deployment of robotic process automation?

By way of overview, according to Richard Hilditch, Engagement Manager for Blue Prism working with Xchanging, *"There are four key workstreams in delivering an automation capability. One is the infrastructure, the second is the operating model, the third is the training and the last one is the actual processes themselves. If you don't have the first three, then you can't deliver the last one."*

From an infrastructure point of view, the lesson is that the client does need to get strong engagement with IT. On the operating model, the further lesson is you do need to define the roles and create a new group. It is an organisational change to bring a robot team in, and a support group is needed to develop and manage the virtual workforce on a day-to-day basis. A lot of training can be done online with a mentor, but better still to have multiple developers who can learn off each other. On business processes to be automated, it is important to define these or their sub-sets and select the ones most amenable to robotisation before you start working.

However, we can suggest a more structured, detailed set of seven steps:

6.4.1. Establish Business-RPA alignment

This requires defining the RPA vision and the expected business benefits against corporate strategy. It raises the question of how far RPA is a tactical weapon, and the degree to which the intention is to evolve RPA into a strategic capability and asset. In our research cases we saw touted and delivered benefits that included increased efficiency and productivity, greater operational agility, reduced operational risk, enhanced IT governance, control and security, business insight. A sample of actual results from three cases was shown in Table 6.1. Not surprisingly, RPA needs a strong business case to proceed.

6.4.2. Define the organisational design and role of Head of RPA

We have seen RPA deployed successfully in decentralised, federated and centralised organisational and IT structures. What matters is deploying RPA initially in ways that fit with the existing structure and culture. However, be sensitised to the issues that arise in doing so. Deployed and organised in single, siloed business units, RPA will give quick wins but will not be scalable across the enterprise – standards can become fragmented and difficult to impose, and duplication of hardware infrastructure may result. In a federated structure low cost, scalable automations across multiple operations functions can be achieved using a central and standard platform. However, recognise that, if the model does not already exist, implementing centralised change and automation delivery management disciplines across multiple operational units can be problematic. A centralised structure has similar advantages as a federated one, and is a good model for RPA where a Centre of Excellence is already established in the organisation., Implementing a Centre of Excellence culture in the organisation, however, is a material investment if the structure does not already exist, and, as with centralised IT structures and IT resources, capability can become a resource bottleneck.

RPA needs an institutionalised project champion responsible for managing and reporting on RPA benefit realisation to the Board. Ideally this will be called the Head of Robotic Automation, for whom a detail role specification will be issued. Not surprisingly this will cover defining and delivering the Robotic Operating Model; acting as the internal evangelist for RPA; developing, managing and delivering on the demand pipeline for process automation; operational management of the virtual workforce; oversight of the technology platform; interacting with IT as required; managing third parties, and internal and external dependencies (e.g. change programmes, software and application upgrades etc.) to maintain business continuity.

6.4.3. Form an RPA governance board to manage the demand pipeline and assess RPA opportunities

As will be clear from earlier parts of this paper, and the case study evidence, RPA governance must be in the hands of interested stakeholders who will include, at a minimum, the Head of Robotic Automation, IT representatives (responsible for managing inward and outward dependencies, and gatekeeping demand on RPA capability from IT) and business unit representatives (who as consumers of RPA services provided by RPA are responsible for managing alignment with business strategy, and accountable for RPA benefits case).

The RPA governance board will be accountable for demand management, demand generation, benefits tracking, continuous improvement initiatives, and forming a delivery steering point as a decision-making forum and escalation point for emerging issues and risks. Managing the demand pipeline sees the governance board managing and generating demand, assessing RPA opportunities, prioritising processes for automation, carrying out impact assessments, and scheduling and reporting on the delivery lifecycle.

6.4.4. Agree the RPA delivery methodology, and the tracking of its correct use

The delivery methodology can be designed in-house, and adapted from a combination of how reengineering and IT projects are delivered. However some RPA vendors now offer a standardised methodology that can be adapted in-house, with the templates and policies embedded in existing client change management methodologies. A standardised delivery methodology – supplied by Blue Prism – is shown in Figure 6.3. One needs also to define the delivery management and tracking approach that ensures optimal usage of the defined methodology. The delivery methodology takes us from process management to defining, designing, configuring, testing and deploying the virtual robotic workforce while accomplishing demand management, operational support in relationship to technical infrastructure, IT security and IT governance.

Delivery Methodology – Key Deliverables

Delivery Phase	Deliverable:	Purpose / Description:
Process Management	Process Assessment / IPA	Define, by process, the feasibility, scope, complexity, effort, and projected benefits
	Business Case	Translates the aggregated results of Process Assessments into a financial case and provides the inputs for project planning (i.e. effort and cost breakdown)
Define	Refined Process Assessment (RPA)	(Optional) Provides further detail and clarification where required on process scope
	Process Definition Document (PDD)	Documents the current process at a keystroke level – forms the requirements for design
Design	Solution Design Document (SDD)	Translates the set of PDDs into an over-arching design to minimise development effort and maximise object reusability
Configure	Release Note	Delivers the Blue Prism Release Package into test (i.e. the output of process development)
	Configuration Test Plan	Generate conditions to test the functionality of the individual Business Objects, Components and Processes along with an initial end to end test
Test	Verification Test Plan	Generate & document test conditions to ensure all relevant scenarios are captured. Step through cases in a controlled manor in the presence of Operational SME's
	UAT Plan	Controlled testing, gradually ramping up the volume based on successful completion, and starting with the processing of a single case
Deploy	Operations Handbook	Provides instruction, information and advice on the running of the specified automated process in a normal daily operational environment for those who will run the process
	Operations Ready (Model Office)	Provides an opportunity to walkthrough the process with all key stakeholders (controllers, Business, IT) to validate the process is ready for live deployment
BAU	Implementation Plan	Outlines the approach, timetable and resources required for releasing the process into the production environment
Technical Infrastructure, Security, Governance	Infrastructure Design	Provides the architecture requirements and proposed solution for supporting the automations – this is a living document that will evolve over time
	Security Policies	Outlines the security policy and procedures that supports the Blue Prism Agility Program with input from Business, IT Security & Access Control departments
	Database Governance	Defines the approach for managing the archiving and maintenance rules to control the size and integrity of the database

RPA Methodology Deliverables

Delivery Management

Operations Support

Figure 6.3: A Standardised RPA Delivery Methodology
(Source: Blue Prism. Reprinted with permission)

6.4.5. Establish the RPA service engagement model required to support operational processes

With the correct support infrastructure in place, RPA optimises the productivity of both human and virtual workforces. Operational support activities include referral and exception handling, business continuity, testing and deployment, systems support, process support and product support. The roles and responsibilities for such tasks need to be assigned across business unit, operational, RPA and IT teams as well as the RPA software provider.

6.4.6. Define the people, their roles and responsibilities, and provide the training they need for operating efficiently in the existing organisational structure

The number of people needed for a strong RPA capability, even at enterprise level, is not large. However who those people are in the RPA delivery and support teams, their skills sets, and their ability to operate in a multi-disciplinary environment, are critical determinants of success. An important part of this is choosing an optimal training/mentoring approach for each role from a mix of modules covering product induction, assessment, controller tasks, developer tasks, and support tasks.

Looking across our case studies, RPA needs distinctive operator roles: A Process Analyst leads opportunity assessments and creates process definitions. A Process Developer will design, develop, test and support RPA solutions. A Test Analyst is needed to provide business process focused testing and auditing of the automated solution. A Process Controller administers, co-ordinates and controls the automated processes in the operational environment. A Service Analyst provides first line support for RPA production processes. Meanwhile, at more senior levels, we have found senior process controllers with expertise in all phases of the RPA development process and associated methodology plus hands-on ability in designing, developing, testing and support of the solutions. A Programme Manager is required to oversee the creation and ramp-up of RPA capability, while an Automation Manager would manage RPA capability to deliver new and support existing processes.

This terminology is indicative, and we have seen clients change the titling of roles, but the titling is less important than the substance and capability that the roles constitute. Note that these personnel will also work with IT support staff, and requisite business unit and Operations staff who will be assigned part or even full time to the RPA team.

6.4.7. Define a scalable, low maintenance technical environment and associated growth strategy

Each RPA supplier will provide/need different technologies, software and components. The key to building a sustainable RPA capability is to create a scalable, low maintenance, technical environment. An example of one is shown in Figure 6.4.

Blue Prism Architecture Components

Blue Prism Interactive Client *(1 per developer / controller)*
- Standard user desktop image with Blue Prism installed
- Used by Blue Prism developers to build and test processes (requires business applications to be installed)
- Used by Process Controllers to monitor runtime resources in live
- Typically provisioned as a data-center secured virtual device but can be a locally installed client or hosted on virtual infrastructure

Blue Prism Runtime Resource *(Typically 1 robot per device)*
- Standard user desktop image with business applications and Blue Prism installed
- Runs automated Blue Prism processes, usually "headless"
- Typically provisioned as a data-center secured virtual device and must be persistent

Blue Prism Application Server (service) *(1 per 100 runtime resources)*
- Windows Server or Windows Client operating system
- Used to schedule processes, authenticate users and encrypt data
- Marshalls database connections

Blue Prism Database *(1 per environment)*
- SQL Server Database, centralized repository that holds process definitions and audit information

*certain automations can support multiple robots per PC

Figure 6.4: Sample RPA Technical Infrastructure Components
(Source: Blue Prism. Reprinted with permission)

It follows from everything we have said in this paper, that as lightweight IT, all RPA technology and its fit with existing architecture, infrastructure and applications, needs to be fully audited for security, risk, resilience, and business continuity in the event of technical issues.

6.4.8. Plan for scaling

We found earlier adopters saw RPA first as mainly a tactical tool. As their knowledge and experience grew they sought to build their RPA capability and utilise it more widely across the organisation. The sorts of growth we see in the organisations portrayed in Table 6.1 are in more recent RPA adopters, now planned for from the beginning. An important part of this process is first initialising RPA use and capability, building that capability so that success can be replicated and ramped up in new processes, then institutionalising RPA as an enterprise capability that can give differentiates performance of strategic value to the business. The case for this is made by a relatively recent client of RPA:

> *"You need to apply the same sort of big enterprise systems discipline to robotics automation tools as you do to anything else. And don't forget – they tend to be running on servers, so you need to really think about it in that enterprise way. You need to consider business continuity and therefore disaster recovery. The business can and should drive the introduction of robotics, but really you need to think through what the long-term implications of scaling RPA usage in your organisation are, and therefore engage the IT department."* **Adrian Guttridge, Executive Director, Xchanging Insurance**

6.5. Conclusion

With RPA there seem to be four top messages emerging from the case studies. Firstly, start with a foundation where you can build globally at an enterprise scale. As one respondent put it, *"Do not build a foundation for a bungalow.*

Build the foundations for an 80-storey high building." Secondly, make sure you have all of the stakeholders involved very early in the process, and ensure security, audit, governance, control, and IT oversight are covered. This will not slow down the ultimate adoption of the application. It will not cost money. But it will mean that if all the stakeholders are involved early on, and the roadmap to success is drawn up based on these stakeholders' involvement, then the organisation is going to be able to build a much more solid foundation and a solid business offering underpinned by resilient IT. Thirdly, do not be tempted by quick wins, or service level or departmental solutions. This is something that needs to start as an enterprise rollout. Even if it does not, in the end, become an enterprise rollout, you have to begin with that concept. Fourthly, if you do these three things, you can build around the RPA, for example at the front end for unstructured data, and later for insight through business analytics.

The deeper you imbed RPA, the more touch points it can add value to. This fundamentally is the reason for thinking of and treating RPA as a platform rather than a tool, and as a programme rather than a one-off, restricted, desktop application that gives a quick, but limited win on its business case. A tool, at the end of the day, is in the hands of an individual and, as assisted (or attended) automation can give you some small gain. An RPA platform, however, represents an enterprise capability, which, when properly founded, the IT function supports, is comfortable with, and even leverages for its own purposes.

Having looked at the in-depth case study evidence, in the next three chapters we draw upon a further valuable sources of evidence, namely the views and RPA experiences of a range of practitioners drawn from client, provider and advisor organisations.

Citations

[1] See papers by Mary Lacity, Leslie Willcocks and Andrew Craig (2015) on *Robotic Process Automation at Telefónica O2*, LSE Outsourcing Unit paper 15/03; *Robotic Process Automation at Xchanging,* LSE Outsourcing Unit paper 15/03. Significant benefits are also recorded by clients at three other major organisations we have researched, namely Leeds Building Society, University Hospitals Birmingham NHS Foundation Trust, and a major utility. See also chapter 5.

[2] See Willcocks, L., Venters, W. and Whitley, E. (2014) *Moving To The Cloud Corporation*, (Palgrave Macmillan, London). Also Lacity, M. and Willcocks, L. (2015) *Nine Keys To World Class Business Process Outsourcing.* (Bloomsbury Press, London). Our research findings on evolving IT function structure and capability towards delivering strategic business value are summarised in Willcocks, L., Petherbridge, P. and Olson, N. (2005) *Making IT Count: Strategy, Delivery, Infrastructure.* (BH Press, Oxford).

[3] We found the high performers in IT in the lower spending range on legacy maintenance, and much more on creating digital platforms and innovating for the business. See Lacity and Willcocks (2015) op. cit.; also Weill, P. and Ross, J. (2009) *IT Savvy: What Top Executives Must Know To Go From Pain To Gain.* (HBS Press, Boston).

[4] See Cullen, S., Lacity, M. and Willcocks, L (2014) *Outsourcing – All You Need To Know.* (White Plume, Melbourne) for a summary of our research on different sourcing options, and a guide to emerging effective practice.

[5] See Willcocks, Venters and Whitley (2014) op. cit.

[6] Across 2011-15 we carried out three in-depth research projects into the cloud experiences and practices of 75 SMEs and large corporations in Europe, Asia-Pacific, and the US. See Willcocks, L. and Lacity, M. (2015) *Cloud Management: Where we are going and how to get there*, Parts 1 and 2 Business Technology Strategies, volume 8 nos. 4 and 5, Cutter IT Consortium.

[7] See papers by Mary Lacity, Leslie Willcocks and Andrew Craig (2015) on *Robotic Process Automation at Telefónica O2,* LSE Outsourcing Unit paper 15/03; *Robotic Process Automation at Xchanging,* LSE Outsourcing Unit paper 15/03; and chapter 5.

[8] See Gozman, D. and Willcocks, L. (2015) *Shadow Boxing Clever,* Professional Outsourcing Magazine, 21, Summer, pages 36-45. Properly implemented, in fact RPA can positively assist regulatory compliance.

[9] One problem mentioned was crashing applications by crowd swarming systems of record. This can occur because users apply their own passwords and IDs.

As stealth IT, the robots do not have their own IDs or their own permissions, so do not identify themselves as robots to other applications. Screen scrape encrypting tools, often labelled RPA, tend to be unmanaged and uncontrolled. This introduces new risks into an operational IT architecture, and raises multiple issue including security, resilience, performance, impact on underlying systems, change control, and user permitted access rights. When sold as part of an outsourcing contract, they create a further latent problem at the end of the contract in that the software tends to be written in freeware code that is non-transportable to another service provider or the client.

[10] Bygstad, B. (2015) *The Coming of Lightweight IT,* Proceedings of the ECIS conference, Munster, May.

[11] See Cullen, S. Lacity, M. and Willcocks, L. (2014) *Outsourcing – All You Need To Know.* (White Plume, Melbourne), chapter 13, for a detailed account of how to deliver business process innovation projects.

[12] See Willcocks, L., Feeny, D. and Islei, G. (1997) *Managing IT As A Strategic Resource.* (McGraw Hill, Maidenhead). Also Willcocks, Petherbridge and Olson (2002) op. cit. Chapter 8.

[13] See papers by Mary Lacity, Leslie Willcocks and Andrew Craig (2015) on *Robotic Process Automation at Telefónica O2,* LSE Outsourcing Unit paper 15/03; *Robotic Process Automation at Xchanging* LSE Outsourcing Unit paper 15/03; and chapter 5.

[14] Weill, P. and Ross, J. (2004) *IT Governance. How top performers manage IT decision rights for superior results,* Harvard Business Press, Boston.

[15] This section draws upon 27 formal interviews, and 25 further less structured discussions with clients, RPA service providers and advisors. It also draws upon Blue Prism's Enterprise Robotic Process Automation Model, and the learning it embodies to October 2015 from working with over 100 clients on RPA development.

Chapter 7

In Their Own Words: Client Responses

What's Inside: *Clients from the Associated Press, the Ascension Ministry Service Center, the VHA, and Virgin Trains share their service automation adoption stories, the business value delivered, and lessons learned. The clients in this chapter implemented different service automation software (from Automated Insights, Blue Prism, Automation Anywhere, and Celaton) but all reported similar business results pertaining to improved staff job satisfaction, improved service quality, the ability to expand services and to increase service volumes. FTE savings occurred but were not the main drivers of automation in these organisations.*

7.1. Introduction

While researching this book, we had the privilege of formally interviewing many thought leaders on the topic of service automation and the future of work. In previous chapters, we analysed, synthesised, and aggregated the stories and lessons from formal interviews, but in this chapter, we invited four clients who have deployed automation in their organisations to be heard '*in their own words*', unfiltered and unedited (see Table 7.1 below and the *Notes on Contributors* on page 19). In this chapter, we first describe their organisations and the questions we asked them. Next, we present their contributions and then we extract some common themes from across the contributions.

Service Automation Stakeholder	Name	Title	Company	Country Headquarters
Client	Lou Ferrara	Vice President	The Associated Press	United States
	A. J. Hanna	Sr. Director Operations Support	Ascension Ministry Service Center	United States
	Michael 'Chet' Chambers	Director of Information Technology and Development	VHA	United States
	Christian Clarke	Head of Customer Relations	Virgin Trains	United Kingdom

Table 7.1: Client Thought Leaders
Contributing to *In Their Own Words*

7.1.1. Overview of the Contributing Organisations

The four clients are from The Associated Press (AP), the Ascension Ministry Service Center (MSC), the VHA, and Virgin Trains. Three of the four companies are based in the United States, which helps to bring diversity when viewed with our sample of UK/European client adoptions discussed in previous chapters.

The AP is a multinational, not-for-profit news agency headquartered in New York City. It has about 3,200 employees and earns over $600 million in revenue each year.[1] Lou Ferrara, Vice President for the AP, shared his experiences with adopting Automated Insights in 2014 to automate corporate earnings reports. His automation efforts increased the volume and quality of earnings reports, and freed his journalists to work on more challenging assignments.

The MSC is headquartered in Indianapolis, Indiana and provides human resources, supply chain, and finance services. The work of the MSC supports 22 Ascension Ministries, 135 acute care hospitals and 120,000 associates, in their efforts to lead healthcare's transformation.[2] As a shared service providing hire-to-retire, record-to-report, procure-to-pay, and direct support services, the MSC was created to reduce costs without impacting care by sharing services – leveraging size and scale was very important to its mission of keeping costs contained.[3] A.J. Hanna, Sr. Director Operations Support, tells below the story of adopting Blue Prism in 2014 to help automate 'swivel' chair processes. Automation improved the quality and response time of services and freed staff to focus on more value-added work.

The VHA is a corporation based in Irving Texas. Founded in 1977, the VHA is a national health care network of not-for-profit hospitals, and UHC, the alliance of the nation's leading academic medical centres, which together form the largest member-owned health care company in the United States. The VHA applies its knowledge in analytics, contracting, consulting and network development to deliver nearly $3 billion in savings and additional value to members each year.[4] The VHA has over 1,000 employees and earns over $700 million annually.[5] Michael 'Chet' Chambers, Director of IT and Development, explained how he adopted Automation Anywhere software to free business staff from time-consuming, dreary activities so they could focus on selling and revenue generation.

Virgin Trains is a train operating company based in The United Kingdom. Virgin, the brand founded by entrepreneur Richard Branson, owns 51 percent, and Stagecoach owns 49 percent. Virgin Trains operates long-distance passenger services on the West Coast Main Line between London, West Midlands, North West England, North Wales and Scotland.[6] The service carries more than 32 million passengers each year. Virgin Trains employs over 3,000 people.[7] Christian Clark, Head of Customer Relations, explained how Virgin Trains adopted Celaton to filter, organise, and route customer correspondence so staff could focus on engaging customers and improving customer relationships.

7.1.2. Questions Posed to Client Thought Leaders

Lou Ferrara, A.J. Hanna, Chet Chambers, and Christian Clarke are pioneers of service automation. Given their experiences as early adopters and thought leaders of service automation, we posed a number of questions to them pertaining to their service automation adoption, business value delivered, lessons learned and the future of service automation in their organisations. The specific questions were:

- **Client adoption:** Briefly describe your service automation adoption story within your organisation. Did you do a proof-of-concept, and if so, when and on what process? What was your initial business case? What were the critical success factors?
- **Business value delivered:** How has service automation delivered on the initial business case in terms of financial (i.e. cost savings, return on investment), operational (i.e. improved quality, faster delivery, better compliance), and strategic value (i.e. strategy enablement, access to new customers, better customer retention)?
- **Lessons learned:** If you had to do your service automation implementation all over again, what three things would you change, and why?
- **Automation and the future of work:** What does the future of service automation look like in your organisation two years from now? How about five years from now?

Below, their responses to these questions are conveyed *'in their own words':*

7.2. Lou Ferrara, Vice President, The Associated Press

Lou's client adoption story:

I began exploring automation technologies for journalism in late 2012, after reading about their development in the media industry. I explored automation with two companies, and ultimately narrowed that to one, Automated Insights, in 2014. We then used it to test several automation efforts. We explored automated sports rankings, for instance, and then I had a eureka moment where

I realised that, by the end of 2014, we could probably automate corporate earnings reports. That moment arrived because I was faced with a smaller staff at the business desk and high demands for earnings reports from customers – though earnings were no longer the top reason customers subscribed to AP business news. I somehow had to produce a high volume of earnings reports with a smaller staff, and it seemed crazy that we would put most of our staff time and energy into something that, while important, wasn't the top reason AP Business existed. The market had changed, and I had to find a way to streamline what we did at a reasonable cost.

At the same time, I saw the opportunity to free staff time – not eliminate jobs – to stop doing mundane work and focus on higher-end journalism, the type of work people get into the news business to do. In fact, not one reporter liked doing earnings reports, so we had an audience that was game for change. The business case was about time, not money directly, but how we use our time and resources.

By early 2014, I had assembled a small team internally – five people – and worked out an agreement with Automated Insights to develop the automated corporate earnings reports. We worked with Zacks Investment Research to obtain the earnings data. We needed structured data that could, in the simplest terms, be pinged by an algorithm from AI and generate an earnings report onto the AP wire. And that's exactly what we did.

In the summer of 2014, we began testing the automation, having editors look over each earnings report automatically generated. We located bugs and had them fixed, and we worked in tandem with Automated Insights and Zacks, both of whom turned out to be great partners and remain so.

After the testing, and realising that they system we created was generally working, we went fully live in October 2014, meaning we only spot checked the automated reports and increased our volume significantly. Throughout Q4 of 2014 we were entirely live with automating earnings reports. By the end of 2015, we will be generating about 4,700 earnings reports automatically each quarter. With humans we were generating about 300 per quarter.

We have freed the equivalent of three full-time employees with automation – time that was spread among all of the staff. By doing so, we have refocused our energies on more higher-end reporting and recalibrated our operations even more for the social and mobile age.

Lou's thoughts on business value delivered:

Automation has been very successful for the AP, on pretty much all fronts:

- We freed time equivalent to three full-time employees.
- We increased our volume of earnings reports by more than 10x.
- We invested in the automation company, Automated Insights, in 2014. The company sold in early 2015 and AP received a 3x return on its investment.
- The AP business news product is better than before because we addressed volume – which was sought by some customers – while simultaneously improving the overall reporting quality throughout the department.
- We have made automation a key driver of other initiatives in the company, as we see the possibility to automate more parts of the AP operations in order to free time and focus on work of more importance for the modern landscape.

Lou's thoughts on lessons learned:

What three things would I change if I had to do it over again? I'm not sure what I would change. It has worked better than anyone expected. If anything, I would have increased our investment in Automated Insights and figured out a way to hold on to the company even after it sold and we profited from that sale. Operationally, I don't see much we would change.

Lou's thoughts on automation and the future of work:

Over the next two years, you will see more items automated from the AP. Some of that will be in the form of stories – as was the case with earnings reports. We are working on automating lower-audience sports, for example, and thus eliminating that work while increasing our volume.

In many other situations, it will involve backend technologies – for instance, the automation of data visualisations using structured data to convey a story in graphical form. Or, automation of different databases our reporters use that will reduce the manual time they have to spend looking for information. Instead the information will be surfaced to them automatically, thus saving time and making the AP news report faster and ahead of its competitors.

We look at automation as a solution, not a replacement, for the future of how news is produced and delivered.

7.3. A.J. Hanna, Sr. Director Operations Support, Ascension Ministry Service Center

A.J.'s client adoption story:

Ascension, the largest non-profit health system in the U.S. and the world's largest Catholic health system, is dedicated to transformation through innovation across the continuum of care. Five years ago, Ascension decided to spend a billion dollars to sort through thousands of ways it did business, identifying inefficiencies and standardising processes. That landmark initiative resulted in $3 billion in savings, freeing up resources to further its

ability to invest in patient care that serves all persons, including the poor and vulnerable.

The Ascension Ministry Service Center has played a key role in that health care transformation initiative. The Ministry Service Center delivers those standardised shared services throughout Ascension in the form of human resources, supply chain, and finance – the most significant enterprise resource planning initiative in health care. In less than four years, the initial innovation of delivering shared services has now moved to optimising those services with Robotic Process Automation, thus enabling more scale and leverage.

The value of a shared service center is the creation of efficiencies and application of economies of scale. As an organisation growing at a rapid pace, we are constantly looking for avenues to make us more efficient and scalable, while minimising the need for incremental increases in staffing. With more growth forecasted, and the pressure increasing to provide more value, we knew that we had to look for alternatives to the current workflow processes. A few of us at the Ministry Service Center had previously worked for organisations that had built in-house 'virtual processors', so the concept of work automation was not new. What was new to us was the growing library of tools springing up that put process automation more firmly in the hands of Operations.

In 2012, we started about an 18-month analysis of the available technology and how we might incorporate it into our organisation. We knew we needed a tool that was as flexible as possible in working with the technology stack that we utilise in the delivery of our services. It was also important to us to be able to have centralised control over any of the work done by the automation.

We developed a proof-of-concept test from a common process within our Human Resources service area. After we narrowed down the list of potential vendors, we invited them to walk through the building of the process with a team of people who would be using the tool in the operations area. This allowed us to assess how it worked with our tools, how easy (or complex) it appeared to be for an end-user, and to compare the relative cost of entry for each tool. (*Authors' note: The MSC selected Blue Prism as its first RPA provider.*)

A.J.'s thoughts on business value delivered:

Service automation has delivered much in the way we would have expected after our discernment process. After choosing a solution, we took a very measured approach to roll out to allow us the time to concurrently develop our protocols and controls. We did this mostly by automating the many 'swivel chair' activities that were a part of our work. (*Authors' note: please see Chapter 2 for an explanation of 'swivel chair' activities.*) Especially in our human resources and payables service areas, clients submit custom data sheets that were being manually entered into the appropriate system. Not only does this take resources away from more meaningful work, but it also is more prone to human error. These initial efforts provided us with the opportunity to train our staff with practical work outcomes. In addition to developing the team's skill set, we have been able to eliminate an estimated 16,000 hours of labour with only eight partial processes. Since many of our processes will always contain some component of human intervention, it also helped us to introduce the operating areas within the Ministry Service Center to how this type of automation can be integrated within their workflows.

We also have been able to realise improvements in quality for the work that has been automated. 'Robots' are not subject to the distractions and loss of attention that can affect a human and cause error. Automating the work has virtually eliminated the re-work component within these processes. The quality of the transaction is now almost entirely based on the quality of the data provided by the client.

The results of these introductory initiatives have proven to us that moving into more complicated automations will provide us the with the labour savings that will allow us to meet our goals of controlling incremental staffing increases, thereby improving our value proposition to Ascension.

A.J.'s thoughts on lessons learned:

Our primary learning, at this point, is that you are better served to segregate the process of automation into distinct components. Our configuration team was gathering and writing business requirements, doing the configuration in the tool, doing the testing and validation, and completing all of our documentation requirements for each automation activity. While this provided the team with a great perspective on the end-to-end activity, it did not allow us to gain the efficiency of someone specialising in each of those functions. It also assumed that the skill sets required to be effective at each stage of the automation lifecycle were transferable.

We have started the process of dedicating the automation team members into business requirements and documentation specialists, process modeling specialist and configuration specialists. This will allow us to increase our output by putting a specific focus on each of the stages of automation.

A.J.'s thoughts on automation and the future of work:

It is our belief that automation is not just the newest fad or hot topic. Automation of work is also not a new concept. The continued evolution of the technology, and the relative ease of implementation into different types of work environments, is changing the way business looks at these tools. Automation integration at the Ministry Service Center will not be just something we do, it will be the WAY we do what we do.

Now that we have a good feel for Robotic Process Automation, we are exploring how to incorporate the entire cycle of intelligent process automation into our work. We believe that there are avenues for us to use natural language processing as a next step on our journey and have started our deliberations on what tools are available in the market. We have also had preliminary conversations about what a full cognitive tool, like IBM's Watson, has to offer in the delivery of our services.

7.4. Michael 'Chet' Chambers, Director of IT and Development, VHA

Chet's client adoption story:

As Director of IT and Development at VHA, I try to give the business the time to do the things that are critical to them, like selling and generating revenue. So if the business is doing back office work that is taking people's time away from doing the things that make the company money, I want those things. Give me those activities and let me automate those functions out of their way. I took the lead in adopting the service automation software from Automation Anywhere because I thought it could help alleviate a problem the business was having. Here was the context:

As one of our services, VHA helps its hospital clients reduce procurement spend by pooling volumes and by working with suppliers to negotiate better deals than any hospital could negotiate on its own. So, for example, we might be buying syringes for all the hospitals. We'll go to the suppliers who sell syringes and ask for bids. Well, the suppliers send us files that contain typical bid data, but we want to know the nitty-gritty details and about the product's attributes. Our business people would have to go out into the public domain and look up all that detailed data on the Internet and extract it into our system. It took a lot of their time. I thought software could do this for them. Previously I had listened to a presentation by Automation Anywhere, so I brought them back in to look at the process. I asked them, *"Can you help me go out and collect data from the public domain and put it into a useable format?"* The answer from them was very much a resounding *"Yes"*. I went back internally to get funding for the project. The VHA funded about $100,000 for the multiple servers and software and $80/hour for staff through the end of the year. That amount only funds about only one FTE. I had one staff member who is extremely bright and she learned the software, but I clearly needed more staff to make a real business impact. So we decided to go find college interns to supplement her automation team. The internship program was about to start a new session at the VHA, and we signed up for one. The intern was a brilliant young man, he goes to Texas A&M, majors in computer science, and minors in mathematics. He picked up the software very quickly. So my staff member and I got together and said: Let's go find some more interns. Let's go find some eager college students that learn for a living and let's see if we can get them up to speed and put them to work in a commercial environment. Well, it worked very well. Automation Anywhere did a good job of providing training for those young interns and we were off and running. We've pulled in over 360,000 items from the Internet using the automation software as of fall 2015.

Chet's thoughts on business value delivered:

The business value of service automation has been great. If you multiply those 360,000 items by the $35,000 average spend of each item, you're looking at about $12 billion dollars in spend that we were able to cover in a few months with the cost of one employee. And that led to the business asking, *"If you can automate that, what else can you automate?"* And that's where automation is going now – we keep finding new processes to automate. For example, we have groups that send people out into hospitals to identify and disseminate best-in-class practices. All of that information comes back to the VHA to be processed. We wrote some scripts to collect that information from the individual's laptop, transport it back here, process it and then return the answers. It's been a huge hit. We've had another situation where a seven-person group spent up to 40 hours a week working on this particular process and the transfer of data up to a shared site for the data to be processed. They were spending 2-3 hours per person times seven people every week. We were able to go in and, in less than a week, automate that function and save a full

FTE's worth of work. So within a few months, we've had an ROI of 6:1 on a very limited exposure. So it's been a great success for us here.

Chet's thoughts on lessons learned:

What I would have done differently? I would have gone bigger faster. Although we've had great success with the interns, I wish we had a few seasoned staff members who were more technical in the beginning to help the interns along. I would have gotten results much faster. I would have put a lot more horsepower behind it from the beginning but understand that we were a grassroots movement. There was no high-level sponsor; there was no big initiative by the company. It was a piece of software that we found and an idea that sparked between my brilliant staff member and me. She and I sat down and asked, *"How are we going to be able to make a meaningful impact with $80 an hour?"* So that's where the college students came from but it would have been great to put a team of ten out there instead of scratching up a team of four or five to make this go. Now over the course of time, I plan on having 20 interns.

Chet's thoughts on automation and the future of work:

We're trying to get everybody off of the treadmill. Imagine the little hamster that just runs and runs and runs and runs on the wheel – we're trying to get our business people off of the wheel. We're trying to give them the time to do the things that they ought to be doing instead of the things that they have to do. In two years from now, I plan on having 30 to 40 percent of the total enterprise-led processes automated. That's a big goal. I plan on freeing up 150 FTEs worth of time with automation; another way to say this is that I plan to add 150 FTEs worth of work to the company by the next two years. In five years, it should be exponential.

7.5. Christian Clarke, Head of Customer Relations, Virgin Trains

Christian's client adoption story:

Virgin Trains is committed to delivering customer service excellence to its growing number of customers – this is one of their main objectives. This growth created  challenges due to the demands of handling an unprecedented volume of customer correspondence. These volumes were a result of a number of factors – the company working hard to improve the customer contact channels and encouraging customer feedback; truly understanding the wants and the needs of the customer; its ever-growing social media profile; delays and disruption to trains (often beyond the control of the company); and ultimately more and more people wanting to sample the great customer experience for which Virgin Trains has become synonymous.

The increasing volume of customer emails alone – which has more than doubled in the last 12 months – placed significant demands on the Customer Relations team. As a result, the department initially found itself using highly skilled individuals for effectively high level data entry. This was not sustainable as it prevented members of the team from actually interacting with customers and other areas of the business, to facilitate first time resolution, which is the primary function of Customer Relations.

Virgin Trains engaged with Celaton to deploy its inSTREAM platform and apply Artificial Intelligence to streamline the labour-intensive administrative tasks of registering customer details and decision making in handling customer emails. All customer emails are now received by inSTREAM. Unique to inSTREAM is its ability to learn the pattern of unstructured content through the natural consequence of processing it. As a result, inSTREAM is able to read, understand meaning/sentiment, categorise and then recognise key information within customer emails as they are received.

Celaton were aware that this level of automation was unchartered waters for Virgin Trains and, as a result, were able to work with them on a proof-of-concept, which ran for three months, to enable them to gain trust and confidence in inSTREAM as a product.

Virgin Trains completed their due diligence and this included an inspection of the data centres and work with Celaton to define the SLA, security, availability and performance characteristics. Their primary requirement, after performance and availability of the service, was scalability and low human intervention. Virgin Trains operate in a sensitive and complex environment and sometimes their resources are tested by events on the railway network. At all times their objective is to respond to customers and provide an amazing customer experience. With inSTREAM they can help to achieve this and can cope with unexpected demands that allow Virgin Trains to exceed their customers' expectations.

Ultimately, success hinged on whether or not inSTREAM improved the lives of customers and staff alike. Crucially it has taken time used on administrative tasks and given that back to the customer, through enabling staff more time to engage with customers and frontline colleagues, to ensure first time, front end resolution of issues wherever possible. On this level we have seen great success in liaising with all areas of our business to make things impossible to complain about.

Christian's thoughts on business value delivered:

Virgin Trains Customer Relations team are not a complaints department – they are resolution centre. As a result everything we do has to be geared toward maximising the time we can spend solving issues and engaging with internal and external customers. By implementing inSTREAM, the daily processing time and manual labour involved in dealing with customer emails was reduced by 85 percent, from 32 'man' hours per day, to four. This has a significant impact on the time it takes to respond to customers and so significantly improves the customer experience. In addition, Virgin Trains are able to provide customers with a faster and more personal response, further improving the quality of service and differentiating them from other train operating companies.

While there were some financial gains, Virgin Trains prefer to use customer satisfaction as their barometer. Crucially inSTREAM has allowed them to utilise the skills and passion of permanent staff more effectively, which has enabled them to create, implement and drive a sustainable long term strategy for Customer Relations, which is already having a positive impact on both the department and Virgin Trains as a whole. inSTREAM is not so much a tool for Customer Relations to use, it has become an important part of the team. This evolution would not have been possible without inSTREAM and the collaborative partnership between Virgin Trains and Celaton.

Christian's thoughts on lessons learned:

We would change very little about our implementation, as it has been extremely successful. However, if pressed I would say that we were a little too reticent in our approach to automation – specifically AI – and that middle men suppliers were often challenging for both Virgin Trains and Celaton. While we would have liked to embrace and forge ahead with the implementation to straddle more areas of our business, that level of financial and resource investment is only possible once you truly trust your collaborators, which comes with time and results, so I don't think we could have done it any quicker. Through our collaborative approach with Celaton we have not only developed inSTREAM, but have created a relationship that has led to evolutions across multiple areas of the business.

Christian's thoughts on automation and the future of work:

Automation is an important innovation, however, like all technology, it is vital that the systems work for us rather than we work around the systems. Technology is moving so quickly that it can be counterproductive to set too many parameters, that way your evolution gets boxed in by your own ideas. As a company, the key question that Virgin Trains always asks is *"What is the right thing to do for the customer?"* This overarching approach allows for a far greater agility in thought and action. For this reason I am reluctant to try and pre-empt where we will be in two or five years, as, given the huge strides we've made in the last 12 months, five years is a lifetime. That being said, inSTREAM is now a fundamental part of the customer service process and Virgin Trains is already planning to expand its use to deal with other unstructured processes such as general correspondence, white mail, feedback and delay related compensation. What I do know is that if it's the right thing to do for our people and our customers we will do it, and I am confident that we will continue on that journey with Celaton.

7.6. Common Themes

Looking across the client responses, there are many similarities and few differences. Like most of the clients in this book, three of the four clients in this chapter launched service automation from within their business operations. One client launched the service automation from within IT. All four picked proof-of-concept cases that were highly visible, gaining interest, and even enthusiasm, from within their organisations as well as attracting attention from media and external organisations. Overall, the main business drivers for service automation were focusing internal staff on more interesting and critical work, doing more work with existing staff resources, and improving service quality. FTE savings occurred, but the freed FTE resources were deployed to higher-value work – none of these organisations laid off staff because of automation. The clients also praised their service automation providers and called them, for example, *"great partners"*. Finally, all four client organisations planned to adopt more service automation in the future. These observations are expanded upon below.

7.6.1. For enterprise clients, service automation initiatives started in either business operations or in IT

Potential service automation adopters often ask, *"Where is service automation launched – in business operations, IT or in outsourcing provider firms?"* In previous chapters, we saw that service automation in the client firms we studied was almost always launched in business operations. Among the client respondents in this chapter, Lou Ferrara (AP), A.J. Hanna (MSC), and Christian Clarke (Virgin Trains) worked and launched service automation in business operations whereas Chet Chambers (VHA) worked and launched service automation in IT. However, this may be an artifact of our client sample. A broader survey of 178 enterprise buyers by HfS in 2015 found automation was based in IT in 38 percent of responding organisations and in business units in 29 percent of responding organisations.[8] Thus, according to the HfS survey, IT more frequently adopts service automation than business operations, so in this sense, Chet Chambers of the VHA may be the more typical client. However, we believe most of the IT deployed automations are automating IT services (not business services).

The HfS sample and our client case studies in this book both found that service automation is happening inside enterprises more frequently than through their ITO and BPO providers. This may just be an issue of visibility, since ITO and BPO providers clearly need to rely on automation (and labour and other resources) to deliver competitive services. Our IAOP survey of BPO/ITO customers did find that clients *"primarily rely on service providers to automate services"*, but the majority of respondents had not (yet) adopted service automation. Certainly in the next chapter, we will see how one provider, Infosys, is embracing service automation as part of an overall value proposition.

7.6.2. Pilot projects were exciting and noticeable

Organisations are naturally sceptical of new technologies because new technologies often over-promise and under-deliver. The phenomenon is so common that Gartner developed the 'emerging technology hype cycle'. Gartner's hype cycle has five phases – an innovation trigger, a peak of inflated expectations, a trough of disillusionment, a slope of enlightenment, and a plateau of productivity. Proof-of-concept cases are an important way to obtain realistic stakeholder buy-in; the organisation needs to see substantial benefits. The clients in this chapter all selected pilot projects on visible processes that delivered much more value than just cost savings to their organisations – they each removed tedious, dull, and monotonous work.

For the AP, corporate earning reports is a major service and its clients relied on the 300 reports generated each quarter and indeed, clients were asking for more companies' earnings to be reported. The task, however, was quite boring for journalists because the data comes in very structured (see top side of Figure 7.1) and does not require any creativity to write the release (see the bottom side of Figure 7.1). By automating this particular process, Lou Ferrara delivered a highly visible success story. His journalists were thrilled to be assigned to more interesting stories and the uniqueness of the context gained Ferrara media attention. Lou's been asked to speak all over the world, including China.[9]

At the MSC, the first thing A.J. Hanna and his team did was a proof-of-concept launch on a moderately complex, moderately high-volume business process of updating employee records. Excel spreadsheets are sent to the MSC from all the member hospitals and the MSC staff had to manually copy and paste updates from the spreadsheets to the HR system of record. The task was tedious. Hanna and his team were able to automate about 75 percent of the task. The Blue Prism software now extracts and loads the new data into the databases, freeing up the MSC staff to do more interesting work. As of December 2014, the automation software had processed 7,474 transactions.[10]

FROM THIS INPUT:	ZERN AN RWIN 0000350698 12 Q3-14 AUTONATION INC 201409 2014-10-28 1 4909 4909 106.700 106.700 0.000 0.000 0.000 0.000 0.000 0.000 0.000 0.000 0.000 0.000 0.000 0.000 0.000 0.000 106.700 -0.200 0.000 0.000 106.500 0.000 106.500 118.500 118.500 0.900 0.000 0.000 0.000 0.000 0.000 0.000 0.000 0.000 0.000 0.000 0.000 0.000 0.000 0.900 0.000 0.000 0.000 0.900 0.900 0.900 0.000 0.000 0.000 0.000 0.000 0.000 0.000 0.000 0.000 0.000 0.000 0.000 0.000 0.900 0.000 0.000 0.900 2014-10-28 07:09 07:02 PR newswires 201409 4799.000 6 100.149 4909.000 2.292 201409 0.860 8 0.010 0.900 4.651 201409 0.855 8 0.009 0.900 5.263

TO THIS OUTPUT:

Slug:	BC-US-Earns-AutoNation
Headline:	AutoNation beats Street 3Q forecasts
Extended Headline:	AutoNation posts 3Q profit, results top Wall Street forecasts
Urgency:	Non Urgent
Dateline:	FORT LAUDDERDALE, Fla.

FORT LAUDDERDALE, Fla. (AP)_AutoNation Inc. (AN) on Tuesday reported net income of $106.5 million in its third quarter.

On a per-share basis, the Fort Lauderdale, Florida-based company said it had net income of 90 cents.

The results beat Wall Street expectations. The average estimate of analysts surveyed by Zacks Investment Research was for earnings of 86 cents per share.

The auto retailer posted revenue of $4.91 billion in that period, also surpassing Street forecasts. Analysts expected $4.8 billion, according to Zacks.

AutoNation shares have climbed roughly 5 percent since the beginning of the year, while the Standard & Poor's 500 index has climbed 6 percent. The stock has climbed almost 6 percent in the last 12 months.

_____

This story was generated by **Automated Insights** using data from Zacks Investment Research. **AN stock research report from Zacks**.

Figure 7.1: RPA Example: Inputs and Outputs for
Corporate Earnings Reports
(Source: The AP. Reprinted with permission)

This pilot was demonstrated to various operations group to show how it works. This helped gain momentum and stakeholder buy-in, with business operations asking, *"What else can we automate?"* Hanna, along with Lee Coulter, the CEO, and Sandor Bahtory, Manager, Business Technology Service, have all gained external attention and are frequent keynote speakers on the topic of service automation.[11]

At the VHA, Chet Chambers saw a real business need – business operations staff were wasting time searching the Internet for product specification data. This task was dreary and high volume, as the VHA purchases hundreds of thousands of products for its members each year. By selecting this painful and visible task, Chambers was able to not only get buy-in, but enthusiasm for more service automation in his firm. He too has gained external attention for his automation efforts.[12]

At Virgin Trains, Christian Clarke saw a real need to focus his staff on engaging with internal and external customers rather than on data entry tasks. As Virgin Trains grew as a company, a tsunami of additional customer email and social media ensued, stretching the existing staff beyond its limits. The staff were spending too much time filtering incoming correspondence, categorising it, and then routing it for resolution. They wanted to spend more time resolving issues with customers. Using automation, Celaton's inSTREAM receives all the correspondence, filters, categorises and routes it. The staff now work on more value-added tasks, such as spending more time with customers and with business operations folks working on the frontlines.

7.6.3. Business results were multifaceted

Of course the service automation business cases at the AP, the MSC, the VHA, and Virgin Trains all included cost savings in the form of freeing up FTEs, but the four clients highlighted other business benefits, like increasing job satisfaction of the staff because they are doing more interesting work, increased service volumes and improved service quality. Each business benefit is discussed below.

All four clients did more work with existing resources. All four of the client organisations – the AP, MSC, VHA and Virgin Trains – were under pressure to take on more and more work with existing resources. The AP, for example, produces 2,000 stories a day, 38,000 videos a year and 1 million photos each year with only a few thousand employees. The AP was losing money in 2012 and hiring more net staff would only hurt profitability. It needed to grow revenue and improve profitability without commensurate increases in staff. At the MSC, it was launched in 2011 to save their non-profit hospitals money by sharing services – keeping costs contained without degrading services was a major imperative. As one of Ascension Health's Board members is known for saying, *"There is no mission without margin"*. Similarly, the VHA had a similar charge to save client hospitals money – doing more with existing resources. Virgin Trains was growing as business, which was great news, but the customer relations team was not increasing staff to keep pace with the number of new customers. It needed to find a way to better handle the increased volumes of customer correspondence and automation met that need.

In all the client firms, service automation helped the organisation to produce more work with existing headcount. At the AP, service automation increased volumes from 300 to 4,700 earnings reports each quarter while freeing up three FTEs. At the MSC, an estimated 16,000 hours of labour, or approximately eight FTEs, according to our estimation,[13] were freed up by service automation. At the VHA, Chambers clearly saved FTEs when the automation software pulled product specifications for over 36,000 items. At Virgin Trains, the daily email processing time was reduced from 32 man hours per day, to four. Over the course of a week, by our estimate, that amounts to freeing up nearly six FTEs for more value-added work.[14]

All four clients used automation to focus staff on more interesting work. Lou Ferrara, A.J. Hanna, Chet Chambers, and Christian Clarke all mentioned releasing staff from the drudgery of repetitive and tedious tasks so that staff could focus on more interesting and critical work. Service automation not only enabled the ability to take on more work in all four client firms, it took over the least desirable tasks. In these organisations, the employees thus welcomed automation. Also a key lesson for stakeholder buy-in: none of these organisations use service automation to lay off staff; each is reallocating the freed up labour for more mission-critical work.

All four clients improved service quality with automation. Humans are actually poorer performers of repetitive work than machines because humans make mistakes when they get bored and tired. All clients mentioned that quality improved as a consequence of service automation because the software executes processes exactly as configured to do so and the humans do what they are most suited for – social interactions and judgments. The remaining data errors, as Hanna noted, was caused by the quality of the data passed into the MSC's control.

7.6.4. All clients will help their organisations adopt more automation in the future

With visible success stories, the AP, the MSC, the VHA, and Virgin Trains are all ramping up their service automation capabilities:

The AP continues to announce its automation capabilities and expansion. In March of 2015, for example, the AP released an article that it would use automation technology to provide thousands of stories about college sports previously not covered by the news organisation.[15] The rollout of the automated game stories was planned to start with the spring Division I baseball, to be followed by Division I women's basketball, Division II and III football, and Division II and III men's basketball. This time, the data that feeds Automated Insights would come from the US National Collegiate Athletic Association (NCAA).

The MSC also had big plans to expand service automation. In December of 2014, immediately following the proof-of-concept case, four processes were in development, five processes were waiting development, and 14 processes were awaiting review for RPA.[16] More recently, the MSC was evaluating natural language processing and cognitive computing in autumn 2015.

At the VHA, Chambers had ambitious plans of freeing up 150 FTEs over the next five years with service automation. At the time of this writing, it was clear that the VHA was close to making some announcements pertaining to more automation deployment, so readers were encouraged by Chet Chambers to contact him for more details.

At Virgin Trains, Christian Clarke noted that the company was planning to expand its use of automation to deal with other unstructured processes, but he was careful to stress that customer satisfaction and engagement drive all business decisions.

7.7. Conclusion

In this chapter we heard the service automation stories of four very different client organisations, using four different RPA providers. Associated Press adopted RPA in response to market changes. Ascension Ministry Service Center adopted automation as part of a larger Ascension Health initiative to achieve $3 billion in savings, freeing up resources thereby increasing its ability to invest in patient care. VHA used automation software to reduce significantly hospital clients' procurement spend. Virgin Trains used automation platform and software to deal with an explosion in incoming data. All four clients reported high business value delivered. All intended to extend their use of present and future service automation software and tools. Their endorsements, as clients of service automation are highly valuable. Their learning confirms and extends what we were discovering amongst clients in chapters 3, 4, 5, and 6.

But what about the views, experiences and approaches of service automation providers? In the next chapter we hear from four companies – Celaton, Blue Prism, IPSoft and Infosys – with an established history of building service automation software, platforms, and supporting services. What automation capabilities do they have, what sort of clients do they serve, what challenges do those clients face, and what value is delivered? Having raised the question in Chapter 1, we also asked their views on the future of work as a consequence of service automation – a subject we will also deal with in detail in the last chapter.

Citations

[1]   Source: https://en.wikipedia.org/wiki/Associated_Press

[2]   Source: http://ascension.org/our-work/subsidiaries/ascension-ministry-service-center

[3]   Source: *Our Journey into RPA with Blue Prism*, presentation at the Automation Innovation Conference, New York City, December 10, 2014.

[4]   Source: https://www.vha.com/AboutVHA/Pages/CompanyInformation.aspx

[5]   Source: https://en.wikipedia.org/wiki/VHA, Inc

[6]   Source: https://en.wikipedia.org/wiki/Virgin_Trains

[7]   Source: https://www.virgintrains.co.uk/about/media-room#/pressreleases/business-is-great-with-virgin-trains-1122674

[8]   Sutherland, C. (2015), *The Raw Truth about Intelligent,* HFS Research White Paper, September.

[9]   Source: *The Impact of Robotic Process Automation on BPO*, presentation at the Automation Innovation Conference, New York City, December 10, 2014.

[10]   Source: *Our Journey into RPA with Blue Prism*, presentation at the Automation Innovation Conference, New York City, December 10, 2014.

[11]   For example, Hanna and Bahtory were main session speakers at the launch of the Institute of Robotic Process Automation in NYC in December of 2014; Coulter has been a featured speaker at many events and webinars such as *Where is the Action Today in Intelligent Automation?,* HfS Research Webinar, August 27, 2015.

[12]   For example, Chet Chambers has spoken at the launch of the Robotic Process Automation Chapter of the IAOP in Dallas on July 9, 2015.

[13]   Calculation assumes an FTE works 2,000 hours per year.

[14]   Estimate calculated as follows: 32 hours per day time 7 days a week (since trains run daily) equals 224 hours per week of work. Assuming an FTE works 35 hours per week, the weekly FTE effort is 6.4 FTEs. After automation, the task was done in 4 hours per day, or 28 hours per week, or .8; this total FTE savings are nearly 6 per week.

15 Sources:

Taibi, C (2015), *Robots Are About To Write Your Sports Coverage*, The Huffington Post, March 4, 2015, available at http://www.huffingtonpost.com/2015/03/04/robots-sports-coverage-associated-press-automated-insights_n_6795648.html

Associated Press (2015), AP, *NCAA to grow college sports coverage with automated game stories*, March 4 2015, available on http://www.ap.org/Content/Press-Release/2015/AP-NCAA-to-grow-college-sports-coverage-with-automated-game-stories

16 Source: *Our Journey into RPA with Blue Prism*, presentation at the Automation Innovation Conference, New York City, December 10, 2014.

Chapter 8

In Their Own Words: Provider Responses

What's Inside: *CEOs from among the top service automation providers – Celaton, Blue Prism, and IPsoft – and the COO from a top global ITO/BPO provider – Infosys – discuss their companies' automation capabilities, challenges they help their clients overcome and the future of service automation 'in their own words'. Like client contributors in the previous chapter, the provider contributors all identified multiple business benefits of service automation, including cost savings, the ability to scale without adding headcount, improving the end-customer's experience, producing consistent, high-quality, fast results that are compliant, and allowing real time visibility into IT and business operations. The providers note that service automation causes disruption in the short-term, but that it has positive impacts on the human experience in the long-term.*

8.1. Introduction

This is the second chapter in the book that invited service automation stakeholders to respond to questions *'in their own words'*. In this chapter, we probed the CEOs from among the top service automation providers – Celaton, Blue Prism, and IPsoft – and one of the top global ITO/BPO providers – Infosys (see Table 8.1 and the Notes on Contributors) to answer a set of questions about their companies' automation capabilities, client challenges, and the future of service automation. In this chapter, we first describe their organisations and the questions we asked providers. Next, we present their contributions. One will immediately note that, despite the apparent newness of 'robotic process automation', 'cognitive learning', or 'intelligent automation', these companies have an established history of building service automation software, platforms, and supporting services. Furthermore, their capabilities continue to evolve, as innovation is an imperative for all four providers. Finally, we extract some common themes from across the contributions.

Representing	Name	Title	Company
Service Automation Provider	Andrew Anderson	CEO	Celaton
	Alastair Bathgate	CEO	Blue Prism
	Chetan Dube	CEO	IPsoft
Global ITO/BPO Service Provider	Pravin Rao	COO	Infosys

Table 8.1: Provider Thought Leaders Contributing to
In Their Own Words

8.1.1. Overview of the Contributing Organisations

The three CEO service automation provider contributors – Andrew Anderson, Alastair Bathgate, and Chetan Dube – are the CEOs of Celaton, Blue Prism, and IPsoft respectively. All of them lead organisations recognised for their service automation capabilities. These companies created the software products that helped to launch the service automation revolution. We are also most pleased to include Infosys in our book because we know from our IAOP survey that many ITO/BPO clients plan to rely on service providers to automate business services (see Chapter 1). Global ITO/BPO service providers must embrace service automation as part of an overall value proposition based on service transformation. Pravin Rao, COO of Infosys, discusses how automation is embedded in Infosys' 'Zero Touch Initiative'.

Celaton is based in Milton Keynes in the UK, and was founded in 2004 from the management buy-out of Redrock software and the acquisition of DG Tech.[1] Its main service automation product is called inSTREAM. This product was introduced to readers in the last chapter, as Christian Clarke described Virgin Trains' adoption of inSTREAM to handle incoming customer correspondence. According to Celaton's website, *"Unique to inSTREAM is its ability to learn through the natural consequence of processing and human interaction. It applies this artificial intelligence to streamline labour intensive clerical tasks and decision-making in a way that hasn't been possible before. Delivered as a service, inSTREAM processes the unstructured (and structured) content that flows into your business every day from customers, such as correspondence, claims, complaints by email, social media, fax post & paper. It minimises the need for human intervention and ensures that only accurate, relevant and structured data enters your line of business systems. It's artificial intelligence, but to our customers it's the best knowledge worker they ever hired and it means better customer service, compliance and financial performance."[2]*

Blue Prism was founded in the UK by a group of process automation experts in 2001, and now has offices in London, Manchester, Chicago and Miami.[3] Blue Prism is credited for coining the term 'Robotic Process Automation'. Blue Prism adoption stories include Telefónica O2 (Chapter 3), Xchanging (Chapter 4), and Ascension MSC (Chapter 7). According to Blue Prism's website, *"We provide an enterprise-strength Robotic Process Automation software platform which is robust, highly scalable, powerful and flexible, designed from first principles to provide organisations with a business owned and IT supported Virtual Workforce. The Virtual Workforce is built, managed and owned by an accredited operational team or Centre of Excellence spanning operations and technology adhering to a comprehensive, enterprise wide Robotic Operating Model. It's code-free and can automate any software in a non-invasive way. In short, it can be easily applied to automate processes in any department where clerical or administrative work is performed across your organisation."*[4]

IPsoft was founded in 1998 in the United Kingdom; the founder and CEO believed that the IT infrastructure of the future would be managed not by people but by expert systems.[5] IPsoft has been widely adopted to automate IT services, and as such, is a welcome contribution to this book. As noted in the last chapter, our research has focused on adoption of service automation in business operations, yet sample surveys have shown that IT functions are indeed the most frequent adopters of service automation.[6] IPsoft has a variety of automation products and services, but one stand-out is 'Amelia'. According to IPsoft's website, *"Amelia is the first cognitive agent who understands like a human. Amelia, our cognitive knowledge worker, interfaces on human terms. She is a virtual agent who understands what people ask – even what they feel – when they call for service. Using the same instruction manuals as, for example, call centre operators, Amelia can be deployed straight from the cloud in a fraction of the time. She learns as she works and provides high-quality responses consistently, every day of the year, in every language your customers speak."*[7]

Representing the global ITO/BPO providers, Pravin Rao is COO and Member of the Board for Infosys. Infosys was founded in 1981 and has since grown to one of the largest global service providers, employing nearly 180,000 employees worldwide. Pertaining to Infosys' overall capabilities, its website says, *"Infosys is a global leader in consulting, technology, and outsourcing and next-generation services. We enable clients in more than 50 countries to outperform the competition and stay ahead of the innovation curve. With U\$8.83 billion in LTM Q1 FY16 revenues and 179,000+ employees, we are helping enterprises renew themselves while also creating new avenues to generate value. We provide enterprises with strategic insights on what lies ahead. We help enterprises transform and thrive in a changing world through strategic consulting, operational leadership, and the co-creation of* *breakthrough solutions, including those in mobility, sustainability, big data, and cloud computing.* "[8]

8.1.2. Questions Posed to Provider Thought Leaders

For these CEOs and COO, we asked questions about their company's automation capabilities, the types of clients served, the challenges clients face, the value delivered to clients from automation, and the future of work as a consequence of service automation. The specific questions were:

- **Automation capability:** Briefly describe your major proprietary automation capabilities. For what is your tool most suited?

- **Clients:** In your business, to what degree are your clients from within operations, like shared services, or from outsourcing service providers? Are you seeing more RPA activity from business operations or IT operations? What are the biggest struggles clients have concerning RPA and service automation? Can you provide a few specific examples of value delivered to clients? For example, financial (i.e. cost savings, return on investment), operational (i.e. improved quality, faster delivery, better compliance), and strategic value (i.e. strategy enablement, access to new customers, better customer retention)?

- **Automation and the future of work:** Beyond your company, how will automation affect the future of IT and business services? What will be a likely effect on jobs? Will more or less work be sourced from traditionally low-labour cost countries? Which countries will likely be most affected? Bold answers are welcome!

Below, their responses to the questions are conveyed *'in their own words'*:

8.2. Andrew Anderson, CEO, Celaton

Andrew's thoughts on Celaton's automation capabilities:

Our Cognitive Learning Technology enables organisations to deliver better customer service, faster, with fewer people. Delivered as a service, inSTREAM applies artificial intelligence to streamline labour-intensive clerical tasks and decision-making, to process unstructured, unpredictable content that organisations receive every day, by email, fax, social media, post and paper.

Despite the ever-increasing choice of media channels, people continue to communicate in an unstructured descriptive way. Whilst this may be easy for other people to see and understand, it is not so for machines and therefore, it requires high levels of manual labour to read, understand and interpret the content into the structured data that can be understood by machines. Unique to inSTREAM is its ability to learn the pattern of unstructured content through the natural consequence of processing it and in collaborating with people. The unstructured nature of correspondence such as complaints, claims, contracts etc., makes handling it one of the most labour-intensive tasks that is subject to delays, errors, misinterpretation and inconsistent judgements.

Andrew's thoughts on client types, challenges, and business value delivered:

Celaton's goal is to work directly with business operations that are seeking to enhance their customers experience and improve business processes. Our target customers have a few things in common: They are mid to large, ambitious disruptive brands who are passionate about their reputation and their customer. Since in STREAM's launch into the market place, our technology has streamlined over 110 processes across 25 brands in the retail, travel, insurance, logistics and central government sectors.

Our product, InSTREAM, enables business operations to allocate internal resources efficiently and without relying on outsourcing service providers. In the last couple of years more companies and their core business operations, such as customer service, accounts and human resources, are looking at ways to improve the way in which large amounts of unstructured data are processed, and are starting to look towards cognitive learning technologies to provide the answer.

Interest from companies in automation and cognitive learning technology is not without hesitation. One of the biggest concerns key decision makers have when committing to automation, is the cost. Companies are often presented with the choice of investing in more staff, outsourcing or technology to solve their business operation problems and often it is easier to find an argument for tried and tested solutions. Technology is often perceived as an expensive option, however once the potential return on investment and productivity benefits of automation solutions and inSTREAM are examined, it becomes a very appealing choice for businesses.

In the last 18 months we have released the latest version of our inSTREAM Cognitive Learning Technology platform and as a result we have increased our client base by 260 percent, increased sales by 37 percent, increased our booked business by 34 percent and our pipeline of projects is now exceeding £4M. Delivered as a service, our inSTREAM technology enables ambitious brands like Virgin, Carphone Warehouse and Asos.com to deliver better service, faster and with fewer people. inSTREAM learns to understand, process and, where appropriate, respond to the plethora of unstructured and unpredictable correspondence that flow into customer service operations every day. On average, our clients realise a 74 percent reduction in operational costs in the area of handling customer correspondence. That saving alone can be significant, but it is the ability to scale without recruitment and still deliver consistent service levels, that enables our clients to achieve growth.

As a result of what we do, our clients have visibility of processes regardless of where they are. This enables our clients to see what their customers are saying in real-time and to recognise and react to key events as they happen. The key advantages are: Real-time visibility of unstructured processes enables better planning; accurate and structured data into BI systems ensures compliance; identification of events in real-time, such as priority customers or suspicious claims.

Andrew's thoughts on automation and the future of work:

At present there is a growing wave of interest from forecasters, analysts and the media on the benefits and negative impact of automation on business services. This interest is largely driven by the expectations of consumers who demand ever-increasing levels of service. Faced with the challenge of serving their customers better, providers are seeking out any competitive advantage to get ahead – and stay ahead – of their competitors.

This pressure from consumers is found in the majority of service industries, including retail, travel, insurance, banking and utility providers; although there are many more. Many of these industries have invested heavily in technology to serve their customers and yet the challenge still remains: How do these systems deal with the ever-increasing volume of customer correspondence through the plethora of media channels available to them? The fact remains that even the modern line of business systems cannot understand what customers are saying without first applying significant manual effort.

Automation, and specifically cognitive learning technology, enables organisations to consume and understand what their customers are saying, regardless of the fact that the content is unstructured and unpredictable. More importantly, the technology is able to learn and so the work force doesn't need to scale to cope with growth or even unexpected surges in demand.

Organisations will be able to realise what customers are saying in real-time and respond appropriately. A growing number of the correspondence received will be able to be dealt with without human intervention, ensuring that customers receive a swift, consistent and personal service. Automation will give meaning to even the most unstructured content. Organisations will be able to realise the value that would otherwise remain buried in unstructured content, providing insights and making sure that relevant information is shared with the right people and systems without delay. The productivity of staff increases, and customer service and reputation improves, which ultimately leads to improvement in financial performance.

People are essential to the success of automation and, in the case of cognitive learning technology, it is their collaboration that teaches what the system learns. This has the potential to reduce the need for people to carry out high volume repetitive tasks and decision-making. By comparison, people take longer to complete tasks and they make mistakes and so it is important that these tasks can be completed faster and more accurately by technology. People are able to focus on the tasks and decision-making that people do better – social interaction with other people.

Certainly, some costly aspects of outsourcing will be reduced as a result of the wider introduction of automation; organisations will be able to take responsibility for tasks that they would otherwise outsource. There will always be a requirement for collaboration with people. Despite all of the advancements automation can provide business services and industries with, the system must be programmed, taught and monitored by people. Contrary to some technology doomsday predictions, we are not anticipating the uprising of the machine and the redundancy of the human race.

As automation spreads globally with the advancement in computer technologies, it is fair to predict no country would be significantly impacted. It is also important to remember that some industries and customers value the human element and personal involvement. Automation merely offers a viable and effective tool to support people in their work.

8.3. Alastair Bathgate, CEO, Blue Prism

Alastair's thoughts on Blue Prism's automation capabilities:

Let me start by saying that Blue Prism is not a tool – it's a platform. Let me explain what I mean by this and, by doing so, explain the technologies capabilities and where it is most suited. Our vision is to provide the enterprise with a Virtual Workforce powered by an 'army' of Software Robots.

Blue Prism is a sophisticated technology platform, which strives to deliver the highest levels of availability and reliability expected of a tightly managed Virtual Workforce of Software Robots. The technology platform and associated Robotic Operating Model and deployment methodologies have been designed and developed over many years working in the world's most demanding regulated industries, to provide high integrity, transactional platforms for executing computer based administrative processes. The Virtual Workforce is multi-skilled, can access and drive any application that an authorised person can (through the applications User Interface just like a person would), and follow business rules (which can be extremely complex) to execute business processes and complete transactions. It's another resource that sits alongside your existing IT applications and your people and offers an alternative to outsourcing.

The robotic workforce is deployed on servers (not desktops) and the platform passes the most stringent requirements for data security – it even passes PEN tests (that's penetration tests which demonstrate the robustness of the platform) – and we are used to performing transactions in highly regulated environments and comply with PCI[i], HIPAA[ii] and other demanding regulations. Blue Prism clients (and there are over 100 of them at the time of writing) are world brands in highly regulated and performant industries such as banking, insurance, telecommunications, healthcare, logistics, retail – in fact there are very few industries where the technology cannot add value.

The processes most suitable for automation share a common DNA. They are digital, they start with an electronic trigger, they follow known business rules (and these can be very complex and nested) and require data to be gathered from multiple systems and data to be written back to multiple systems. When you think across all the departments in your enterprise and look at any areas where teams of admin people are performing 'manual' computer-based processes, think what impact a Virtual Workforce of Software Robots could have, as they can perform the majority of that work in a systematic and automated fashion, with all the benefits of accuracy, efficiency and effectiveness this brings.

Alastair's thoughts on client types, challenges, and business value delivered:

Blue Prism clients are an interesting mix and maybe if we look at the 30+ clients who have signed up to use Blue Prism software robots this year, it gives us an interesting view of who is buying into the vision of the Virtual Workforce. Around 80 percent of the clients are end-user enterprise organisations with the majority of owners sitting in shared services or centralised process improvement functions. The majority of buyers are the business owners who are working with their internal IT and procurement partners to investigate and acquire a Robotic Process Automation capability. The other clients include a number of the technically savvy BPOs whose heritage is in technology-based solutions rather than off-shored labour. These partners are providing innovative and technology-led propositions to the ever-demanding clients

---

i   PCI stands for Payment Card Industry; it is a data security standard that ensures that all companies that process, store or transmit credit card information maintain a secure environment.

ii HIPAA stands for Health Insurance Portability and Accountability Act of 1996 who are looking for the benefits of automation and process excellence from their service providers.

Unlike traditional process automation technology, the benefits are rapidly realised and accurately measurable. Why is this? The most obvious reason is that you are taking a known process, with known metrics, and you have a very clear before and after scenario. In many cases a less than six month pay back and ongoing savings of 50 percent to 80 percent.However, not all Blue Prism projects are about cost reduction; many clients are looking to increase their capacity without adding additional headcount – doing more with the same – and improvements in accuracy and right-first-time processing to increase customer satisfaction and reduce churn. Straight Through Processing, which enables an enterprise to connect new offerings (like mobile customer access) to the systems of record without the need for costly and time-consuming integration. In this sense Software Robots and the Virtual Workforce can be thought of as 'digital labour' – filling the gaps in the digital landscape and connecting and orchestrating technical assets to create the 'frictionless enterprise'.

As for the challenges adopting an enterprise RPA capability, there is no such thing as a free lunch. If something seems too cheap and too fast to be true, then it probably is. Some organisations who take their first look at RPA are initially wowed by how quickly a basic script generation technology can 'automate' a process, where in fact all it is doing is running a recorded script against a simple process flow. This is not something suitable to put live in a regulated transactional environment. So, our main challenge is to help clients understand that a Blue Prism Virtual Workforce is all about working to establish a viable, long-term, strategic capability for the enterprise, which requires thoughtful construction and deployment. This is what we call our Robotic Operating Model and we believe it is as important as the technology platform itself.

Once a Virtual Workforce capability has been established, the operations teams can create and deploy new processes in a fraction of the time and at a fraction of the cost than was previously possible. This vision of the 'zero latency enterprise' is a powerful capability which organisations can leverage to increase market share and become more competitive.

Alastair's thoughts on automation and the future of work:

There are many elements to this debate, but there seems to be two main sides with opposing views. On one side we have the technical optimists that believe automation and digitalisation of work will lead to increases in economic growth, new jobs, less hours of working, more fulfilling and interesting careers and overall improvements in our quality of life. The other side of the debate seems to believe that the machines will bring mass unemployment, riches to the few and generally weaken our quality of life.

My personal view is the former. Having been involved in process automation and making businesses more efficient, I have seen the benefits of automating processes that are not a good use of human skills – just as we have seen horses replaced by the internal combustion engine and children are no longer put up chimneys to clean them. Automation of routine administrative work frees us as agricultural automation and mechanisation has freed us from working the land.

Every generation has seen a new technology that has driven mass change and the end result has seen net benefits to all in society – the rising tide carries all boats – but the argument for this latest change, driven by robotics and cognitive technologies, is that the rate of change will be much quicker than before and because we are in a 'virtual' world, this time the physical attributes that have slowed us down before do not exist. Robots have massive limitations in the physical world but, with new technologies like Blue Prism, they are essentially un-constrained in the virtual world.

The US in particular seems very worried by the impact of automation – maybe a simple solution would be for Americans to work a 30 hour week and let the robots do the other work? The economy can afford it if robots are doing the work. The other economies and geographies that will be dramatically effective by digital labour will be the geographies that have built large corporations on the back of labour arbitrage, driven by low cost labour and fast telecommunications. Many in the Business Process Services industry see a seismic shift already occurring and it will be fascinating to see how business models based on physical labour move to ones based on virtual, digital labour.

8.4. Chetan Dube, CEO, IPsoft

Chetan's thoughts on automation capabilities:

Our mission is to leverage expert systems to build a more efficient planet. We apply our autonomic proficiencies (IPcenter) to automate infrastructure management processes. We apply our cognitive capabilities (Amelia) to automate business processes.

IPcenter uses Artificial Intelligence – 'virtual engineers' – to manage IT and handle many routine functions through an automated process.

Amelia is a cognitive agent who understands like a human. Amelia can absorb the mundane tasks that knowledge workers have been doing for years. She can be applied to help desk environments and can handle end user requests – for example, a forgotten password. Amelia can understand the context of requests and solve problems.

There are a lot of tools and companies that provide IT management services, but they are mostly human generated automation. Manual automation is an oxymoron. It dilutes the efficiencies automation is supposed to drive. Our automation is rooted in deep machine learning and leverages AI techniques to absolve us of the manual chores.

Chetan's thoughts on client types, challenges, and business value delivered:

In your business, to what degree are your clients from within operations like shared services or from outsourcing service providers?

Service providers have tremendous pressures to reduce costs of the end user service. They are looking to automation to solve problems that they used to address with labour arbitrage. We are seeing a service provider demand for automation capabilities to change their cost environment as they provision their services. There's the ever-increasing demand for the enterprises that either buy this technology themselves, learn it and use it – or hire a service provider that is using automation at the heart of its services.

Are you seeing more RPA activity from business operations or IT operations?

IT operations are the early adopters of automation technology. Business operations were previously always conducted by people (or cheaper people) with few BPMS tools that lent structure to operations. Lately, automation has become the dominant trend, displacing the labour arbitrage trend of last decade. While the need for ITO automation continues, there is a burgeoning demand for business operations automation, where the market is a factor bigger than the ITO market.

What are the biggest struggles clients have concerning RPA and service automation?

The biggest struggles concerning RPA are the true value realisations. A service capability gap continues to increase as applications complexity and velocity of change outpace the rate of automation. Manual processes required to generate automation form the weakest link in the chain and undermine the efficiency curves.

Can automation itself be automated? Can the infrastructure and business operations of tomorrow be self-governing and self-healing through autonomic and cognitive processes? Expert systems technology has become available that can deliver to that mandate.

The next issue facing RPA adoption is organisational change and human fear. People are afraid that automation will replace their jobs.

We need to understand that there is going to be a human reaction, like there was in the labour market in the manufacturing and automotive industries. Consider the people in the auto factories who began watching the robotic approach to putting lug nuts on tyres. It didn't take them long to figure out that they were going to lose their jobs to those robots, who can function faster, more reliably and at less expense. Those who continued to succeed in the industry got training and moved up the ladder, for example, as finishers of the cars.

In the same way, knowledge workers are going to have to step up and will probably have to be retrained to take on more complex tasks and roles. The more we automate, the more we elevate human roles. It's a big shift in how we're going to do things.

Can you provide a few specific examples of value delivered to clients?

In the customer service environment you can greatly reduce the amount of time the customer needs to be on the phone to have something resolved. Automation provides speed of access into the customer service centre and the speed of response and resolution.

We have enabled a large media services company to streamline its IT operations and save over 40 percent annually. Automations have taken on repetitive tasks and, as a result, the company has seen a substantial reduction in customer handling time and access to the service centre.

Chetan's thoughts on automation and the future of work:

Beyond your company, how will automation affect the future of IT and business services?

Automation will create a more efficient world. Man is shackled by the ordinary today. Automation will be the faithful servant that will free man from the boredom of chores and allow him to extend his horizons in creative dimensions. We use 10 percent of our creative brain today. Imagine a world where we had the liberty to engage more gainfully in value creation.

Automation is changing the way business is conducted. Companies need to be digital in their nature, in terms of efficiency and how they're run. This is going to change the way we operate our businesses going forward.

What will be a likely effect on jobs? Will more or less work be sourced from traditionally low-labour cost countries? Which countries will likely be most affected?

Automation always trumps outsourced labour. Automation, as opposed to labour arbitrage, allows businesses to better manage their environments at much lower costs and to be much more responsive, agile and rapid.

Even if I'm paying a very low wage, automation can beat the lowest priced labour. That's going to impact the labour players like India, who have made a business out of labour arbitrage. They're going to have to rethink the services they provide. It won't be those first level issues that they hire people to quickly train to work on a support desk. Those jobs are going to be automated. The new kinds of jobs will be elevated roles in technology and support.

We are going to see a resurgence of hiring as companies understand that now, IT infrastructure is how a company operates. Companies need knowledge workers who understand not only how the infrastructure works, but how to can save money, do more with it and be more proactive.

Low cost, labour arbitrage solutions will start falling by the wayside as companies re-evaluate the kinds of hiring they should be doing inside of their organisations. People in countries like India, Mexico and Romania are going to have to change their skill sets in order to stay relevant. Countries and people that are proactive will have leverage over those that are laggards.

The human brain is the ultimate Darwinian engine. When mundane chores are no longer available, man will be forced to elevate his game and retool his skills to be productive in an automated world. When automation delivers 60 percent more value, the luddites need to ask if we have a choice of turning against such an automation tide. We need to embrace the automation tide that is coming. It will lift all embracing companies' ships.

8.5. Pravin Rao, COO and Member of the Board, Infosys

Pravin's thoughts on automation capabilities:

At Infosys, we are completely re-imagining the concept of services. In doing this, we are rethinking software, platforms and services – and people – and how they come together in entirely new ways. Service automation is a fundamental part of this effort and a major area of focus for us. We are calling it the 'Zero Touch Initiative'. As part of this, we are leveraging AI and knowledge-based techniques to solve ticketing problems with

Infosys Automation Platform(IAP), automating not merely the business processes but also the experience in BPO, through Panaya automating application maintenance and application testing. All these levers are about driving efficiencies into our service lines for productivity gains across our client portfolios as well as for internal use.

Pravin's thoughts on client types, challenges, and business value delivered:

Infosys RPA platform is proven, capable, robust and non-intrusive. Tasks that require human expertise or human judgment are executed by machines using advances in artificial intelligence, deep learning, big data, and natural user interfaces, combined with unprecedented computing power and connectivity.

- IAP is helping improve productivity in IT operations across our industry verticals. IAP has helped resolve 15 percent to 20 percent of tickets with zero intervention.
- Knowledge-based engineering (KBE) automation approach adopted for the design of an aircraft structural component has reduced the cycle time and effort by more than 30 percent.
- Using Panaya, we bring agility to the enterprise. We have been able to reduce changes to ERP Time To Market by as much as 30 percent, and costs by as much as 50 percent.

Pravin's thoughts on automation and the future of work:

As markets expand and the technology landscape changes, disruptions come from unexpected places. This leads to the creation of new business models and the appearance of new buyers and influencers who reshape the market dynamics and ultimately the very fundamentals of value creation in an ecosystem. Automation is one such disruptive force in the technology landscape that has the potential to rewire the rules of the game. Further, it is our belief that technology makes people more productive, as their abilities are amplified by technology. So, with automation we are likely to see a temporary reorganisation of work as people take on higher order jobs. This will likely be coupled with a redistribution of labour as it adjusts to the new market dynamic.

8.6. Common Themes

Looking across the provider responses, there were differences and similarities. As far as differences, each respondent focused on his company's unique service automation capabilities. As we have noted throughout this book, service automation is best conceived as a continuum of capabilities; each provider has its 'sweet spot' within it. Furthermore, the 'sweet spots' will evolve over time and the entire service automation continuum will push the boundaries of what is automatable. As for similarities, each provider contributor reported that service automation has a rich set of business benefits. By our assessment, based on their contributions, we classified all provider contributors as technology 'optimists', in that service automation was seen to elevate rather than enslave humanity. Some of these differences and similarities are expanded upon below.

The biggest customer challenge is the initial business case, and often times, decision-makers focus too narrowly on costs. Andrew (Celaton) notes that decision makers have concerns about costs and they have to assess whether to invest in more staff, outsourcing, or technology to solve a business problem. Technology is often (wrongly) presumed to be the expensive choice. Alastair (Blue Prism) also acknowledged that costs often drive decisions, but warns customers that, if it seems too cheap to be true, then it probably is. Chetan (IPsoft) also mentioned that business value realisation is the major challenge, but that fear of change is the next biggest issue. How can these challenges be met? Throughout this book, we have shown that service automation frequently starts with a grass-roots pioneer who champions a highly-visible proof-of-concept that garnishes buy-in – and even enthusiasm – for service automation. Change management is a perennial challenge, but using service automation to free existing staff from dreary tasks to focus on more decision-making tasks and on more social interactions was successful in all the cases examined thus far in our research.

Providers identified that business benefits are multifaceted. Like client contributors in the last chapter, provider contributors reported that business benefits of service automation are multifaceted. The provider contributors all mentioned cost savings (examples were given of cost savings between 40 percent to 80 percent), but also stressed that service automation allows organisations to scale services without adding headcount, improves the end-customer's experience, produces consistent, high-quality, and fast results, and allows real time visibility into operations. Provider contributors also stressed that service automation solutions are compliant and secure.

Providers are optimistic that automation will improve the human experience. Several provider contributors noted that technology in general – and service automation in particular – creates market disruptions in the short-term. In the long-term, all shared optimistic visions of the future. Andrew (Celaton) wrote, *"The productivity of staff increases and customer service and reputation improves which ultimately leads to improvement in financial performance"*. Alastair (Blue Prism), acknowledges that he sides with the technology optimists who *"believe automation and digitalisation of work will lead to increases in economic growth, new jobs, less hours of working, more fulfilling and interesting careers and overall improvements in our quality of life"*. Pravin (Infosys) wrote, *"technology makes people more productive as their abilities are amplified by technology"*. Chetan (IPsoft) sees that man can choose his fate and urged us all *"to embrace the automation tide that is coming. It will lift all embracing companies' ships."*

8.7. Conclusion

This chapter heard from a small number of provider voices, but these were senior executives from amongst the market leaders. It is interesting that most of them saw clients as experiencing the business case as the major challenge. In our cases of actual implementation, clients found their business cases for service automation were easily met and mostly surpassed. Providers also report in this chapter that clients experienced multifaceted business benefits from adoption. Providers emerged as very positive on what automation brought to the human dimensions of work.

The next chapter extends these insights but from an advisor perspective. Advisors can influence clients and providers in terms of strategy and effective practice, but also gain insight into how service automation pans out in specific settings using various automation tools. As we shall see, advisor insights are very rich indeed. Change management emerges as a major client challenge, in their experience. They observe different practices as to who drives automation adoption. They see automation definitely affecting outsourcing in terms of pricing models, value proposition and location decisions. They see automation affecting job numbers in certain jobs, but also increasing demand in others. In our last chapter we will deal in detail with the theme of the future of work.

Citations

[1] Source: http://www.celaton.com/company

[2] Source: http://www.celaton.com/instream

[3] Source: http://www.blueprism.com/about-us

[4] Source: http://www.blueprism.com/our-products

[5] Source: http://www.ipsoft.com/about-ipsoft/

[6] See for example Sutherland, C. (2015), *The Raw Truth about Intelligent,* HFS Research White Paper, September

[7] Source: http://www.ipsoft.com/what-we-do/amelia/

[8] Source: http://www.infosys.com/about/#

Chapter 9

In Their Own Words: Advisor Responses

What's Inside: *Service automation practice leads from top advisory firms – The Everest Group, KPMG, Horses for Sources (HfS), Alsbridge, and Information Services Group (ISG) – responded to questions pertaining to client service automation adoption, effects on outsourcing, automation tool capabilities, and the future of work as a consequence of automation. Overall, advisors report that clients are challenged to distinguish hype from reality and need help traversing their automation journeys. Advisors report that IT is ahead of business operations in automation; whereas many business operations are still automating structured tasks, IT is moving into natural language and machine learning very quickly. Automation is affecting outsourcing's pricing models, value proposition, and location decisions. Finally, the overall effect on jobs will likely be much less demand for low-skilled jobs, partly offset by a rise in higher-skilled jobs.*

9.1. Introduction

This is the third and final chapter where we requested service automation stakeholders to respond to questions *'in their own words'*. For this chapter, we invited five thought leaders from the advisory community to speak of their experiences. We are pleased that service automation practice leads from several top advisory firms – The Everest Group, KPMG, Horses for Sources (HfS), Alsbridge, and Information Services Group (ISG) – contributed (see Table 9.1 below and the *Notes on Contributors* on page 19).

Name	Title	Company
Sarah Burnett	Research Vice President	Everest Group
Cliff Justice	Leader of US Shared Services and Outsourcing Advisory	KPMG
Charles Sutherland	Chief Research Officer	HfS Research
Derek Toone	Managing Director, Robotic Process Automation	Alsbridge
Rob Brindley	Director, Robotic Process Automation and Media Industry	ISG

Table 9.1: Advisor Thought Leaders Contributing to
In Their Own Words

Advisors are a powerful stakeholder group who highly influence practice. Advisors help clients develop an automation strategy – usually within a bigger context of service transformation. Advisors also help develop requests for proposals, evaluate provider responses, guide the selection of automation tools (where clients are doing-it-themselves) or assist clients to select providers with proven automation capabilities. Advisors assist in proof-of-concept tests, help clients build automation capabilities and prepare the organisation for the changes caused by automation, among other services. Advisors also help service providers, for example with an automation strategy, or crafting new pricing models as services increasingly shift from human to robotic fulfilment, to name just a few of their services. They observe different practices as to who drives automation adoption. They see automation definitely affecting outsourcing in terms of pricing models, value propositions and location decisions. They see automation reducing employment numbers in certain jobs, but also increasing employment in others.

In this chapter, we first describe their organisations and the questions we asked advisors. Next, we present their contributions, and finally we extract some common themes from across the contributions.

9.1.1. Overview of the Contributing Organisations

The five advisors – Sarah Burnett (Everest Group), Cliff Justice (KPMG), Charles Sutherland (HfS), Derek Toone (Alsbridge), and Rob Brindley (ISG) – are all service automation experts. They each work for some of the world's leading advisory companies.

The Everest Group was founded by CEO Peter Bendor-Samuel in 1991 and is headquartered in Dallas Texas. Bendor-Samuel's vision was *"to assist the then nascent outsourcing and global services industry to evolve more powerful and effective mechanisms to create and capture value."*[1] Since then, the Everest Group has grown to a global advisor firm with offices in Toronto, London, Gurgaon, Montevideo, and New York City. It advises in Enterprise IT as a-service, strategic sourcing, business transformation, service optimisation, and service provider consulting.[2]

KPMG was formed in 1987 when the Dutch firm KMG and the English firm Peat Marwick joined forces. Today, KPMG is one of the largest professional services companies in the world earning around $25 billion annually, and employing 162,000 people. KPMG has three lines of services: audit, tax, and advisory.[3] Its advisory practice focuses on *"improving business performance, turning risk and compliance efforts into opportunities, developing winning strategies and creating, enhancing and preserving value are at the core of what we do for leading organisations everywhere."*[4]

HfS Research was founded by CEO Phil Fersht in 2010. Today, Fersht leads a multi-disciplinary group of analysts, with a core team of 17 industry experts. HfS's research and advisory services help buyer and provider organisations with digital transformation of operations, cloud-based business platforms, services talent development strategies, process automation and outsourcing, mobility, analytics and social collaboration.[5]

Alsbridge was founded in 2003 as the Trowbridge Group and became 'Alsbridge' in 2005 after the merger with ALS. Alsbridge acquired

ProBenchmark and TAG in 2009, Telwares in 2012, and Source in 2015.[6] Today, Alsbridge is headquartered in Addison, Texas, employs 300 advisors in the US, Canada, European Union, and APAC. The CEO is Chip Wagner. Alsbridge provides advisory services for benchmarking, intelligent process automation, IT asset management, network, outsourcing, transformation, cloud, and vendor management and governance services.[7]

Information Services Group (ISG) was founded in 2006 by Chairman and CEO Michael Connors. ISG acquired TPI in 2007, Compass and STA Consulting in 2011, and CCI Consulting in 2014. ISG is based in Stamford, Connecticut, operates in 21 countries, earns over $200 million in annual revenue, has more than 900 employees.[8] ISG provides services that inform, assess, design, execute, and operate technology and business solutions.[9]

9.1.2. Questions Posed to Advisor Thought Leaders

Given the depth and breadth of the advisor community's experience with service automation, we posed a number of questions to them pertaining to client adoption, effects on outsourcing, automation tool capabilities, and the future of work as a consequence of automation. The specific questions were:

1. **Client adoption:** In your practice, what are the biggest struggles clients have concerning RPA and service automation? How do you advise them to overcome these struggles? In your practice, are most adoptions being driven by clients within their own organisations or through outsourcing relationships? Are you seeing more service activity from business operations or IT operations?
2. **Automation and outsourcing:** How does/will RPA and service automation affect outsourcing relationships? How are clients addressing RPA/service automation in request-for-proposals and renewal decisions? How are providers incorporating automation in their proposal responses, proposed pricing models, and post-contract delivery? How will RPA/service automation affect location decisions? Will more or less work be sourced from traditionally low-labour cost countries?

238

3. **Tool capabilities:** How do you help clients select the right RPA/ service automation tool? Do you see real differences in capabilities across the tools and providers? Do you see evidence of 'RPA or automation washing' – software vendors marketing old tools as new?
4. **Automation and work:** How will automation affect the future of IT and business services? What will be a likely effect on jobs? Which countries will likely be most affected?

Below, their responses to these questions are conveyed *'in their own words'*. At the end of the chapter, we summarise the common threads among their responses.

9.2. Sarah Burnett, Research Vice President, Everest Group

Sarah's thoughts on client adoption:

Client adoption has largely been tactical to address specific business process requirements. Once started on automation, some organisations adopt it as an enterprise capability that they deploy again and again to address different requirements. Typically, organisations that get to this stage will have developed an automation strategy, and gained enough experience, to have best practice methodologies or even a centre of excellence.

But getting started is often the most difficult step. To address this, the automation champion has to get approvals from both senior business stakeholders and IT. Many start with a proof-of-concept to showcase the power of automation and then gain support from all stakeholders. In fact, Everest Group recommends this approach to its clients (see Figure 9.1).

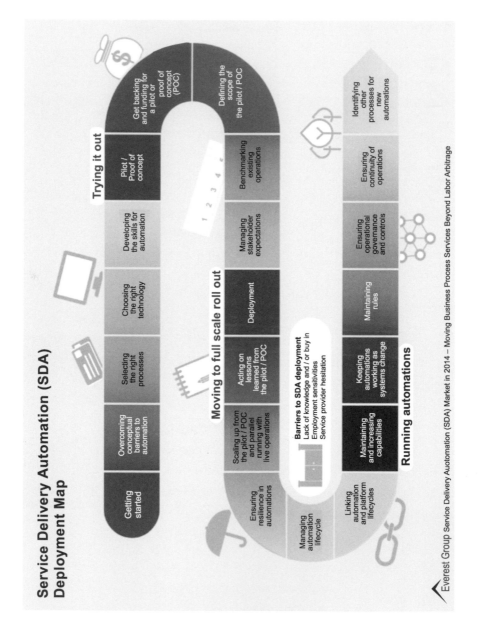

**Figure 9.1: Everest Group's Service Delivery
Automation Deployment Roadmap**
(Source: Everest Group. Reprinted with permission)

Some will run dual proofs-of-concept with different automation technologies – for example, robotic process automation and business process management tools – to find the most efficient solution for their requirement.

Challenges after the first automation is deployed include ensuring the best configuration for the run time environment and optimisation to get the most out of the deployment.

In the world of business process services, adoption has largely been driven by clients. However, over the last year, we have seen more and more service providers commit to automating some of their services. The majority of the service providers today have automation programs in progress to automate more of their existing clients' business processes. These initiatives are driven by the need to show improved operational efficiency and continuous improvement.

We are seeing a huge emphasis on automation in IT services and an increasing shift towards cognitive automation with machine learning. This is the evolution of a few years of IT automation – some might even say that it is more mature than business process automation.

Sarah's thoughts on automation and outsourcing:

Automation will change the way that outsourcing contracts are fulfilled, as well as the location of service delivery. It is already changing the commercials of contracts. As delivery teams shrink, we will see more outcome and transactional pricing blended with other models for service delivery. Over time, we might also see a shift from offshoring to near-shoring or re-shoring, as automation replaces some aspects of labour arbitrage. It will not replace all FTEs and there will still be an advantage to arbitrage, for example, cheaper overheads for automation. It is the mix of locations that is more likely to change.

Already, we are seeing some clients only send out invitations to tender to service providers who offer a high degree of automation in service delivery. This type of requirement will rise steadily over time and as large contracts come up for renewal.

In the next 18-24 months, we expect to see automation, and in particular, the type that is enabled by natural language processing and machine learning, to open up new opportunities for business process services. These will include document-based service opportunities, such as legal services and financial fraud detection and prevention.

Sarah's thoughts on tool capabilities:

There are different types of tools for different requirements, such as contact centre and back-office. We advise our clients that they can have a portfolio of automation tools. These would often be in addition to traditional workflow, document management, and other software such as activity monitoring.

Everest Group is delving deeper into the latest technologies. We are in the process of completing an extensive service delivery automation technology assessment report that will include comparison and positioning of third party business process automation software tools. We have assessed a wide range of the newer style of automation tools already and have more underway. These include robotic, cognitive, and tools that rely on plug-in architecture and cascading style sheets (CSS)[i] to automate processes. Our clients will be able to refer to this report, as well as our service provider research findings and experience, to help them find the best solution for their needs.

The buzz in the market about RPA has boosted the market for other types of automation technologies too. For example, a plug-in architecture software vendor told us that he is getting more and more business thanks to RPA. There has been some degree of RPA-washing among technology and service providers, but we are starting to see a shift of emphasis to cognitive tools.

---

[i] Cascading Style Sheets (CSS) are a mechanism for adding styles such as fonts, colors, and spacing to web documents.

Some RPA technology vendors and also service providers are today touting their new machine learning capabilities.

Sarah's thoughts on automation and the future of work:

Automation in IT has been going on for some time. This is being accelerated due to increasing adoption of cloud and models such as 'Software as a Service', 'Platform as a Service', and virtualisation. In addition there is the rise of 'software defined' infrastructure, network, and storage. The nature of a software-defined environment makes automation a necessity.

There is already much scripted automation in IT, but increasing complexity is driving the need for artificial intelligence. This is leading to more investment in machine learning tools as technology vendors and service providers alike compete in this market.

Current automation technologies, combined with machine learning, are continuing the long path towards infrastructure operations, which require essentially no human management. We aren't there yet, but it now appears unavoidable for any modern infrastructure environment.

9.3. Cliff Justice, Leader of U.S. Shared Services and Outsourcing Advisory, KPMG

Cliff's thoughts on client adoption:

Clients are focused on understanding the landscape of capabilities, the processes and functions within the organisation that can be impacted, and the business case for embarking on such an effort. Additionally, they want to understand the magnitude of organisational change that needs to occur to achieve a particular outcome and whether there is an appetite for it. There is a tremendous amount of hype and confusion around basic robotic automation and where 'cognitive' technologies and artificial intelligence fit in. Our clients ask us to help discern hype from reality and help them vet the capabilities.

We take clients through a structured internal assessment to understand where automation could have an impact and then evaluate the relevant technologies and change management strategies that would be needed for success. There are technologies that are suited for different settings, and they have different objectives and price points. Additionally the organisation must be ready to make the changes necessary to execute effectively in an automated environment. We have tools that help objectively assess their organisational readiness and impact to people and culture. We also have people who are specialised in configuring the technology and integrating it within the process.

Concerning whether adoptions are being driven by clients within their own organisations, or through outsourcing relationships – it's a mix of both. Providers have been implementing this technology for years to improve effectiveness in their outsourcing contracts, but today we are seeing clients learn more about this technology and bring on internal expertise to experiment with the capabilities to determine the best sourcing solution. There are classes of automation, with the first and most common class being the rules-based automation with no machine learning or cognitive capabilities. These tools need to be 'trained' and managed, and exceptions to the programmed process must be resolved by a human. Over time, the bots are taught to recognise exceptions to the process and more scale can be added and as long as the basic process remains the same, necessity for human intervention is reduced. Cognitive technologies are the game-changer: They learn from humans who provide expert knowledge as well as their own trial and error and interactions with other humans. Cognitive technology can inform either human workers or robotic automation tools to make a decision and take a particular course of action.

There is more interest in automation from business operations and clerical activity than from IT operations. IT operations automation has been around for a while, but is improving with cognitive and machine learning capabilities from companies like IPsoft. The business operations side has more white space and opportunities for automation, which is fertile ground for technologies like Blue Prism or Automation Anywhere. There are also many companies building advanced, industry-specific applications on cognitive platforms, like IBM Watson.

Cliff's thoughts on automation and outsourcing:

RPA and service automation will ultimately have a material impact on the profitability of providers and savings of the clients. The question will be what if the clients decide to do it themselves, and the value add that the provider brings to the table. Additionally, RPA makes location less relevant for the processes that are served by automation. It is delivered in the cloud or locally. See KPMG's white paper on the topic: *How robots can improve legacy sourcing agreements.*[ii]

Cliff's thoughts on tool capabilities:

We are tool-agnostic. We have a process that is similar to selecting software or an outsourcing vendor. We look at client priorities and objectives, do a deep dive of the processes, and scope and evaluate the solutions based on their ability to achieve the objectives. We look at the client's internal capabilities to manage and deliver and compare that to the solution and support that the service provider or technology provider is bringing to the table.

And yes, absolutely, we see evidence of 'RPA washing'; We see real differences in capabilities across the tools and providers. This is a new market with emerging technologies. Some are more mature than others. There is a

---

[ii] http://www.kpmg-institutes.com/content/dam/kpmg/sharedservicesoutsourcinginstitute/pdf/2015/robotics-improve-legacy-sourcing.pdf

range of capabilities moving from 'bots' that can carry out programmatic tasks, to cognitive agents, which can parse natural language and infer intent, and probabilistic answers. As these come together, we see a new class of intelligent, cognitive automation forming.

Cliff's thoughts on automation and the future of work:

I have called service automation the 'death of outsourcing' – as we know it, anyway. As this evolves, this will impact those areas the most, which have generated value and savings by lifting processes performed developed countries with high wages and shifting them to a low cost country. Unfortunately for some service providers and countries, this type of work makes up a material part of the outsourcing and offshoring industry. Many service providers are successfully getting in front of this and offering automated, digital solutions and moving away from labour arbitrage as the primary lever. However the impact will be material. Many of the global service providers have proven to be very innovative and introducing advanced autonomic solutions. Ultimately, this will create a better, stronger industry with a higher value proposition than simply low cost labour but there will be some turmoil along the way.

9.4. Charles Sutherland, Chief Research Officer, HfS Research

Charles' thoughts on client adoption:

As 2015 draws to a close, it seems that almost every conversation about IT and Business Process Outsourcing (BPO) at some point turns to the effect that automation, and in particular Robotic Process Automation (RPA) is having – and could have – on service providers, third-party advisors, RPA software vendors and the enterprise clients that are affected by this technology. This pervasiveness

of automation was captured in a recent study that HfS Research conducted amongst 178 enterprise buyers of IT and business services showed that 11 percent of respondents had already acquired some to extensive hands on experience in RPA with a further 52 percent showing an interest in still learning more about it for their business.

At HfS, we have been following this for several years now and have held at least 100 briefings and presentations on RPA with service providers, RPA vendors and advisors in the last year alone. However, in most of these conversations we have observed that the opinions and change management issues of operations leaders, functional executives and C-suite enterprise buyers of RPA, are being largely overlooked. In short, RPA began more as an offering from the software vendors, services providers and consultants – eager to find an edge to sell more cost-reduction capability to clients beyond traditional wage-arbitrage outsourcing, than demand-pull from buyers keen to automate their processes and eliminate manual tasks but the reality is changing.

We interviewed 16 early enterprise adopters of RPA in 2015 to understand why they had implemented RPA, how they got the organisational buy-in to implement this today.

The top three reasons for implementing RPA now amongst early adopters:

1. The annual cost reductions from the existing BPO platform were below what was needed by the business and something had to be found to kick-start accelerated savings.

2. A lack of time and/or available support from internal IT to be able to transform the existing application environment with new software that simplified processing and/or improved the overall quality of delivery.

3. Neither I nor my service provider can easily ramp up resources I

need for even simple tasks when we get hit by incoming volume volatility and seasonality spikes (found at the operational and functional level).

How to get organisational buy-in for RPA? Because RPA may be deployed outside of IT (and also by an external service provider within their own operations while certainly benefiting the enterprise client), it isn't always easy to get the necessary broader organisational buy-in required to test the capability – let alone moving to a broader production regime. HfS interviews with these early RPA adopters resulted in several suggestions for how to overcome resistance and obtain organisational buy-in for RPA:

1. *Start small*. Don't jump in with both feet in RPA until you, as an operational or functional leader, have really tested out where you see it has potential based on your own knowledge of the process(es) and the experience of your service provider. With that in mind, don't get carried away by the hype of potential total savings before you have seen it in action.

2. *Bring IT in under the umbrella as soon as you can*. Your enterprise IT function may see RPA as a threat (or an unwanted distraction from their own programs), but you need to bring them along – and not by leaning on the C-suite to do so – as without their active support with regard to the planning and management of the existing underlying application structure, it will be nigh impossible to get this done successfully and then maintain the benefits over time.

3. *Look to a service provider that has a long-term vision for automation as a capability*. In 2014, the IT/BPO industry was just coming to terms with RPA and many service providers went through a journey from seeing this as a tactical contract based capability to a strategic cross-client, cross-process capability. Wherever possible, understand how your service provider(s) sees RPA, understand their strategic vision on automation, and share that back with the rest of your enterprise, including your executive sponsors that will

be part of this effort.

4. ***Get this done within the existing contract, where possible***. Your service provider may be super willing to undertake RPA if your existing arrangement is fixed-fee or transactionally-priced, but also work with them to incentivise this opportunity under FTE-based contracting arrangements as well, which may require bringing in senior executive sponsorship.

Charles' thoughts on automation and outsourcing:

RPA and Intelligent Automation solutions are already impacting the outsourcing market today. All of the major service providers are budgeting for and building new capabilities in automation across IT and business service delivery at the same time as they are changing their solution and commercial models to reflect this new reality. Every outsourcing contract that is up for renewal is being subjected to an automation applicability review because if the incumbent service provider doesn't do this, competitors willing to do this analysis and build it into their pricing today will replace them. While much of the attention of late has been on the impact that RPA will have on Business Process Outsourcing, we have also seen potentially even more momentum building for automation impacts in Infrastructure and Application Outsourcing.

Charles' thoughts on tool capabilities:

In our role as industry analysts, HfS is not advocating one RPA solution over another to the market today. Instead, we are focused on defining and communicating the business benefits to be achieved across the full range of what we are calling the HfS Intelligent Automation Continuum, that runs from macros through RPA to Autonomics, Cognitive Computing and Artificial Intelligence (see Figure 9.2). Each of these technologies segments has a contribution to make and increasingly we see both enterprises and service providers combining these to create the most impactful solutions.

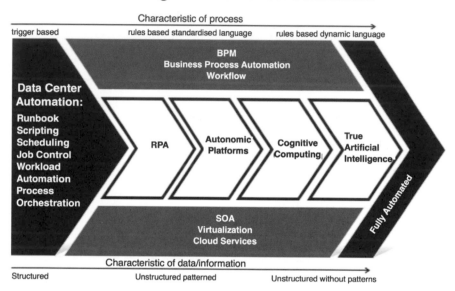

Figure 9.2: The HfS Intelligent Automation Continuum
(Source: HfS. Reprinted with permission)

Charles' thoughts on automation and the future of work:

HfS believes that we are just beginning to see the impact of Intelligent Automation on IT and business services, and that it will, over the next five years and beyond, have a dramatic impact on the current structure of employment in these services. Already we are seeing service providers and large shared service centres changing their talent acquisition and career development models to recognise that there will be less demand for lower end, often entry-level, task-oriented jobs in the future. A few early adopters are going beyond this as well and looking at how they redesign their delivery floors to account for lower future requirements for human agents in many roles and how the remaining human agents will interact with robotic and cognitive technologies in their working environment as well.

Given the sheer size of the IT and business services workforce in India and the Philippines, already many of the most significant impacts will be felt there first – especially in Tier II/III/IV delivery cities where the current work is more task-oriented than knowledge or judgment-based. Our view is that jobs in the call centre industry will be dramatically reduced in aggregate over the next decade perhaps by 30 percent to 50 percent from current levels, but we expect to see more of a neutral overall impact on other IT and business services role as low-end work gets swapped out for higher end roles and augmentative solutions.

9.5. Derek Toone, Managing Director, Robotic Process Automation, Alsbridge

Derek's thoughts on client adoption:

One of the first hurdles clients face is education on what is possible and how to distinguish between the different forms of service automation available. With so many emerging and evolving technologies and all of the market hype, many clients have a hard time distinguishing between products, and/or mistakenly believe one product has the features of another, which can result in the misapplication of a sub-optimal product to a business need/objective.

Creating an automation strategy aligned with business goals; assessing and prioritising processes for automation; balancing process reengineering with process automation; building the business case; and implementation roadmap, are common struggles most clients have. But one of the key challenges that most clients fail to take into account and/or adequately address is assessing their organisational readiness and successfully incorporating transition management, organisational design and change management, communications, operational alignment and the development of a future state operating model to manage the combined human and digital workforce.

In Alsbridge's practice, we advise clients on leveraging service automation both directly and via their outsourcing relationships. As of mid-2015, we are seeing business operations more often adopting RPA directly than through a BPO player, and conversely IT operations more often leveraging service automation as part an ITO service. Alsbridge's Intelligent Automation Practice includes Six Sigma Black Belts, organisational change management SMEs, and automation architects from leading outsourcing providers and automation software vendors. These professionals leverage our data-driven methodology, tools and templates to help clients overcome these challenges and optimise outcomes based on their goals.

Derek's thoughts on automation and outsourcing:

Advances in service automation are affecting ITO relationships in dramatic fashion. To unseat competitors, ITO providers are leveraging service automation to materially lower their price while simultaneously enhancing service quality. However, we have seen responses that push the envelope and introduce risk into the deal by making commercial commitments on technology innovations around which that the service provider has not yet matured their capability.

In BPO deals, which tend to have a higher percentage of FTE-based pricing, we are seeing slower adoption of RPA and service automation. The operational maturity of RPA-enabled BPO solutions varies materially between leading outsourcing providers. Those few BPO providers who have embraced RPA are capable of delivering stunning results in terms of cost, speed and accuracy, which enables them to more easily shift to transaction-based and/or outcome-based gain-share pricing with clients.

If adopted, RPA/service automation, will materially affect location decisions for services which have previously relied heavily on availability and cost of labour for a given skill-set. For outsourced services, RPA/service automation will not entirely eliminate the need for labour and, if a given skill set is readily available in a lower cost location that will continue to be a business driver for using that location. However, as labour becomes a smaller component of overall service delivery, then the weight of the counterbalancing factors (e.g., language, time zone, culture, IP security, etc.) will begin to more often tip the scale in favour of using onshore service delivery.

Derek's thoughts on tool capabilities:

Alsbridge is tool agnostic, and helps clients to select the optimal RPA/service automation tool based on careful analysis of their objectives, IT environment, business processes characteristics and constraints unique to their business or industry. There are meaningful differences between capabilities and features across the different tools in the market, which are all currently being generically referred to as 'RPA'. Some are easier to deploy and manage; others provide a higher degree of audit and security; some come with pre-configured automations while others do not; some are better at dealing with unstructured data than others; some have a higher degree of transaction processing horsepower for a lower price; the degree to which each has achieved 'narrow artificial intelligence' varies – the list of differences goes on and on.

'RPA washing' absolutely occurs – not only from the software vendors, but also the outsourcing providers. Old tools being paraded under a new banner – sometimes they've at least been updated to mimic RPA functionality, but even so they've yet to be tested and refined over hundreds of implementations.

Derek's thoughts on automation and the future of work:

In their current incarnation, RPA/service automation tools will reduce the need for human labour to process many transactions performed manually today. In some cases, this will eliminate a job in its entirety, but more often it will free up the human worker from performing some portion of their daily tasks and enable them to perform higher value-added activities. This, of course, is dependent on two factors: (1) the availability of higher value-added activities to be performed and (2) the capability of the human workers to perform them. Overall, the likely effect on jobs will be the elimination of those involving rote, repetitive processing, and a higher focus on the value human workers who can deliver results in jobs requiring creative thinking and subjective decision-making. Any countries whose economies are dependent on jobs in the former category, without the ability to shift to the latter, will be adversely affected.

9.6. Rob Brindley, ISG Director, Robotic Process Automation and Media Industry

Rob's thoughts on automation:

Automation is not new. Information Technology (IT) professionals have been developing and deploying technology to automate the supportability of information systems for more than forty years. Job control language (JCL) is an early example of how IT used Robotic Process Automation (RPA) to manage batch jobs on the mainframe. Historically, the challenge for IT in its adoption of RPA was due to the fact that compute and storage capability were  not as economically feasible as the low cost of labour to perform IT business processes. Over time, as IT has become a more substantial component of the success of an organisation's business model (but still not its core capability), businesses began to turn to outsourcing to provide a cost-effective solution. This was the beginning of the commoditisation of IT processes.

To leverage this shift in demand, outsourcing firms, such as IBM, CSC and EDS (now HP), optimised common processes to provide their customers more efficient and affordable IT services. For business models of all types, global outsourcing was the next step in the evolution of making IT cost effective. This shift followed the similar and more mature trajectory of the manufacturing industry, which had long sought the benefits of global outsourcing of well-defined processes previously performed internally.

So what has changed?

Compute processing power, storage capacity and self-diagnostic capabilities have become considerably less expensive over the last few years, enabling companies to use technology to perform highly repeatable and significantly more complex IT business processes. IT can now apply this processing power to a wider range of business processes to optimise more complex areas of IT service delivery. The wide adoption of process standardisation, as put forth by the International Organisation for Standards (ISO), Software Engineering Institute (SEI), Information Technology Infrastructure Library (ITIL) and Control Objective for Information Technology (COBIT), has made it easier for outsourcing firms to commoditise their IT delivery across industries and business models.

Process standardisation and less expensive compute processing power have come together, and the IT industry now finds itself in a position to reap the benefits of automation like never before. Trailblazing industries, such as manufacturing – which has used robots in the automobile assembly line for many years – serve as examples of how automation can be leveraged to make highly repeatable and standardised processes more efficient. RPA is making itself known in other ways, too, like in the connected washing machine that can alert the manufacturer via the internet to ship a replacement part or schedule preventive maintenance. Or like the front door deadbolt lock that allows access via a smartphone app. We use it even in the basic act of resetting our passwords in our online banking accounts.

Today, RPA is achieved through IT's ability to process millions of events per second to determine which require attention and which do not. Sophisticated algorithms and statistical analyses – without human intervention – can determine if a probable-event solution is needed to resolve what would be a business-impacting event, all while logging the activities within the Incident Management System (IMS). If the resolution of the event fails to deploy successfully, the system can deploy an alternative event solution. If the system exhausts all solution options, it can activate the escalation process within the IMS to engage humans for restoration of the business-impacting event and tag it as an incident.

RPA is like an archer with five arrows in his quiver. The archer's target is the event and each arrow is a potential solution to the event. The archer works from a set of sophisticated algorithms and statistical analyses to determine the order in which he should shoot the arrows at the target. If the archer has an arrow that will resolve the event, he will shoot the right arrow to hit the bullseye. If the archer does not have an arrow to resolve the event, he will elevate the event to an incident to seek assistance for restoration.

The RPA market is flush with technology providers and new ones are entering every day. This hyper-market state is similar to the cloud computing clamour we experienced not too long ago. The market will continue to saturate with outsourcing providers and niche RPA technology providers until leaders emerge and providers rationalise and consolidate into a mature industry. Though many RPA providers offer a low-cost entry fee as a tactic for winning market share, enterprises are learning to practice prudence as they work to first understand the RPA provider business model and how it might fit with theirs.

Rob's thoughts on automation and the future of work:

There is no question that automation technologies will alter world economics. Taken in both its virtual and physical forms, RPA represents one of the most significant disruptive events in the world today. RPA is likely to bring changes that will be even more significant than those brought about by the Industrial Revolution. Information Services Group (ISG) research indicates that automation technology will have a $5.2 to $6.7 trillion annual economic impact by 2025. ISG also estimates that, by this same year, the deployment of automation technology will equal the output of 110 million to 140 million full-time equivalents.

RPA's greatest impact during this period will be on performing those highly repeatable tasks in functions such as system monitoring, event management, capacity provisioning, software distribution, self-healing, enablement of self-help, preventative rerouting of workloads and release and change management. In one case study, when an enterprise deployed RPA technology into its environment to perform system monitoring, it saw measurable gains in stability, reliability and scalability of its environment, which it was able to see without what would have been the costs associated with growing its IT organisation.

Consumers of RPA will use various approaches to realise its benefits, including self-deployment and engagements with outsourcing providers, RPA technology providers or consultancies. Regardless of approach, a well-developed strategy will be imperative. Those who engage thought leaders, such as consultancy and outsourcing providers, in the early stages of market development will be best able to realise the long-term business benefits of achieving business goals, return on investment and competitive advantage.

The idea that the IT industry could use RPA to improve stability, scalability, reliability and, ultimately, reduce costs is, indeed, an exciting proposition. Because of its capability and affordability, RPA is very likely to embody the next wave of outsourcing as companies leverage it for both reactive and proactive processes.

While current RPA technology is focused on the event-and-incident-management side of the equation, driving the effort to turn complex reactive practices into standardised processes, some RPA providers are working on proactive practices. This work is providing additional capability to the non-IT consumer in, for example, performing self-help password reset through a service catalogue, and to the IT consumer, for example, in issuing service requests to build out an environment via an application development on a virtual machine. The future is limited only by human imagination, social impact and economics. A few RPA providers have already developed early cognitive capability that can handle a service desk call, pleasantries and all. Of those, some are already exploring the next generation of artificial intelligence and neural networks.

Advanced outsourcing providers are acknowledging the disruptive long-term impact and are beginning to integrate RPA into their solutions to reduce operational cost and improve sustainability, reliability and service level achievement. ISG research shows global Tier 1 outsourcing providers are currently incorporating RPA technology into their solutions and Tier 2 providers are not far behind. However, only limited deployment of RPA has been applied to existing outsourcing engagements, which is most likely due to the low return on investment for the provider. Customers whose outsourcing engagements contain innovation provisions are best positioned to realise the benefits of RPA.

Of course, despite the potential upside, a CIO must ensure his or her investment in RPA will bring a return over the long term. Some technology providers offer very low entry fees, but because IT business processes are becoming more complex, both horizontally and vertically, and because they are subject to change, it's possible that future maintenance costs could render RPA a poor value proposition. CIOs who have a strategy, practice operational discipline and are custodians of technology in the context of their organisation's business objectives will be the most well-prepared to realise the benefits and manage the cost to achieve the business benefits.

Just as the archer needs more and ever-sharper arrows in his quiver, the CIO needs to ensure processes are solid, well defined, repeatable and resistant to change before considering them as worthy of an RPA investment. The IT professionals of tomorrow will not only need to understand IT, but they will also need to know how to apply process engineering principles to truly optimise the candidate processes for RPA. If they do not, they will need the skills to work with their business partners to define and achieve repcatable, scalable processes so that they can realise efficiencies in the future. ISG research indicates that the increased adoption of RPA could create hundreds of thousands of new high-skill employment opportunities, but the larger effect could be a mass redefinition or elimination of jobs and the widespread application of economic assistance and retraining for tens of millions of people.

We are in new territory – and it is changing before our eyes. Many technology firms have rushed to debut their latest and greatest RPA product or service, and the marketplace has not yet rationalised itself into a neat list of proven, high-quality RPA name brands. Meanwhile, CIOs must cut through the market noise and serve as stewards of technology for their organisations. They must ask specific and relevant questions: How repeatable are the processes? How commoditised is the environment? What are the intellectual property rights? What is the total cost of ownership? How do I migrate from my legacy environment to an environment that can realise the benefits of RPA?

CIOs must sharpen their golden arrow, seek first to fully understand the potential of RPA and then aim carefully for the specific benefits that will help them best leverage it for customer value creation.

9.7 Common Themes

Looking across the advisor responses, there were many similarities. Overall, advisors see evidence of 'automation washing' and a lot of hype, buzzwords, and a dizzying array of service automation choices. Consequently, many clients have difficulty getting started – how do they distinguish between the hype and reality? How do they prepare their organisations for the changes automation requires? How does automation affect their outsourcing relationships? The advisors' insights into these questions and other issues are explored below. Most interesting, perhaps, is their views on service automation and the future of work.

Advisors see evidence of 'service automation washing'. The terms 'RPA washing' and 'automation washing' refer to the phenomenon of companies spending more resources on advertising and marketing claiming to have new service automation capabilities than actually building new automation capabilities. Although none of the advisors chose to elaborate, several advisors noted that they have seen some evidence of 'service automation washing'. This causes confusion in the market, and leads to one of the biggest service automation challenges for clients: distinguishing hype from reality.

Distinguishing hype from reality and change management are the biggest adoption challenges for their clients. Clients are facing a plethora of choices about service automation and can get lost among the hype, options and buzzwords. Rob Brindley noted that the RPA market is *"flush with technology providers and new ones enter the market every day."* As far as hype, Charles Sutherland has frequently criticised the hype about bloated cost savings. Cliff Justice and Derek Toone also said that clients need help distinguishing hype from reality. Sarah Burnett noted that all this makes 'getting started' the biggest client challenge. Once a few insiders have worked through these issues, broader issues of change management become the next big hurdle. Charles Sutherland noted that the change management issues are being overlooked and that it isn't always easy to get the necessary buy-in for an enterprise automation capability, which Charles calls a 'broader production regime'. Derek Toone notes that organisations sometimes underestimate their readiness for change management and all that encompasses from creating an aligned automation strategy to developing a future state operating model.

Several advisors, including Sarah Burnett and Charles Sutherland, echoed what we found in the adoption stories presented in Chapters 3, 4, 5, and 6: Service automation often begins as a grass roots effort by a local champion. After a successful proof-of-concept, organisations then see the value and aim to build enterprise capabilities.

IT is ahead of BP in terms of service automation. The advisors agreed that IT is the more mature adopter of service automation technologies. In particular, Rob Brindley offered a comprehensive history of automation and global sourcing of IT – IT has led all the major market shifts. Cliff Justice and Sarah Burnett also noted that many business operations are just getting started with the automation of structured tasks, whereas IT has already done so and is moving quickly to cognitive and machine learning. Derek Toone really sees differences in ITO and BPO providers, where ITO providers are already leveraging service automation to reduce prices and increase service quality, whereas some BPO providers that rely on FTE-based pricing seem slower to adopt automation. These observations are worth highlighting since this book has focused upon service automation in business operations, and thus largely ignored the automation revolution in IT infrastructure services.

Automation changes outsourcing. One of the boldest assertions came from Cliff Justice when he wrote, *"I have called service automation the 'death of outsourcing' as we know it"*. So, what will change? According to all the advisors: service automation is affecting pricing models, value propositions, and location advantages.

For decades, the main cost component of an outsourced service has been the providers' labour – a provider's labour arbitrage advantage was a major source of value and justified FTE-based pricing. Because service automation replaces some or even much of that labour, it requires pricing mechanisms that are based more on outcomes and transactions. Indeed, Sarah Burnett already sees these shifts in her clients' outsourcing contracts. Charles Sutherland encourages clients to get service providers to automate within existing contacts, but warns clients that they will need to incentivise providers if the current contract is based on FTE-pricing.

According to the advisors, automation will affect location decisions more and more as service delivery will increasingly be done through combinations of machine and human labour. As the relative size of a delivery team shrinks, the value of low-cost locations diminishes. Sarah Burnett thinks the mix of offshore/nearshore/reshore locations will change. Derek Toone sees that, as labour becomes a smaller component of service delivery, onshore service delivery becomes more attractive. Cliff Justice believes automation makes location less relevant, particularly as automation moves to the cloud.

As far as shifting value propositions, the advisors all note that providers have either (a) already leveraged automation or (b) are planning to leverage automation as soon as possible. Rob Brindley predicts that there will be a shakeout among providers *"until leaders emerge and providers rationalise and consolidate into a mature industry."*

Clients and providers will have a portfolio of automation tools. Also supporting a major theme of this book, advisors note that clients and providers adopt, or will adopt, a plethora of service automation capabilities, including robotics, natural language processing, and machine learning. The advisors stressed that different automation tools are suited for different tasks. Early adopters frequently began by automating structured tasks, but note that natural language processing and machine learning will happen quickly. Advisors all stressed that they are not advocates for particular products, but work with clients to find the best tools that meet their needs.

Automation will reduce the number of FTEs needed in low-skilled jobs and increase demand for people with automation and other higher-skilled capabilities. In general, the advisors did not predict massive unemployment, but instead saw that the workforce composition would change. Charles Sutherland noted that demand for labour for lower-end, entry-level tasks will diminish – as much as 30 percent to 50 percent in call centres. He sees that service providers and shared services organisations are already altering their talent acquisition and career development practices to account for the future of work – where human agents with higher-level skills interact with robotic and cognitive technologies. Derek Toone concluded, *"the likely effect on jobs will be the elimination of those involving rote, repetitive processing, and a higher focus on the value human workers who can deliver results in jobs requiring creative thinking and subjective decision-making."* Perhaps the boldest estimates came from Rob Brindley – he estimated that service automation will do the work of as many as 140 million FTEs by 2025. While service automation could create hundreds of thousands of new high-skill jobs, millions of people would require retraining or assistance.

9.8. Conclusion

In this chapter, five highly experienced advisors gave us rich insights as to what was happening in the automation space, and the likely impacts on clients, outsourcing and the nature and future of work. The advisors, found, as we did, that there is still much education of the market needed to help clients distinguish the automation hype from the reality. Interestingly, they found clients wrestling most of all with change management. They recommend that clients adopt a portfolio of automation tools. The advisors also see large future impacts on outsourcing content and practices down the line. Their observations on automation and the future of work set the stage for our more comprehensive treatment of this theme in the next, final chapter.

Citations

[1] Source: http://www.everestgrp.com/about-us/leadership/peter-bendor-samuel

[2] Source: http://www.everestgrp.com/services/

[3] Source: https://en.wikipedia.org/wiki/KPMG

[4] Source: http://advisory.kpmg.us/

[5] Source: http://www.hfsresearch.com/about

[6] Source: http://www.alsbridge.com/about-alsbridge-inc/

[7] Source: http://www.alsbridge.com/services/

[8] Source: http://www.isg-one.com/web/about/company/

[9] Source: http://www.isg-one.com/web/services/

Chapter 10

Lessons and the Future of Automation and Work

What's Inside: *This chapter summarises the lessons learned from the survey, case studies, interviews, and 'in their own words' contributors. These lessons help clients define a service automation strategy, launch a successful service automation initiative, prepare the organisation for the changes that service automation induces, and build an enterprise-wide service automation capability. The chapter then provides a framework that examines the latent assumptions people hold about the relationship between man and technology. Finally, the chapter then considers the evidence of the effects of service automation on the future of work.*

10.1. Introduction

> *"An ultra-intelligent machine ... will be built and ... it will be the last invention that (we) need make."*[1] **Irving John 'Jack' Good, mathematician, 1965.**

> *"Technology is a useful servant, but a dangerous master."* **Christian Lou Lange, Nobel Peace Prize lecture, 1921**

As befits a final chapter, we bring together the findings from our research on service automation, then relate the study to the bigger picture of which service automation constitutes just one part, namely automation, robotics and the future of work. We summarise the findings on service automation in thirty lessons derived from our interviews, case study and survey work. We then take a detailed look at where service automation developments fit into the bigger picture of technological developments over the next ten years.

We suggest that diverse optimistic, pessimistic and relativistic approaches are regularly taken, on where the technology will lead. In the two quotes above, Jack Good is philosophically clearly an optimist, while Christian Lou Lange a relativist. Our own sceptical view is that the first task should always be to examine the evidence available, before coming to provisional conclusions as to what is happening and what the future could be. We attempt to do this in what follows.

On automation, robotics and the future of work, we point out that there have always been anxieties about technological development, but ask whether it is different this time. Acknowledging the power of the technologies in train, and also their limits, we look at the evidence for the darker side of digital, and raise the ethical and socially responsible question whether with these technologies 'can' translates so seamlessly into 'should'? We then look in detail at the evidence for the impact of automation and robots on the future of work, job numbers and job types. Then finally, in predictive mode, we take a macroeconomic perspective to automation, robots and the future of work, anticipating a mixed scenario with four major developments on a one to five year horizon, and, on a six to ten year horizon, a further six developments. But let's first concentrate on the multiple lessons learned from conducting the primary research for this study.

10.2. Lessons Learned

This book captures a year's worth of learning about service automation based on various research sources, including a survey we conducted in 2015 (see Chapter 1), in-depth client case studies and formal interviews (Chapters 3 to 6), and written contributions from clients, providers, and advisors *In Their Own Words* (Chapters 7 to 9). In this section, we collect the lessons learned from these various sources about defining a service automation strategy, launching successful service automation initiatives, preparing the organisation for the changes service automation induces, and building enterprise-wide service automation capabilities. We also summarise five common service automation outcomes.

10.2.1. Service Automation Strategy Lessons

According to management guru Alfred D. Chandler[2], **strategy** is *"the determination of the basic long-term goals and objectives of an enterprise, and the adoption of courses of action and the allocation of resources necessary for carrying out these goals."* Clients must develop an automation strategy which defines it long-term goals and how service automation fits into a larger picture of transforming business services.

In Chapter 1, we described how high-performing business services enable organisations by delivering low-cost and high-quality services that are scalable, flexible, secure, and compliant. Organisational leaders use multiple transformation levers to achieve high-performance business services, including centralisation, standardisation, optimisation (i.e. process redesign to reduce errors and waste), relocating to low cost destinations and, of course, automation. Thus, it is within this broader business context that service automation strategy formulation must occur.

Across the survey, formal interviews, and *'in their own words'* contributions, a number of lessons pertaining to service automation strategy emerged (see Table 10.1). First, strategic service automation requires cultural adoption by the C-suite to get the most strategic benefits (*Lesson 1*). Certainly, the Xchanging case highlighted this lesson, as Xchanging's corporate motto is *"technology at our core"* and its robotic process automation capability was prominently featured in its 2014 corporate annual report to shareholders. The C-suite from the European utility also embraced service automation, talked about it with other divisions, and saw it as a lever for improving the customer experience as well as reducing operating costs. Second, service automation requires strategic alignment with the business (***Lesson 2***). While C-suite support is vital for legitimisation, there is also serious work to be done to align service automation initiatives with business operations and with the IT function. When creating a service automation strategy, the business cases for the first set of projects should include multiple expected benefits (***Lesson 3***). If clients only expect cost savings, they might miss opportunities to improve customer experience and employee satisfaction.

			Client Case Studies				In Their Own Words		
	Lessons Learned	C1: Survey	C3: Telefónica O2	C4: Xchanging	C5: Mature Capabilities	C6: RPA and IT	C7: Clients	C8: Providers	C9: Advisors
Strategy	1. Strategic service automation requires cultural adoption by the C-suite			√	√	√			
	2. Service automation requires strategic alignment with the business					√			
	3. Business cases for service automation includes multiple expected benefits	√	√	√	√		√	√	
	4. Understand that service automation is a continuum of many tools and platforms suited for different types of services; Beware of hype			√		√		√	√
	5. Consider RPA as a complement to enterprise systems and other automation tools.		√	√					
	6. Consider carefully the best sourcing option	√	√	√	√	√			√

Table 10.1: Lessons Learned About Service Automation Strategy

The next three lessons speak to the many choices clients have to make. Clients need to understand that service automation is a continuum of many tools and platforms suited for different types of services (***Lesson 4***). In Chapters 1 and 9, two service automation continuums were presented to readers. Our book predominantly addresses the part of the automation continuum pertaining to tools that automate structured processes, most commonly known as Robotic Process Automation (RPA). A number of providers and advisors in Chapters 8 and 9 spoke to the other end of the service continuum that includes other technologies with natural language processing, machine learning, and 'true' artificial intelligence capabilities. Additionally, RPA complements other technologies and Systems of Record, like enterprise planning systems and customer relationship management systems (*Lesson 5*). While many like to think that their Systems of Record can perform end-to-end processes, much of the work being done by humans actually involves 'swivel-chair' processing, where humans are taking inputs from one system, processing the inputs with structured rules, and passing the outputs to Systems of Record. RPA is well-suited for these tasks.

Clients must also consider carefully the best sourcing option for service automation (*Lesson 6*). Clients can buy service automation licenses directly from a service automation software provider, buy service automation as part of an integrated service delivered by a traditional BPO provider, or acquire from the new breed of RPA outsourcing providers. In the future, clients will increasingly cloud source robots.

10.2.2. Service Automation Launch Lessons

We learned six lessons about successful service automation launches (see Table 10.2). Across our various sources, one common experience was that the service automation initiative was launched by a grass-roots pioneer who was willing to take some risks (*Lesson 7*). That person believed that automation could transform services, but he/she had to prove it to the sceptics through a proof-of-concept. The most powerful proof-of-concepts were performed on processes visible to the organisation – something that employees, managers, and external customers would notice; something that eased a pain-point and improved the service in an exciting way (*Lesson 8*). Of course, this visible process must also be 'automatable' (*Lesson 9*). A general lesson

269

learned was that clients initially selected processes (or sub-processes) for automation that were mature, standard, rules-based, and had high-volumes. Clients also reported that it was best to standardise and stabilise processes before automation (*Lesson 10*). As clients built automation capabilities, they explored other ends of the service automation continuum, and may, like Virgin Trains in Chapter 7, seek to automate unstructured and unpredictable processes.

	Lessons Learned	Client Case Studies					In Their Own Words		
		C1: Survey	C3: Telefónica O2	C4: Xchanging	C5: Mature Capabilities	C6: RPA and IT	C7: Clients	C8: Providers	C9: Advisors
Launch	7. Take some risks	√					√		
	8. Proof-of-concepts should be visible, exciting, and noticeable	√	√	√	√	√	√		
	9. Develop criteria for the 'automationability' of processes	√	√	√	√				
	10. Standardise and stabilise processes before automation			√		√			
	11. Test service automation capabilities with a controlled experiment	√				√			√
	12. Lean on service automation providers for training and knowledge transfer	√	√	√	√	√			

Table 10.2: Lessons Learned About Service Automation Launches

As for tool selection, one client (Telefónica O2) and some advisors, recommended testing service automation capabilities with a controlled experiment (*Lesson 11*). When teams automated the identical process with different tools, they could directly compare fit, capability, and value. Training internal staff to use the tools for automation required anywhere from two weeks to a few months. Clients all reported that they leaned heavily on service automation providers for training and knowledge transfer – at least initially (***Lesson 12***). Another common theme from clients was that the providers were *"great partners"* during the launch stage of automation.

Lessons Learned	C1: Survey	Client Case Studies				In Their Own Words		
		C3: Telefonica O2	C4: Xchanging	C5: Matue Capabilities	C6: RPA and IT	C7: Clients	C8: Providers	C9: Advisors
Organizational Readiness/ Change Management — 13. Service automation needs a sponsor, a project champion and piloting		√	√	√				
14. Let business operations lead		√	√	√	√			
15. Bring IT onboard early		√	√	√	√			
16. Service automation must comply with the technology function's governance and architecture policies		√	√	√	√			
17. Pay careful attention to internal communications--send the right message to staff		√	√	√		√		√

Table 10.3: Lessons Learned About Change Management

10.2.3. Service Automation Change Management Lessons

As the advisors noted in Chapter 9, clients often underestimate the change management requirements for service automation. Five lessons help (see Table 10.3). Like all organisational changes, service automation needs a sponsor, a project champion and piloting (***Lesson 13***). A sponsor was the executive willing to write the cheque for service automation whereas the project champion was the person with the political clout who removed obstacles stemming from people or processes. Sometimes these roles were embodied in the same person. As noted many times in this book, we studied business operations automation, not IT automation (i.e. the automation of IT services). Given our focus, we learned that clients should let business operations lead the service automation initiative (***Lesson 14***). However, business operations must bring IT onboard early (***Lesson 15***) and must comply with the technology function's governance and architecture policies (*Lesson 16*). Recall that bypassing IT nearly got one of our pioneers fired (see Chapter 3).

Clients need to pay careful attention to internal communications by sending the right message to staff (*Lesson 17*). In our client stories, service automation was never used to layoff internal staff, and this helped garner stakeholder buy-in and even stakeholder enthusiasm. We can envision that some organisations, however, will face tough economic times and may need to use automation to layoff some workers. Prior research on other job-reducing practices – like outsourcing and offshoring – found that communicating the intended effect on jobs early in the process was by far the best practice.[3] Delaying communication caused staff members to panic and to sabotage the outsourcing/offshoring initiatives because many employees overestimated the effects on jobs. The best time to announce intentions was when the organisation was ready to search for service providers.

10.2.5. Lessons on Building an Enterprise-wide Capability

The ultimate goal for many clients in our study was to build an enterprise-wide automation capability (see Table 10.4). Mature service automation capabilities have evolved beyond proof-of-concepts initiated in a single business unit to create an organisation-wide competency. Although there are several ways to govern a mature service automation capability, we have found that a Centre of Excellence (CofE), that serves as a shared organisational resource, is a recommended practice (*Lesson 18*). In addition to a CofE, a Governance Board can work with a CofE for demand management, demand generation, benefits tracking, and continuous improvement initiatives (*Lesson 19*).

Staffing a CofE requires organisations to rethink talent development and the skills needed for an enterprise automation capability (*Lesson 20*). Chapters 5 and 6 devoted sections to discuss the skills required for service automation. The European Utility looked to recruit RPA developers from among the operations staff who possessed a strong understanding of the business, a logical mind, and preferably had a systems analysis background. For the control room staff who operate the robots after they are in production, the European Utility looked to recruit people who were organised, methodical, logical and had a consistent approach to work. One client in Chapter 7 suggested that it was best to create automation specialists rather than automation generalists. Several advisors reported that they are already seeing evidence of the effects of automation on talent management.

	Lessons Learned	C1: Survey	Client Case Studies				In Their Own Words		
			C3: Telefónica O2	C4: Xchanging	C5: Mature Capabilities	C6: RPA and IT	C7: Clients	C8: Providers	C9: Advisors
Build an Enterprise-wide Capability	18. Establish a Center of Excellence				√	√			
	19. Form a Governance Board for demand management, demand generation, benefits tracking, and continuous improvement initiatives				√	√			
	20. Rethink talent development for skills needed for an enterprise automation capability				√	√	√		√
	21. Evolve the composition of automation teams over time		√	√	√	√			
	22. Prototype continually as service automation expands to new business contexts				√				
	23. Reuse components to scale quickly and to reduce development costs			√	√	√			
	24. Multi-skill the robots			√		√			
	25. Build a scalable, robust IT infrastructure		√	√	√	√			

**Table 10.4: Lessons Learned About
Building an Enterprise-wide Capability**

While in launch mode, we noted that clients leaned heavily on their service providers for training and knowledge transfer. As clients gained experience and as they started to disseminate automation more broadly, they evolved the composition of automation teams to rely less on service providers (*Lesson 21*). The automation teams were comprised of internal staff, and providers shifted to more advisory roles.

A mature service automation capability is constantly learning. It has several feedback loops that serve to strengthen the capability over time. The first feedback loop continually improves the automated processes as the CofE continues to work with the business units to potentially automate more functionality of a live process. It is in a continual state of 'prototyping' as service automation expands to new business contexts (*Lesson 22*). The second feedback loops increases the CofE's productivity as more reusable components are added to and taken from an automation library (*Lesson 23*) and, as robots are multi-skilled, they are never idle (*Lesson 24*). As automation scales, so must the IT infrastructure seamlessly scale (*Lesson 25*).

10.2.5. Service Automation Outcomes

Because we studied actual service automation adoptions, we have good evidence as to the outcomes achieved. Although presented as 'lessons learned', to continue on the theme, they are more aptly described as 'findings' (see Table 10.5). Across research sources, clients reported that business results from automating services were multifaceted and included FTE savings, FTE avoidance, improved service quality, the ability to expand services and to increase service volumes, and improved staff job satisfaction (*Lesson 26*). Why did the internal staff's job satisfaction increase? Because service automation was used to focus internal staff away from dreary, boring, and repetitive tasks to more interesting tasks requiring judgment, empathy and social interactions (*Lesson 27*). Service automation was so successful in client firms participating in this research that all the clients we interviewed planned to automate more services in the future (*Lesson 28*). Although only a few clients mentioned automation as it relates to outsourcing, the survey and advisors all found that service automation will increasingly change outsourcing's pricing models, value proposition, and location attractiveness

(*Lesson 29*). Stepping outside of an organisation, several research sources – most notably providers and advisors – see service automation as a short-term disruption that will ultimately have positive long-term effects on the economy (*Lesson 30*).

		Client Case Studies				In Their Own Words		
Findings	C1: Survey	C3: Telefónica O2	C4: Xchanging	C5: Mature Capabilities	C6: RPA and IT	C7: Clients	C8: Providers	C9: Advisors
26. Business results were multifaceted and included FTE savings, improved staff job satisfaction, improved service quality, the ability to expand services and to increase service volumes		√	√	√	√	√	√	
27. Service automation was used to focus internal staff on more interesting tasks requiring judgment, empathy and social interactions.		√	√	√	√	√	√	
28. More service automation was planned for the future	√	√	√	√	√	√		
29. Service automation changes outsourcing's pricing models, value proposition, and location decisions.	√				√			√
30. Service automation is a short-term disruption that has positive long-term effects		√	√	√	√		√	√

Table 10.5: Service Automation Outcomes

(Left margin label spanning rows 26–30: **Outcomes**)

Having covered what was learned about service automation from early adopters and thought leaders, the last issue we address in this book is: What effect will automation have on the economy and the future of work? To frame this discussion, we first describe three general philosophical assumptions about the relationship between technology and humanity.

10.3. Three Philosophical Views on the Nature of Technology and Humanity

When people are asked to predict the effects of service automation on the future of work, responses often range between two extremes. On one extreme, we hear the promises that automation will 'liberate' humanity by freeing us from the drudgery of tedious work and by creating new and exciting industries, filled with high-paying jobs that will elevate the quality of life for all. On the other extreme, we hear the warnings that automation will enslave humanity, lead to massive unemployment and create greater income disparity. Where do these notions come from? Very likely, anyone espousing either extreme position can evoke evidence from history to support their arguments. We propose that data is not the driving support for these positions, but rather that our views are shaped by the underlying, and often latent, assumptions about the relationship between technology and humanity. Therefore, it is prudent to consider these assumptions before reviewing the 'evidence' as to the future that automation and robotics may bring. Here we draw on a framework of three philosophical, *a priori* views on technology – the optimistic, pessimistic and relativistic – initially proposed by Rudy Hirschheim (1986).[4] Hirschheim applied these three views to assess the social implications of office automation, such as word processors, but thirty years later, the framework remains relevant to the discussion on today's service automation, or indeed any technology.

In general, the optimistic view holds that automation technologies increase the productivity of everyone, create more jobs than it destroys, and the new jobs require advanced skills that warrant higher wages (see Table 10.6). Optimists point to that fact that we could not envision the great industries that would be spawned from previous technologies like steam engines, electrical power, the computer, and the Internet, but hindsight suggests – optimists argue – that new technologies always led to more prosperity, so we can safely assume the same will hold for today's automation technologies. Technology is presumed to increase communication and bring people close together. Need evidence? The number of Facebook users surpassed 1 billion in 2012. Technology is presumed to increase democracy – optimists can point to the enabling power of social media on the Arab Spring for evidence.

With its roots in Marxism, the pessimistic view argues that 'owners' of

	Optimist	Relativist	Pessimist
Automation effects	Humanity is liberated	Humanity determines the effects	Power is centralised — powerless humans are enslaved
Who wins?	Everyone	Those who participate in the design and application	Owners and managers
Who loses?	No one	Marginalised populations who do not participate	Workers and those who cannot adapt
Motto	"Rising tides raise all ships"	"We decide our own fates"	"Our primary responsibility is to our shareholders"
Total effect on employment numbers	More jobs created	It depends	Jobs destroyed
Effects on job skills and wages	New jobs require greater skills, warranting higher wages	It depends	Fewer jobs lead to more employment competition, which lowers wages
Effects on democracy	Increases democracy	It depends	Decreases democracy; technology used to segregate and control

Table 10.6: Three Philosophical Views on the
Nature of Technology and Humanity

capital and the 'managers' they hire as proxies, use technology to increase revenues and profit margins for the owners and seek to reduce their reliance on labourers. The owners and managers justify their positions by claiming their primary fiduciary responsibility is to their shareholders. There is an undercurrent of social Darwinism – businesses and people who do not adapt will fail, or more specifically, owners and managers say, *"If we do not adopt automation, our competitors will beat us and we will fail."* As for displaced workers, the social Darwinian argument extends to them as well: unemployed workers who can adapt to the changes caused by technology through education and training will find better jobs in the future. It's up to them. Pessimists also see that the quality of communication between humans is diminished when mediated by technology. Yes, the pessimist may argue, we have more social connections through social media, but the social ties are quite weak.

Need evidence? CNN recently sponsored academic research that examined the effects of social media on the lives of teens.[5] They found that many teens check social media over 100 times a day; the behaviour is called 'lurking'. The researchers found a direct correlation between lurking and stress.

The relativistic position lies between the two extremes. The relativistic position holds that technology can have either positive or negative effects, depending on how humans choose to implement them. A relativist is *"concerned with developing criteria for social and ethical acceptance of automation."* The relativist position is the moderate view, but it does not escape one huge political implication of: Who decides on the rules? Hirschheim (1986), argued that relativists believe the only way to answer this question is through participation. Participation *"allows the interests of individuals who must use the new technology to be protected. It is based on the belief that individuals have the right to control their own destinies".*[6] He goes on to note that participation by the people whose jobs are affected by technology will lead to positive perceptions of the technology. Need evidence? The Xchanging case study in Chapter 4 showed that the workers who participated with the RPA automation, welcomed the changes it brought to their jobs.

An understanding of the underlying assumptions of the optimistic, pessimistic and relativistic views provides a good framework for assessing the recent debates on the effects of automation, robotics, and the future of work.

10.4. Automation and Robotic Futures

Jack Good was a British mathematician who worked in World War II with Alan Turing at Bletchley Park, England, on cracking the German Enigma code. In 1965, he created the vision, which has since become popularised and extended as that of the technological singularity (see the Great Singularity Dilemma in Chapter 1). Here are his words, *"Let an ultraintelligent machine be defined as a machine that can far surpass all the intellectual activities of any man, however clever. Since the design of machines is one of these intellectual activities, an ultraintelligent machine could design even better machines; there would then unquestionably be an 'intelligence explosion,' and the intelligence of man would be left far behind. Thus the first ultraintelligent machine is the last invention that man need ever make, provided that the machine is docile enough to tell us how to keep it under control."*[7]

Good speculated (his words) that, as probable as not, an ultraintelligent machine would be with us by the end of the 20th Century. As we saw in Chapter 1, Ray Kurzweil, in *The Singularity is Near* (2005), postponed this event (and his optimism) to the late 2020s or after.

10.4.1. Present Anxieties: Different This Time?

Undoubtedly many concerned, articulate and variously informed voices have been cautioning against an unconditional acceptance of recent and future developments in information and communications technologies. Partly this is a reaction to how pervasive these technologies already seem to be, particularly in the developed economies. Here Joel Mokyr and his colleagues[8] are useful for pointing out that, from generation to generation, technology has been often portrayed as alien, incomprehensible, increasingly powerful, threatening, and possibly uncontrollable. And indeed, going back a long way in time, the ancient Greek myth of Prometheus is nothing if not a cautionary tale of the uncontrollable effects of technology. Mokyr et al. (2015) point out that these worries about technological change have often appeared at times of flagging economic growth from the time of the Industrial Revolution, through the Great Depression, to the present day.

Two of the recurring worries base themselves on an 'optimistic' view that technology will continue to grow and probably accelerate. This leads to the fear of widespread substitution of machines for labour, which in turn could lead to technological unemployment and a further increase in inequality in the short run, even if the long-run effects are beneficial. A second worry has been anxiety over the moral implications of technological progress for human welfare, broadly conceived, for example the dehumanising effects of changes in work, or of the elimination of work itself. A third recurring concern is based on a more pessimistic premise, that the epoch of major technological progress may be behind us. Thus following the Financial Crash of 2008, Robert Gordon (2012) argued that economic growth and productivity will be too slow because of insufficient technological progress in the face of six 'headwinds' facing developed economies.[9] While these three anxieties have proven largely groundless, at least in the longer term, Mokyr et al. (2015) do ask the question: Will this time be different?

They stress the limits of our imagination where technological progress is concerned. Computers and robots are unlikely to have an absolute and comparative advantage over humans in all activities. The future will bring product innovations that will combine with new occupations and services not currently imagined. Present discussions on technological disruption focus on existing occupations being disrupted, but have much less insight into the emergence of as-yet-non-existent jobs of the future. These authors are also sceptical that a horizon is relatively near for the end of technological progress, or for the widespread satiation of consumer demand. Moreover, for them, *"the modern anxieties about long-term, ineradicable technological unemployment or widespread lack of meaning because of changes in work patterns, seem highly unlikely to come to pass. Technological advance will continue to improve the standard of living in dramatic and unforeseeable ways."* But fundamental economic principles will continue to operate. Scarcities will be with us – most noticeably of time itself. However, the path of transition to this economy of the future may be disruptively painful for many workers and industries, as historically, such transitions have tended to be.

10.4.2. On the Darker Side of Digital

While Mokyr and colleagues would seem to offer a balanced view, a lot of modern commentators present a less sanguine perspective on where ICTs, automation and robotics are taking us. With digitisation the major perils highlighted in the literature relate to **acceleration, employment, security, privacy** and **environmental sustainability**.[10]

As can be seen from the book titles, Benjamin Noyes (*Malign Velocities*), Paul Virilio (*The Great Accelerator*), Judy Wajcman (*Pressed For Time*), and Scott Patterson (*Dark Pools: The rise of AI trading and the looming threat to Wall Street*) – all of these well-informed commentators make strong cases demonstrating not just the positive, but also the adverse accelerationist impacts of advanced digital technologies.[11] Exponential technological acceleration creates complex, dynamic systems where the principles and insights of chaos and complexity theories increasingly apply. Major tensions arise between capability, control and unanticipated consequences. Even writing in 1980, David Collingridge noted that by the time undesirable consequences are discovered: *"technology is often so much a part of the whole economic and social fabric that its control is extremely difficult."*[12] Maybe the flash crash of May 6th 2010, when the Dow Jones Industrial Index at the New York Stock Exchange (NYSE) dropped over 600 points in a matter of minutes, gives us some insight and signal as to where we might be heading more generally, given widespread usage and dependence on automation and robotics.

Recall that the flash crash occurred, at best guess, because of the effect of one large trade being magnified by the anomalies of computerised trading. Computers automate the buying and selling of orders according to algorithms; the trading of one computer influences that of others; these form complex systems that interconnect also with human actors, that are part of environmental influences and the broader complex adaptive systems that make up the world's financial markets. But the blessings of interconnectivity can also result in disasters. In fact, occasional and unpredictable erratic behaviour is normal for complex systems. The flash crash could be seen as a confluence of factors that led to a very low probability event representing one possibility within the distribution of possible events. But the problem we are left with, as pointed out by Wendel Wallach[13], is that *"in the world of high frequency trading, the sheer complexity of the system, combined with how quickly it acts, can speed up the likelihood of a low probability event occurring."* Researchers of large-scale accidents and failures invariably point to prior signals, tremors and forewarnings. How far was the 2010 high frequency trading 'flash crash' a small portent or microcosm, for what is to come on a much larger scale with societal-wide impacts as a result of accelerationism?

Meanwhile a plethora of reports and publications have been produced on the disruptive, likely adverse, impacts on employment numbers, skill types and occupations: not least the intelligent and sobering books focusing primarily on automation and robotics by Martin Ford and Nicholas Carr, while Wendell Wallach raises many concerns while contextualising robotics in a larger historical and societal view.[14] We will look at this concern in detail below and make some predictions about the future, since it is the main anxiety raised around the current round of automation and robotics.

Informed concern on digital security and privacy can also be found in very recent work by Marc Goodman, Zygmunt Bauman and David Lyon and Edward Lucas.[15] On security, the damage caused by reported cyber crime alone has risen steadily reaching, in some estimates, a global cybercrime figure of over $100 billion by 2013. This is in all probability a big underestimate of the actual cybercrime, which one would expect to increase dramatically with the interconnectedness and exponential use of ICTS. In 2014 90 percent of US companies admitted their networks had been materially breached in the previous 12 months. The proposition is that digitisation and automation give birth to wider networks and consequently new security issues, resulting in changed behaviours, rising damage, and changed societies. As Eugene Spafford memorably put it: *"The only true security system is the one that is powered off, cast in a block of concrete, and sealed in a lead-lined room with armed guards."* On privacy, as one of many possible examples, consider Google. Shoshana Zuboff[17] has written eloquently on *'Big Other: Surveillance capitalism and the prospects of an information civilisation'*. She points out that Google operates four uses from its massive number of computer mediated transactions. These four uses are: data extraction and analysis; new contractual forms as a result of better monitoring; personalisation and customisation; and continuous experiments. The surveillance capability offered by this global architecture of computer mediation is seemingly limitless. It creates a 'Big Other' made up of uncontested, often non-transparent mechanisms of extraction, commodification and control that effectively distance people from their own information, behaviour, and oversight, while creating, for Google, new markets of behavioural prediction and modification. According to Zuboff, this surveillance capitalism challenges democratic norms while departing in key ways from the centuries-old evolution of market capitalism. Such arguments can also be applied to emerging use of big data and business analytics, which are also highly dependent on the information and technology architectures and infrastructures now being developed on a corporate, governmental, and indeed global, basis.

A number of researchers also acknowledge that ICTs have both positive and negative effects on environmental sustainability, with the net effects being a matter of some debate.[18] For example, the Global eSustainability Initiative in 2009 offered data that indicated the potential of ICTS to indirectly reduce total energy consumption by 15 percent by 2020[19]. Lorenz Hilty and Bernard Aebischer suggest a number of moderating influences on the adverse environmental impact of ICTS at three levels: The life-cycle of the technology, i.e. its production and consumption; the micro-impacts of technological changes on societal production and consumption more broadly; and the long-term macro-impacts on institutions and economic structures[20]. At the same time, a large body of literature highlights significant negative effects. A Rebound Effect operates with ICTS whereby, while energy efficiency is increased, this is significantly outweighed by the overall increased energy consumption from dramatically more computation and more devices deployed. While presently ICTS may seem to represent a small amount of total energy consumption, a sharp rise could see ICTS represent as much as 17 percent of the total by 2020.[21] Finally, critics point out that just because opportunities for environmental sustainability are increasingly available, this does not mean that they are seized. Corporates, for example are driven primarily by financial returns rather than environmental protection concerns, and we would suggest that the relationship between sustainable practices, reputation and longer term financial health need to be much more widely explored in many business sectors.

10.4.3. Ethics and Social Responsibility: Does 'Can' translate into 'Should'?

In the face of these possibilities, not surprisingly ethics and social responsibility has been on the agenda for some time. For robotics, an early science fiction response saw Isaac Asimov produce what became his four laws:

1. A robot may not injure a human being, or, through inaction, allow a human being to come to harm.
2. A robot must obey the orders given to it by human beings, except where such orders would conflict with the First Law.
3. A robot must protect its own existence as long as such protection does not conflict with the First or Second Law.
4. A robot may not harm humanity, or, by inaction, allow humanity to come to harm.

They form a useful debating start point, and have been extended by many commentators, but few experts in Artificial Intelligence see them as a practical basis for an ethical robotics. In Asimov's stories the laws are made to fail in ways that perhaps teach us how any attempt to legislate ethics in terms of specific rules is bound to fall apart, contain ambiguities and paradoxes, and have various loopholes. Perhaps better to focus on the behaviour of the people behind the robots. Less glamorously, and possibly more usefully, in the UK in 2011, the Engineering and Physical Sciences Research Council (EPRSC) and the Arts and Humanities Research Council (AHRC) published a set of ethical principles for designers, builders and users of robots in the real world: *"Robots should not be designed solely or primarily to kill or harm humans; humans, not robots, are responsible agents; robots are tools designed to achieve human goals; robots should be designed in ways that assure their safety and security; robots are artefacts; and they should not be designed to exploit vulnerable users by evoking an emotional response or dependency. It should always be possible to tell a robot from a human; it should always be possible to find out who is legally responsible for a robot."* There are problems with inconsistencies between several of these principles including how easily they can be implemented in practice. In many ways these principles demonstrate the difficulties of arriving at an ethical basis for robotics. However, designed for robotics practitioners, these principles do intend to convey several useful messages: that robots have immense positive potential for society; that responsible robot research should be encouraged; bad practice hurts us all; addressing obvious public concerns will help us all make progress; we, as roboticists, are committed to the best possible standards of practice; that we need to understand the context and consequences of our research and so need to work with experts from other disciplines; we should consider the ethics of transparency: Are there limits to what should be openly available?; and we need to correct erroneous accounts in the media.[22]

Even from this brief review, it becomes very clear that with ICTs, automation and robotics, 'can do' does not seamlessly convert into 'should do'. Neil Postman put it succinctly, and perhaps timelessly, in five ideas about technological change we need to heed.[23] *"First, we always pay a price for technology; the greater the technology, the greater the price. Second, there are always winners and losers, and the winners always try to persuade the losers that they are really winners. Third, there is embedded in every great technology an epistemological, political or social prejudice. Sometimes that bias is greatly to our advantage, sometimes not..."* The computer, perhaps, will degrade community life, exacerbate inequality, or perhaps the reverse?

"Fourth, technological change is not additive, it is ecological – which means, it changes everything. And fifth, technology tends to become mythic – that is, perceived as part of the natural order of things, and therefore it tends to control more of our lives than is good for us." Michel Foucault perhaps summed it up best. Talking of technologies, power and knowledge he said: *"my point is not that everything is bad, but everything is dangerous ... If everything is dangerous, then we always have something to do."*[24]

10.5. Robots and the Future of Work

When it comes to the future of work and jobs, how will automation and robotics pan out? This subject is central to the book, so we deal with work futures in detail here. Work can be classified into four types: (1) routine manual, (2) routine cognitive, (3) non-routine manual, and (4) non-routine cognitive. A Deloitte 2015 study looked at changes in the UK labour force since 1992 – a period marked by accelerating uses of ICTs[25]. It found routine manual jobs numbers (e.g. metal making and treating process operatives) were down 70 percent and routine cognitive job numbers (e.g. bank and post office workers) were down 66 percent over the period, the impact of technology being significant substitution. On the other hand, manual non-routine jobs (e.g. care workers and home carers) saw job numbers increase by 168 percent, with limited opportunities for technology substitution. Meanwhile non-routine cognitive workers (e.g. business analysts, management consultants) saw job numbers up 365 percent, Technology emerged as having strong complementarities with cognitive non-routine tasks. For the 1992-2014 period the study found technology substituting for labour as a source of energy, raising productivity and shrinking employment. At the same times jobs were created in the sectors driving technological change, and in knowledge-intensive sectors. Technological change also lowered expenditure on essentials, creating new demand and jobs. Will this pattern continue into the next ten years?

10.5.1. Jobs in the Next Two Decades

Our combined work on RPA, cloud and digitisation, throws interesting light on the likely future. Following a cost-saving agenda, the obvious candidates for outsourcing and offshoring have been routine manual and routine cognitive work. Of these, routine manual work could be mostly automated in the next seven years, and likewise much non-routine manual work – through robotics – over the next 10 years. Meanwhile, routine cognitive work is being automated through the application of big data and business analytics, while even non-routine cognitive work is seeing inroads from the increasing use of algorithms.

What does this add up to? An excellent, and much quoted, 2013 study by Carl Frey and Michael Osborne called *The Future of Employment: How Susceptible Are Jobs to Computerisation?* suggests that, just looking at 702 occupations in the USA, about 47 percent of jobs are under serious threat of automation over the next 10 years. Serious job losses are most likely in office administration, logistics and transportation, construction, and sales and service. All four types of routine and non-routine work are at risk in these major areas of the economy. What jobs are less at risk? Consider what computers are less good at: tasks involving manipulation, dexterity, perception, meta-cognition, pattern recognition, substantial contextual and historical information, and/or creative or social intelligence. Interviewed in mid-2015, both Frey and Osborne felt that developments over the two years since they published their paper only lent further evidence to their claims.

In a November 2014 Deloitte report Frey and Osborne extended their analysis for the United Kingdom and London.[26] They concluded that 35 percent of current jobs in the UK and 30 percent in London are at high risk of disappearing over the next two decades as a result of technology. These jobs are in manufacturing, office and administrative support, sales and service, transport, construction and extraction. However for 43 percent of UK jobs (and 51 percent for London), the risk of automation is low to non-existent.

The jobs last at risk are in skilled management, financial services, computers, engineering and science, education, legal services, community services and media and healthcare. For the UK as a whole, jobs paying less than £30,000 are nearly five times more likely to be lost to automation than jobs paying over £100,000. For London the ratio is more than eight times. The number of jobs at risk in London is relatively low, mainly because a large proportion of the workforce is already in high skill roles that technology cannot easily replace. Deloitte's research shows that, compared to other major cities worldwide, London has the highest number of people working in knowledge-based industries (1.472 million in 2013 compared to New York – second with 1.163 million).

We saw above that Frey and Osborne identify three significant 'bottlenecks' to automation that reduce the risks to jobs: the skills of perception and manipulation; creativity; and social intelligence. The 2014 Deloitte report also point to new jobs being continually created, as certain job types are lost. However, there is also a growing concern over recent developments in Machine Learning and Mobile Robotics, associated with the rise of Big Data, which allows for computers to substitute for labour across a wide range of **non-routine tasks – both manual and cognitive.**[27] For example, driver-less cars may do away with non-routine manual tasks in logistics and transportation. In the creative economy advances in Mobile Robotics (e.g. machine vision and high precision dexterity) will have implications for making and craft activities. Data mining and computational statistics could see algorithms causing cognitive tasks to be automated or at least data-driven, with implications for non-routine tasks in distribution, marketing, education and content programming. How far can creativity in jobs be eroded, and no longer be a bottleneck? In their 2015 study of this issue Hasan Bakhshi, Carl Frey and Michael Osborne[28] found that creativity is inversely related to computerisability. Furthermore, on their estimates, as many as 24 percent of jobs in the UK, and 21 percent in the USA have a high probability of being creative, including a wide range of occupations in education, management, computers, engineering, science, arts and media.[29] They also note that the digitisation of the economy is likely to further increase the demand for creative skills. What is less clear from the several Frey and Osborne studies, is how jobs may change their structures as a result of automation and robotics, rather than be lost altogether.

10.5.2. Automation and Work: Other Studies

The debate around robotics replacing jobs has been a little overheated and needs to be tempered by considering what robots can do over the next 10 years. In the next decade, robotics will best be commercially applied in stable environments – where there are relatively unambiguous rules; where limited human intervention and exception handling are needed; where easy comparisons can be made with current manual costs of work; where benefits are going to exceed the costs substantially in the short to mid term; and where transactions are either high volume or low volume but high value. A 2015 Forester Research study also suggests that recently the old spectre of technological unemployment has been raised once more, with the new spin: *"robots that will take your job"*. The authors argue that nightmare scenarios rest on some critical flaws. The worst-case scenarios are put forward, playing off cultural and psychological anxieties. The scariest numbers attach to the least firm dates. Job loss estimates receive the headlines, unlike job creation estimates. Historically we have adapted to greater changes in labour markets. The changes will be over a long time period, not overnight.

Forester research suggest that robots will engage in increasingly impressive but strictly delimited activities, such as: solving optimisation problems; augmenting human intelligence; reinvigorating legacy software systems (RPA) and legacy physical spaces; taking on menial tasks; reducing errors; and automating routinised tasks. For customers automation will drive powerful self-service solutions. Employees will be augmented and complemented by robots. Human jobs will focus on tasks that need complex intelligence, occur

289

infrequently, require aesthetic judgement or special service, involve higher order value and human decision-making. Looking just at the USA the study suggest that, as a result of automation, 22.7 million jobs will be lost between 2015 and 2025 (e.g. bank teller), but 13.6 million created (e.g., robot service technician). Meanwhile the really interesting suggestion in the study is that by 2019 automation will change every job category by at least 25 percent (e.g. a physician using IBM Watson for a second opinion). In other words, over the next five years, the greatest change for workforces will be in job and work transformation rather than job loss.

David Autor[30] extends this last proposal by pointing out that *"jobs are made up of many tasks, and that while automation and computerisation can substitute for some of them, understanding the interaction between technology and employment requires thinking about more than just substitution."* With an economist's hat on, it also requires thinking about price and income elasticities for different kinds of output, and about labour supply responses. Following Michael Polanyi's observation that *"we know more than we can tell"*, there are also underrated and powerful limits to enunciating explicit rules or procedures for computers and robots to follow.[31] Autor's own conclusion is that some tasks in current middle-skill jobs are susceptible to automation, but many middle-skill jobs will continue to demand a mixture of tasks from across the skill spectrum. In many cases it will be difficult, or not necessary to unbundle the more routine technical from the more skilled tasks. Like Forrester Research, he can see how jobs will persist, even if their content and task balance changes. For both studies, however, the catch lies in whether the US education and job training system can produce the kind of workers that will thrive in the middle-skill jobs of the future.

10.5.3. Jobs and Robotic Process Automation

How does RPA fit into this broader context and time line? On RPA's effects on jobs within client firms, so far we have found that FTE reduction did not equal layoffs. Instead, client adopters redeployed displaced workers, did more work with the same number of people, or avoided hiring new workers internally. The number of FTEs required to perform a process was certainly reduced, but the employees freed from the work, now performed by robots, were redeployed to other tasks. When automation reduced the number of FTEs needed to perform a job, redeploying displaced workers within the organisation emerged as a sound human resources practice. Preventing redundancies is a suggested policy within client firms so that staff members embrace automation rather than fear it. Employees have to believe that their jobs will get better because of automation. RPA is best used to release humans from tedious tasks to focus on more valuable work. RPA was also best embraced when it was used to help to reduce the backlog of work and to add new services that previously could not be added because of resource constraints. Companies deploying RPA have also avoided hiring more workers. Within client firms, the real effect on jobs comes from FTE avoidance. RPA was used to avoid hiring new workers. This is where the reduction in jobs might well be seen in the overall economy, rather than at particular organisations deploying RPA.

FTE reduction did occur in outsourcing provider firms. In several of the cases we studied, clients used RPA to reduce FTE headcounts in the outsourcing provider firms. Probably this is less politically sensitive so clients will do more of this. In two cases offshore processes were reshored, but no new jobs were created onshore – they were done by the robots.

10.5.4. The Bigger Picture Revisited

Looking at the bigger picture, much depends on the choices senior managers make about the relationship between processes, technologies and people. In the past, faced with Shoshana Zuboff's 'automate or informate' dilemma[32], all too many executives have chosen to displace workers rather than think through how technology and humans can also work together symbiotically, and empower workers in discretion, judgement and decision-making. In practice RPA can be deployed using either an automate or informate strategy, or both. Tom Davenport and Julia Kirby (2015)[33] have also suggested a more nuanced approach to job design in the light of advances in automation. With an augmentation mindset, managers and knowledge workers themselves may come to see robots and automation as a way of augmenting human skills, with the 'smart machines' collaborators and co-workers, in solving business problems and delivering service. Davenport and Kirby suggest five ways of working with these machines. Put simplistically, **Stepping Up** involves becoming a big picture manager, beyond the machine's capacity. **Stepping Aside** plays to the human strengths that are not about purely rational, codifiable cognition. **Stepping In** sees the knowledge worker monitoring and modifying how the software runs and its results. **Stepping Narrowly** involves the knowledge worker specialising in an area for which no computer program has yet been developed. With **Stepping Forward**, the knowledge worker builds the next generation or application of smart machine. Our own take on this issue? Like Davenport and Kirby, we see the future of operations as less pre-determined than many think: *"Contrary to today's worst fears, robotics could facilitate the rise, not the demise, of the knowledge worker."* But much depends on the imaginations of managers expanding as rapidly as their automation toolkits[34].

10.6. In Predictive Mode

In this final section we allow ourselves to ruminate over the evidence we, and others, have assembled so far, and to reflect on the most frequent questions we get asked when we present our work. While futurology has been a profession since ancient times, it has its limitations – especially where technology is concerned. Commenting on the microchip in 1968, an engineer at the Advanced Computing Division at IBM supposedly asked: *"But what is it good for?"* In 1981 Bill Gates, founder of Microsoft thought that *"640K ought to be enough for anybody"*. Ken Olson founder of Digital Equipment said, in 1977: *"There is no reason why anyone would want a computer in their home."* Given that these were all knowledgeable proponents of computer technology, interested in talking the market up, one can see how easy it is to get it wrong. Therefore the usual warnings on the dangers of predicting where technology will lead have to apply in what follows.

10.6.1. Robots – More Complicated Than You Think …

Well, yes the robots really are coming, but there are several scenarios on work organisation and jobs going forward, and it would be a mistake to assume a steady state, which many extrapolations are more or less based on. In fact many things are moving:

- The data explosion means that organisations are dealing with an accelerating amount of data even if not growing themselves, for example in a stagnant or slow growth market place. RPA is a part solution amongst many others, to this inevitable data growth.
- Will RPA replace offshoring? The predictions are that the offshoring market will continue to grow over the next 5-10 years, with or without RPA.
- RPA will have limits to its applicability, and so far we have seen that it needs to be both set and overseen by humans, who also need to make many judgement calls. There are jobs that surround RPA to make it function, and there also jobs that will be less touched by RPA, especially those involving cognitive non-routine work.
- Accelerating economic growth will see faster adoption of RPA, but will also see greater demand for labour for specific types of skills – there are always skills shortages announced in a range of areas, and these increase in times of economic growth. Lack of economic growth could actually stifle the application of RPA, unless there are huge pressures on cost savings.
- Our work is looking at an emergent usage, but automation through ICTs also has a thirty year history and the interesting question is whether the application of automation is going to see continuity of the existing pattern on job loss, or whether this technology, this time, will be transformative of the jobs scene – with Frey and Osborne's (2013) extrapolations turning out to be accurate. Our own view is

that automation and robotics, in combination with an array of related technologies, will lead to significant net job loss across developed and emerging economies, but that a parallel, development will be the transformation of existing jobs – as suggested by David Autor and Forrester research (see above).

10.6.2. Impact of SMAC and RPA on Outsourcing

We are regularly asked about the likely timing and impact of social, mobile, analytic and cloud (SMAC) technologies and RPA on IT outsourcing. Taking a broad view, we predict that SMAC in combination with advanced robotics, the Internet of Things, and the automation of knowledge work, will lead to organisations becoming fundamentally digital operations or what we call 'cloud corporations', by 2025. How do these developments affect outsourcing over the next five years? Will these disruptive technologies change outsourcing as we know it?

The first thing to say here is that, as at 2016, 60 percent of IT and 80 percent of back office business process work is still done in-house. So, there is still plenty of room for outsourcing to grow. Judging from client responses to a number of our surveys, this growth is precisely what is going to happen across the 2016-2020 period. We expect the ITO market to grow by about 5 percent per year and the BPO market by about 8 percent per year, over the next five years. Outsourcing will continue to grow, and the 'embeddedness' of existing contracts, signed for anywhere between three to ten years, will slow down the new technology impact.

That said, we see real disruption in this overall growth pattern. Outsourcing will increasingly change its character, as providers themselves adopt new technologies and build and offer services based on them. Through 2015, RPA and other service automation tools were increasingly appearing in renewed and newly signed contracts. Our research suggests that a number of disruptors will impact the traditional outsourcing scene more forcefully.

Cloud computing vendors, such as Amazon and Google, and cloud platform providers, such as IBM and Microsoft, have enough market clout to move on from impacting SMEs to move up the value chain with larger corporations. SaaS could seriously impact outsourcing as an option in many important back office functions such as accounts payable, indirect procurement, payroll, and benefit administration. Using software over the Internet, companies may spend much more time serving themselves through their own managed services. Robotics-driven vendors operated at the bottom of the BPO stack as of 2015. Yet, if the 20 percent to 30 percent promised cost reductions, and the other benefits detailed throughout this book based on robotics do materialise, the technology will find bigger markets. We have researched SMEs who were born in the cloud who are unlikely to switch out of their cloud computing and automation environments. We will see many more of these SMEs coming along over the next five years.

Our 2012-2016 studies that fed into the book, *Moving to the Cloud Corporation,* found majors like Proctor & Gamble, Johnson & Johnson, the Commonwealth Bank of Australia, and News Corporation well into implementing their cloud computing strategies. Many other majors are likely to follow suit in the next five years. All these trends imply less outsourcing or at least a change in its character. The cloud providers themselves have been very aware of the coming change, and they have been already responding. Undoubtedly, the next round of contract renewals, across 2016/17, will see providers adjusting their services to reflect these developments.

As we have seen, a typical estimate from our most recent case study research is that robotics provides a 20 percent to 30 percent cost reduction. If robotics meant a universal reduction in full-time-equivalent employee costs of say 25 percent, and labour-intensive outsourcing providers' total revenues are growing only by 5 percent to 6 percent annually at the moment, then unless they themselves adopt automation, overdependence on cheap labour will put them into economic difficulties. However, several outsourcing providers have a head start in automation. Moreover, there are clearly definable limits to the applicability of robotics and thus their impact on jobs and outsourcing practices.

If the above scenario is correct, then client companies will be able to lose a lot of headcount – not through outsourcing but through automating. Meanwhile, outsourcing providers may combat the automation-based insourcing threat by offering cheaper automated solutions of their own. The likely outcome on a 10-year horizon is to see a slowing down of outsourcing growth among service providers, who will also be moving increasingly from labour arbitrage to automated service offerings.

10.6.3. Automation, RPA and Jobs - A Macroeconomic Perspective

What does this add up to at the macroeconomic level? This is difficult to assess because the world does not sit still, but if clients are using robots for low-level tasks, fewer people will be needed in those job categories – the FTE avoidance will hit these job categories. But what new job categories may emerge? That is the very interesting question. We are aware of Carr's 2014 book on the dangers of the changes in the nature of work that we may build into how we adopt these technologies. Also of Martin Ford's two books, *Lights in The Tunnel* (2009) and *The Rise of the Robots* (2015), on drastic job loss that will accompany automation. We suggest a more nuanced future. On a horizon of 1 to 5 years, we anticipate a mixed scenario:

1. RPA will begin to seriously change the delivery of services, substituting technology for people, which alters the economics of service delivery, causing labour to be less of a factor and making labour arbitrage less important.

2. The domestic/reshoring/in-house 'tides' will rise; with their superior 'ease of engagement', and with the need for the remaining humans to be near the action to handle exceptions, complexity and new services. This will make reshoring and 'domestic' insourcing and outsourcing more advantageous vis-

à-vis most forms of offshoring, whether outsourcing or captive.

3.   A backlash will occur against the impacts of automation, especially in terms of threat to jobs – which will become a symbol for the workforce and economic health generally – in both domestic and offshore locations,

4.   The outsourcing and offshore outsourcing markets will continue to grow globally at anything between 5 percent to 12 percent per annum, depending on function/process outsourced. Leading providers will increasingly seek automation as a core capability for delivery of services. Leading advisory firms will shift capabilities from assisting clients with outsourcing decisions to optimising service delivery that will increasingly rely on automation and may or may not involve external sourcing.

On a horizon of 5-10 years these factors will kick in and be *game changing* in impact. We anticipate:

5.   Through automation, much more in-house, domestic outsourcing and reshoring of business and IT services will occur. Automation will move from routine manual and routine cognitive, to non-routine manual, and non-routine cognitive types of task. Automation will breed further automation as humans can no longer fit into the systems and processes being devised.

6.   Through automation, providers competing against clients (in-house sourcing) and other providers (outsourcing) will use automation to reduce costs and improve process metrics – e.g. responsiveness, timeliness, quality, defect levels, ease of use.

7.   Through automation, issues around socially-responsible sourcing/ outsourcing and work design rising in importance and profile, raising internal issues of management ethos; and external issues of reputation management in the marketplace.

8.   Changes in client-supplier relations and types of contracting will occur.

9.   At the same time, automation will not stop the rise in offshore and domestic outsourcing, as there is still so much work that will be open to outsourced options, which providers will work hard at making attractive. We anticipate a continued growth in ITO and BPO markets globally.

10.   The impact of robotics is hot in current debates, but this must be seen within a much larger context. Our own research studies on cloud computing and service automation, with 2025 as our horizon, suggest that a range of technologies will operate in combination with cloud and with each other to create massive impacts – on individuals, organisations, and on business, economic and social life. On jobs our provisional work suggests the overall impact of these technologies in combination will be for every 20 jobs lost, 13 will be created but that additional job creation will come from two factors and their interactions not factored enough into many studies: the data explosion and the growth of bureaucracy and regulation.

10.7. Conclusion

By 2016 service automation had hit a sweet spot in terms of market take-up. The relevant tools were not just relatively easy to apply, but a maturing body of practice had made them much easier to introduce into organisational structures. Work processes and the role of the IT function had become much clearer, and client organisations had learned to build internal RPA/automation capability and how to scale in terms of number of transactions as well as across new processes. Furthermore, as we saw in this book, multiple benefits seemed to flow from applying automation and robotics to certain (the right) processes or sub-processes. Using the many lessons learned along the way, client organisations were experiencing their strong business cases being delivered on in practice. Many further developments were in train, invested, as we saw, with terms like 'autonomic platforms', 'cognitive automation', 'intelligent automation', and 'true artificial intelligence'. It is also important to understand that, while many robotic devices may be self-contained,

298

robots do not need to be embodied in the conventional sense of the word, or located in one place. Performing any given task requires four resources – energy, awareness, reasoning and means. A robot may draw on electrical energy, but could draw upon a network of sensors distributed throughout the environment of interest. The means can consist of a mix of interchangeable and disconnected motors, actuators and tools, while the logic driving this can be anywhere – as we have seen with drone aircraft. This means that robotics may well interconnect with other technologies in new and unexpected ways.

In this book we have sought to indicate both possibilities and limits to what robots can do in the arena of service automation. On possibilities, these are set by human imagination and build capability, along with socially and politically established boundaries and will. We have also addressed the anxieties and concerns many people have on the bigger picture issue as to where advanced ICTS and automation will lead. In a recent book called *Humans Need Not Apply*, Jerry Kaplan[35] raised once again the danger of us *"becoming roadkill on the information superhighway."* We have tried in this book to give a balanced and informed view as to where the benefits from the new technologies are, how they can be gained, while also warning that the potential downsides of the uses of these technologies need to be managed very carefully at individual, organisational and societal levels.

With digitisation, generally the major perils we highlighted relate to acceleration, employment, security, privacy and environmental sustainability. Undoubtedly in the next ten years we are going to see much transformation in the nature of work, as even newer technologies and newer applications come on stream and become pervasive. It should be recalled that all this will be at human instigation. Not all developments will be bad., but whether you take an optimistic, pessimistic or relativistic view, all developments will be potentially dangerous. Therefore for the stakeholders in the technological future, each and every one of us, there will always be work to do.

Citations

1   Good, I. J. (1965). Speculations Concerning the First Ultraintelligent Machine. *Advances in Computers,* Volume 6.

2   Chandler, A. (1962), *Strategy and Structure: Chapters in the History of the American Industrial Enterprise.* Cambridge, MA: MIT Press.

3   See Practice 4 on pages 20-22 in Lacity, M. and Rottman, J. (2008), *Offshore Outsourcing of IT Work.* (Palgrave Macmillan,United Kingdom).

4   Hirschheim, R. (1986), *The Effect of A Priori Views on the Social Implications of Computing: The Case of Office Automation, Computing Surveys,* 18, 3, pp. 165-195.

5   http://www.cnn.com/2015/10/02/health/acronyms-teens-social-media-being13/

6   Hirschheim, R. (1986), *The Effect of A Priori Views on the Social Implications of Computing: The Case of Office Automation, Computing Surveys,* 18, 3, pp. 165-195.

7   Good, I. J. (1965). Speculations Concerning The First Ultraintelligent Machine. *advances in Computers,* Volume 6.

8   Mokyr, J., Vickers, C., Ziebarth, N. (2015) *The History of Technological Anxiety And The Future of Economic Growth: Is This Time Different?, Journal of Economic Perspectives,* 29, 3, 31-50.

9   Gordon, R. (2012) *Is US Economic Growth Over? Faltering Innovation Confronts The Six Headwinds, NBER Working Paper, 18315.*10; Kalthoff. F. (2015) *Dark Side Of Digital: An overview of perils from digitization, as a new perspective on the Information Society Discourse.* Unpublished MSc dissertation, (London School of Economics, London.)

10 Kalthoff. F. (2015) Dark Side Of Digital: An overview of perils from digitization, as a new perspective on the Information Society Discourse. Unpublished MSc dissertation, (London School of Economics, London.)

11 Noys, B. (2014) *Malign Velocities: Accelerationism and Capitalism.* (Zero Books, Winchester);

Wajcman, J. (2015) *Pressed For Time: The acceleration of life in digital capitalism.* (University of Chicago Press, London); Virilio, P. (2012) *The Great Accelerator.* (Polity Press, Cambridge); Patterson, S, (2013) *Dark Pools: The rise of A.I. trading machines and the looming threat to Wall Street.* (Random House, New York).

12 Collingridge, D.(1980) *The Social Control of Technology,* (Frances Pinter, London).

13 Wallach, W. (2015) *A Dangerous Master: How to keep technology slipping*

beyond our control. (Basic Books, New York).

[14] Ford, M. (2015) *Rise Of The Robots: Technology and the threat of a jobless future.* (Basic Books, New York). Also Ford, M. (2009) *The Lights In The Tunnel.* (Acculant Publishing, New York). Also Carr, N. (2015) *The Glass Cage: Where automation is taking us.* (The Bodley Head, London). Also Wallach, W. (2015) *A Dangerous Master: How to keep technology slipping beyond our control.* (Basic Books, New York).

[15] See Goodman, M. (2015) *Future Crimes: A journey to the dark side of technology – and how to survive it.* (Bantam Press, London); Lucas, E. (2015) *Cyberphobia – Identity, trust, security and the Internet.* (Bloomsbury Press, London); Bauman, Z. and Lyon, D. *Liquid Surveillance.* (Polity Press, Cambridge).

[16] Quoted in Kalthoff. F. (2015) Dark Side Of Digital· An overview of perils from digitization, as a new perspective on the Information Society Discourse. Unpublished MSc dissertation, (London School of Economics, London.)

[17] See Zuboff, S. (2015) *Big Other: Surveillance Capitalism and the Prospects for an Information Civilization, Journal of Information Technology,* 30, 1, 75-89.

[18] Hilty, L. And Aebischer, B. (2015) ICT Innovations For Sustainability. *Advances in Intelligent Systems and Computing,* vol. 310, pp. 36-48; Hilty, L. (2008) *Information Technology and Sustainability: Essays on the relationship between ICT and sustainable development.* (Book on Demand, Norderstedt).; Dutta, S. and Mia, I. (2010). *The Global Information Technology Report 2009-10: ICT for sustainability.* (Palgrave Macmillan, London).

[19] Global eSustainability Initiative (2009) *ICT Sustainability Through Innovation,* GeSI Activity Report, Brussels.

[20] Hilty, L. And Aebischer, B. (2015) *ICT Innovations For Sustainability, Advances in Intelligent Systems and Computing,* vol. 310, pp. 36-48; Hilty, L. (2008) *Information Technology and Sustainability: Essays on the relationship between ICT and sustainable development.* (Book on Demand, Norderstedt).

[21] Pickavct, M., Vereecken, W., Demeyer, S., et al. (2008) *Worlwide Energy needs For ICTS: The Rise of Power-aware Networking, International Symposium on Advanced Networks, and Telecommunications Systems,* Mumbai, December 15-17th.

[22] Engineering and Physical Sciences Research Council (2011), *Principles of Robotics: Regulating Robotics In The Real World.* Produced from a joint research workshop with the Arts and Humanities Research Council, September 2011.

[23] Postman, N. (1998) *Five Things We Need To Know About Technological Change.* Talk delivered in Denver Colorado March 28.

[24] Quoted in Willcocks, L. (2004). *Foucault, Power/Knowledge and Information Systems: Reconstructing The Present.* In Mingers, J. and Willcocks, L. (eds.) *Social Theory and Philosophy For Information Systems* (Wiley, Chichester).

[25] Stewart, I., De, D. and Cole, A. (2015) *Technology and People: The Great Job-creating Machine.* (Deloitte, London).

[26] Deloitte (2014). London Futures - *Agiletown: The Relentless March of Technology and London's Response.* (Deloitte, London) November.

[27] The examples are from Bakshi, H., Frey, C. and Osborne, M. (2015) *Creativity Vs. Robots: The Creative Economy and the Future of Employment.* (Nesta, London) April.

[28] Bakshi, H., Frey, C. and Osborne, M. (2015) *Creativity Vs. Robots: The Creative Economy and the Future of Employment.* (Nesta, London) April

[29] The authors say that 21 percent of US employment is highly creative – that is has a probability of more than 70 percent of being creative, and give examples of these creative occupations as artists, architects, web designers, IT specialists and public relations professionals. They suggest that in the USA 86 percent (UK 87 percent) of workers in the highly creative category are found to be at low or no risk of automation.

[30] Autor, D. (2015) *Why Are There Still So Many Jobs? The History and Future of Workplace Automation. Journal of Economic Perspectives*, 29, 3, 3-30.

[31] David Autor calls this 'Polanyi's Paradox', after Michael Polanyi author of the book *Personal Knowledge (1958 – Chicago Press, USA),* which raise the importance of tacit knowing in human activity.

[32] Zuboff, S. (1988) *In The Age of The Smart Machine: The Future of Work and Power.* (Heinemann Professional, New York).

[33] Davenport, T. and Kirby, J. (2015) Beyond Automation. *Harvard Business Review*, June.

[34] See Lacity, M. and Willcocks, L. (2015) *What Knowledge Workers Stand To Gain From Automation. Harvard Business Review, The Future Of Operations,* June

[35] Kaplan, J. (2015) *Humans Need Not Apply: A guide to work and wealth in the age of artificial intelligence.* (Yale University Press, New Haven).